IMAGES
of America

JAMESTOWN

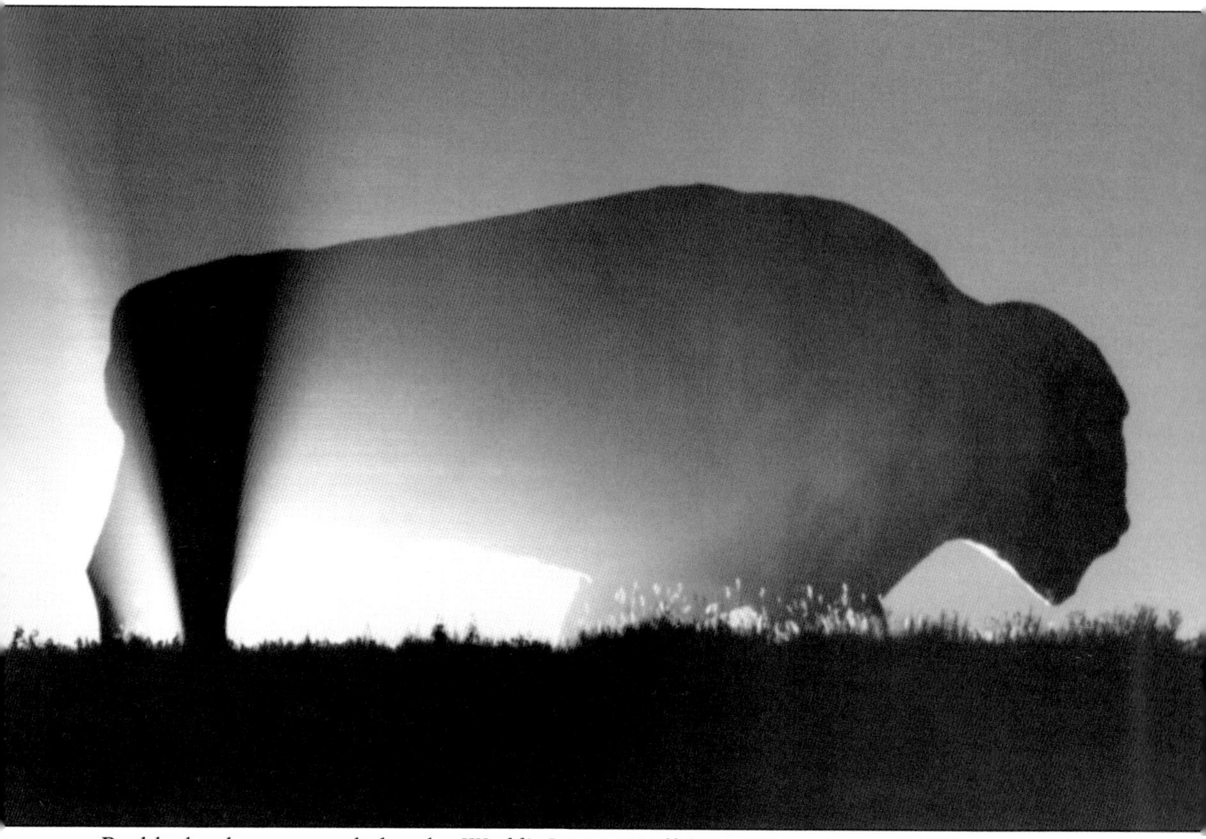

Backlit by the evening light, the *World's Largest Buffalo* glows in silhouette as it overlooks the city of Jamestown in 1984. (Photograph by Tom Domek.)

On the Cover: This early automobile wrecker served H.W. Lyons Buick in downtown Jamestown. The dealership, located in a service station, operated until the 1940s. (Photograph courtesy of Dave Robertson.)

IMAGES
of America

JAMESTOWN

Tom Domek, Journé Domek,
and Keith Norman

ARCADIA
PUBLISHING

ISBN 978-0-7385-9987-8

Published by Arcadia Publishing
Charleston, South Carolina

Printed in the United States of America

Library of Congress Control Number: 2012955337

For all general information, please contact Arcadia Publishing:
Telephone 843-853-2070
Fax 843-853-0044
E-mail sales@arcadiapublishing.com
For customer service and orders:
Toll-Free 1-888-313-2665

Visit us on the Internet at www.arcadiapublishing.com

Tom would like to dedicate this book to his brother and sister, Lance and Barbara—wonderful sidekicks, and great friends as well.

Journé would like to dedicate this book to her family and their deep roots in Jamestown.

Keith would like to dedicate this book to his wife, Jane, who stands beside him through every project, triumph, and challenge.

Contents

ACKNOWLEDGMENTS

The authors would like to thank the following people and organizations for their generous cooperation in research for this book and for the use of images: Kenneth Horton, Dave Robertson, Lenard Cave, the Jamestown Parks & Recreation Department, Mary Faith Young, the *Jamestown Sun*, Fay (Kupper) Domek, Charles Kourajian, Leonard Rude, Thelma Hennings, the Stutsman County Memorial Museum, Nina Sneider and the Buffalo City Tourism Foundation, Felicia Sargeant and the National Buffalo Museum, and Anne Denholm and the North Dakota Farmers Union.

Introduction

This book is not the last word on Jamestown, whose history is too massive and too complicated for a work such as this to provide a comprehensive understanding of the city and its rural surroundings. Instead, this book offers a partial photographic and narrative history. It might help to think of each photograph as a shard of broken glass and to view the entire collection of photographs as a mosaic that offers a representation of Jamestown not found anywhere else.

Photography is an art form that, when done well, presents a mood and offers the viewer innumerable ways to enter into and depart from an image. It ignites the imagination, provides a visual roadway into one's memory, and grants communities of all kinds the opportunity to discuss ideas, moments, and concepts.

Most of the photographs herein were not taken by professional photographers, but by amateur shooters whose main concern was likely just capturing a moment in time for their families and friends. That does not decrease the interest in the images or their importance in understanding the history of Jamestown. Instead, these photographs often show a more authentic slice of everyday life than the posed scene of a professional portrait. They work on the senses and preserve details of bygone days. Some are artfully rendered; others, perhaps less so, but as a whole, these photographs represent good times and bad, high points and low, and can transport viewers back into dream worlds of yesterday and into daydreams of the present.

Photographs play an important role in the preservation of history. That history might encapsulate an epic era, such as the American Civil War or the suffrage movement. But a photographic history of less sweeping topics, like a small city's growth, is important as well. Hopefully, these images and accompanying captions help form a narrative thread that offers readers a better understanding of Jamestown's history.

European Americans first established a foothold in the area in 1872 as survey and construction crews of the Northern Pacific Railroad worked their way across the plains. That year, Fort Seward was built to protect those workers, and it served as a frontier military post until 1877. In 1883, the Northern Pacific Railroad drove its golden spike in Montana. Jamestown was no longer a town along a dead-end railroad, but a growing community providing service to a transcontinental railroad.

Jamestown was a railroad center, a farming community, and later, a hub for manufacturing and business. Its people built homes, churches, schools, and businesses. Government functions, such as the North Dakota State Hospital, also contributed to the vitality of the community, which continues today. Jamestown's principal transportation routes are now Interstate 94 and US Highway 281, serving as a crossroads for the trucks that move the goods of this country. Farm crops have changed from the wheat, barley, and oats of the homesteader to the corn and soybeans of the modern farm. The community is still home to the North Dakota State Hospital, and several clinics as well as Jamestown Regional Medical Center have been added.

In the 1950s, Jamestown branded itself as the Buffalo City. The *World's Largest Buffalo*, a mammoth concrete sculpture of a bison, serves as a centerpiece for the community and as a tribute to the region's western heritage. The National Buffalo Museum and a live herd of buffalo (including rare albino animals) have cemented the city's identity. All of these things have come together to create the community celebrated in this book.

The authors are very grateful to those individuals and organizations that opened up their photograph archives for use in these pages. Their generosity cannot be understated. The authors waded through thousands of images, and because of the great number of quality photographs, decided to focus primarily on images extending just into the early 1950s (though the city's more recent years would undoubtedly make for an interesting study, as well).

One

Etched from the Plains

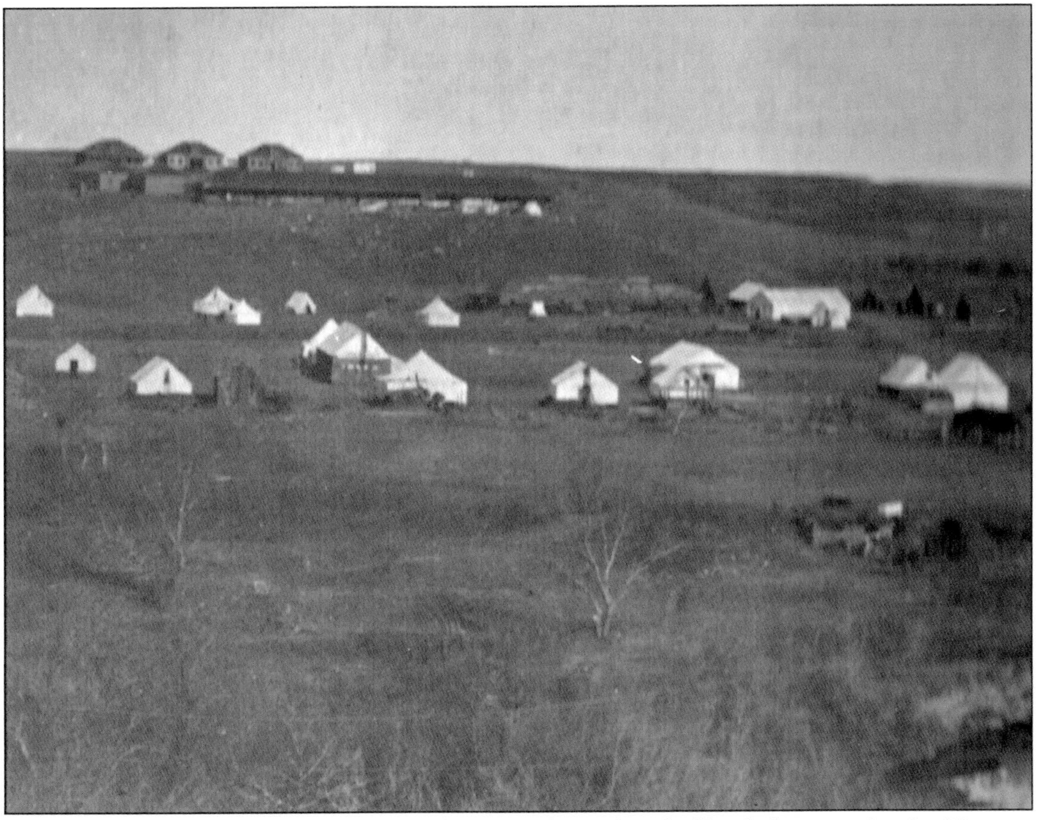

This photograph, possibly taken by Northern Pacific Railroad official photographer Jay Haynes, shows the officers' quarters of Fort Seward. The buildings were duplexes that offered living space for two officers and their families. Fort Seward existed from 1872 to 1877, when it was decommissioned. (Photograph courtesy of the Fort Seward Historic Site.)

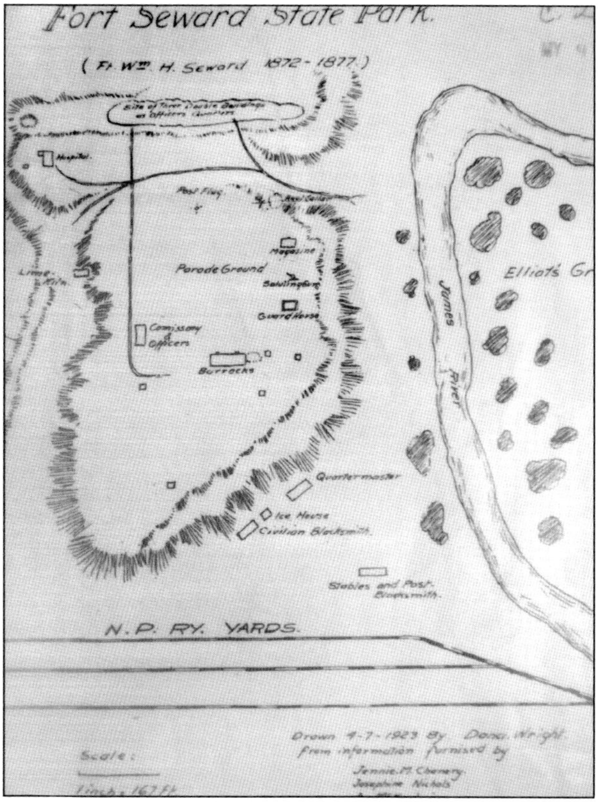

Although Fort Seward is a state historic site, it has never been a state park as indicated on this map. It is now the site of the tallest flagpole in North Dakota and a memorial to North Dakota veterans. (Image courtesy of the Fort Seward Interpretive Center.)

Members of the North Dakota National Guard line up in this photograph taken by C.L. Judd in 1899. Judd photographed the drills conducted when the guard returned from the Philippines after the Spanish-American War. (Photograph courtesy Lenard Cave.)

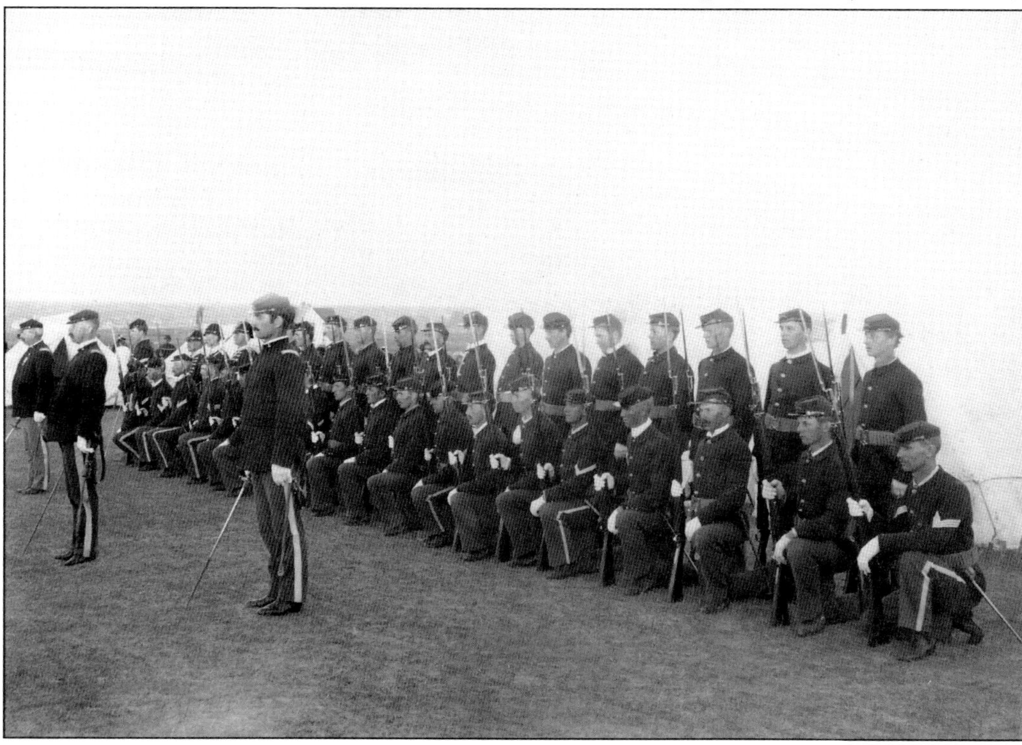

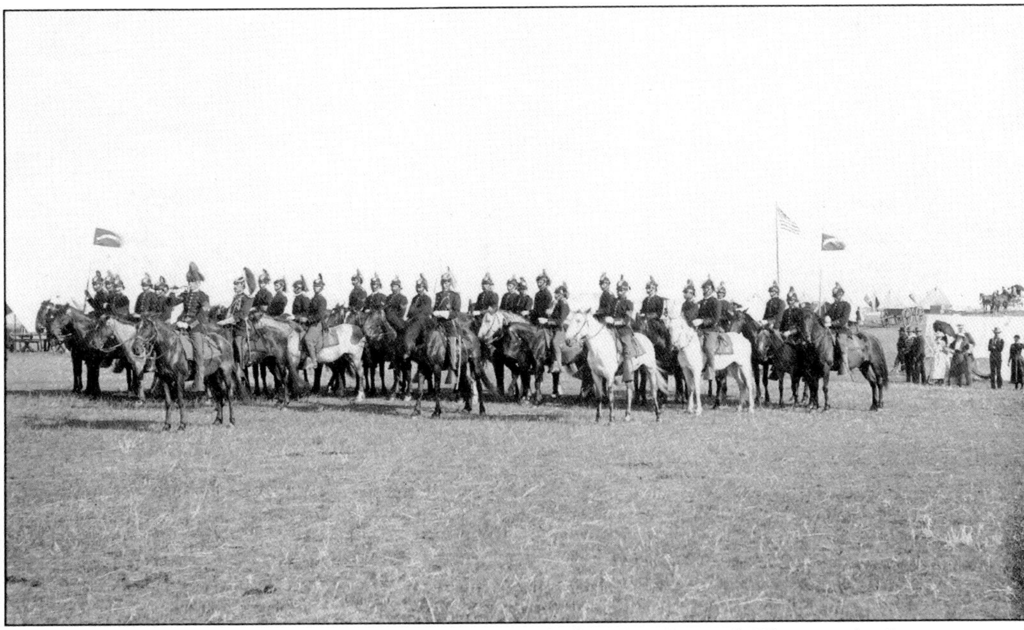

Mounted officers line up for review during an 1899 drill at Fort Seward. The men had just returned from the Philippines and service in the Spanish-American War. This image is part of a collection of photographs taken at the drills by C.L. Judd. (Photograph courtesy of Lenard Cave.)

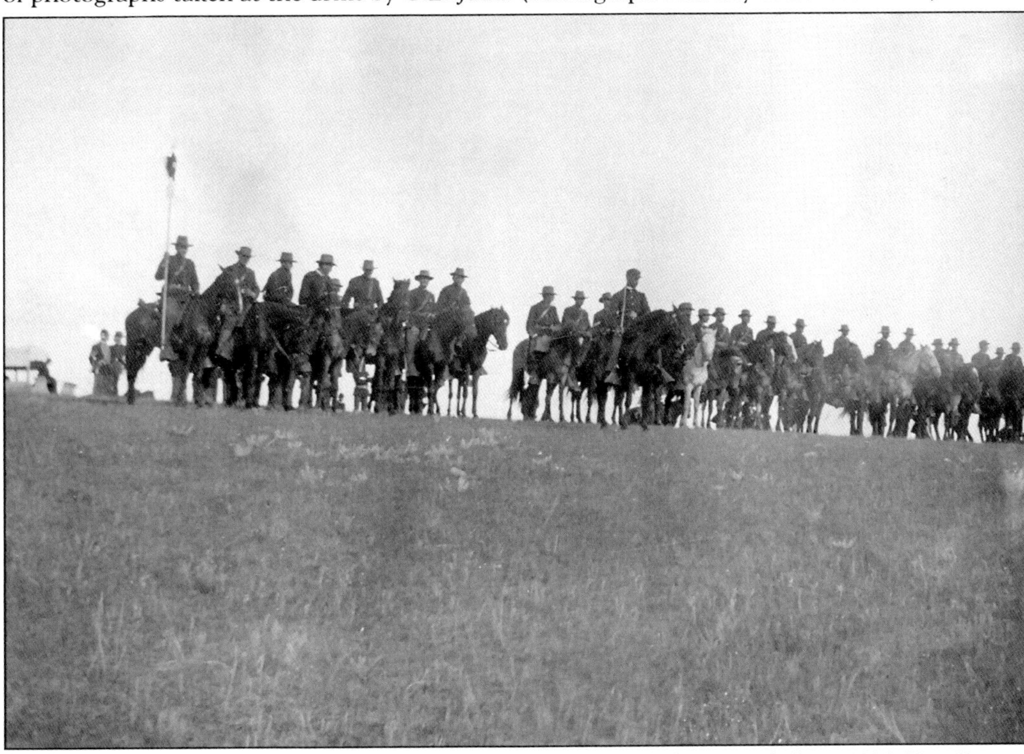

Cavalry line up during a drill at Fort Seward in this C.L. Judd photograph from 1899. Fort Seward had been decommissioned in 1877, but the grounds were still used by the territorial and North Dakota National Guard for several years. (Photograph courtesy of Lenard Cave.)

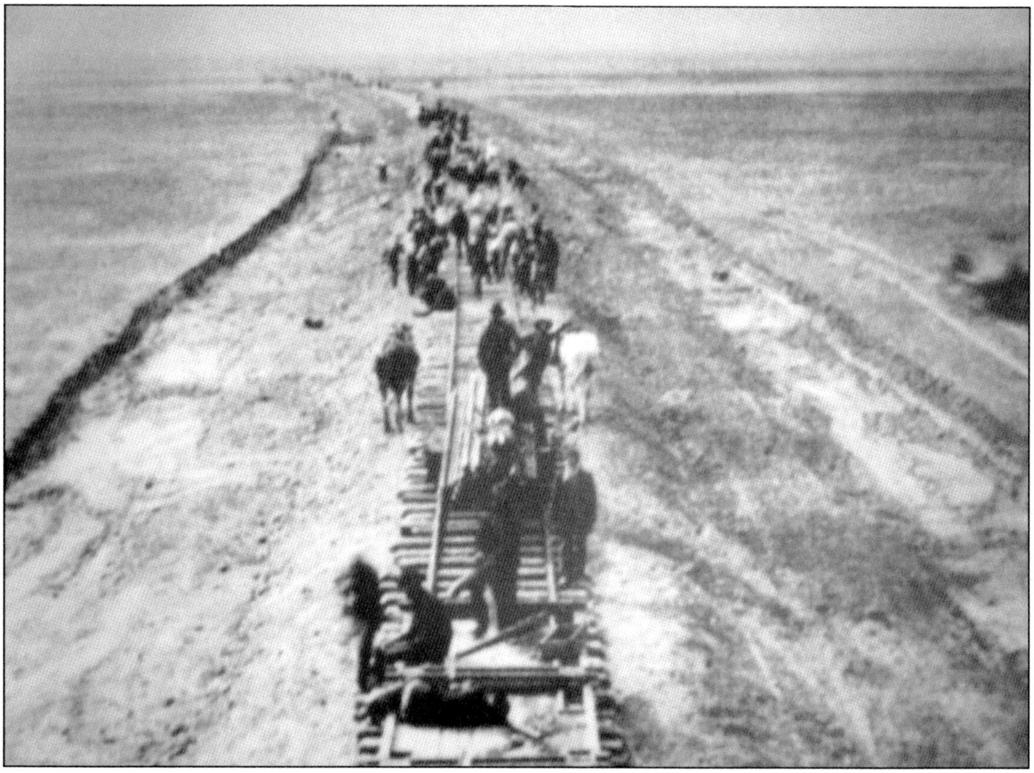

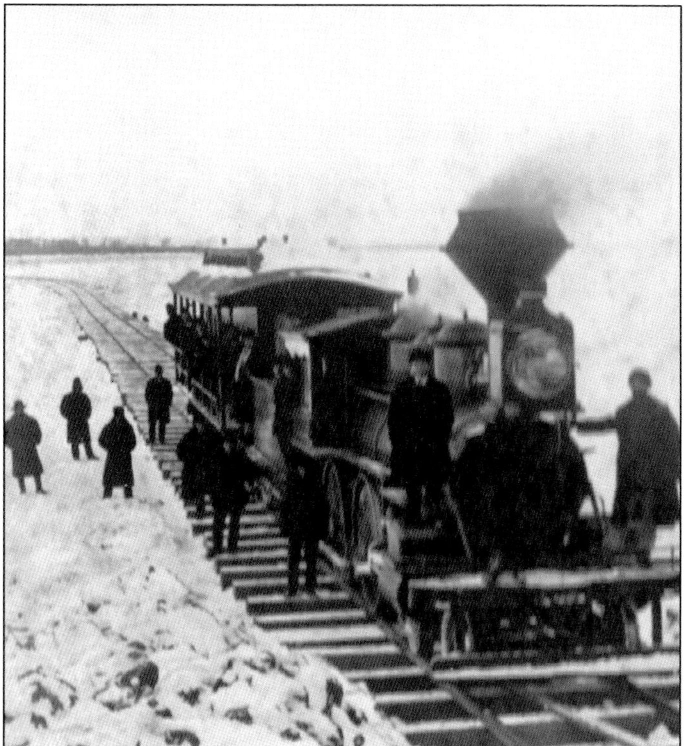

Here, railroad gandy dancers (track workmen) are seen laying ties and rail, probably to the west of Jamestown. In the earliest years, when hostilities still simmered between settlers and American Indian tribes, the US cavalry would often protect railway workers from attack. (Photograph courtesy of the Stutsman County Memorial Museum.)

The Northern Pacific Railroad, a land-grant railway, arrived from the east, reaching the tiny hamlet of Jamestown in 1872. This photograph was taken by the Northern Pacific's official photographer, F. Jay Haynes. (Photograph courtesy of the Stutsman County Memorial Museum.)

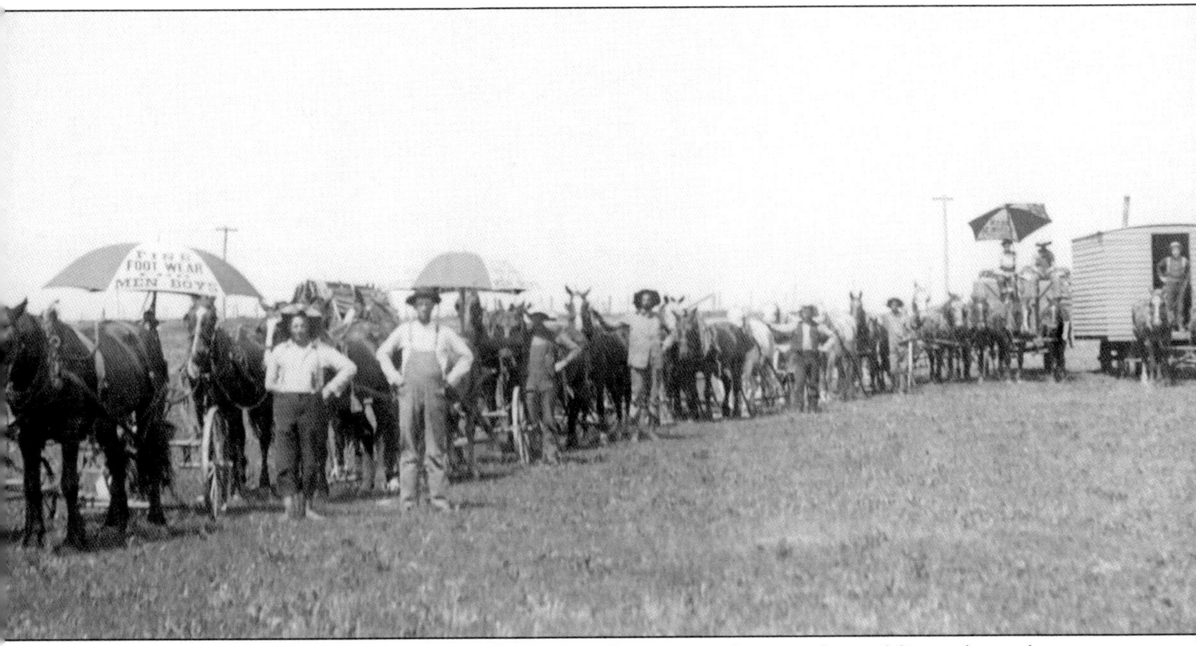

Seen here in 1912, this Northern Pacific Railroad crew stands near the rail line where they are building a firebreak along the track. Sparks and ash from coal-fired steam engines often ignited prairie fires, as did journals that grew hot from the friction of the rotating steel wheels on railroad cars. (Photograph courtesy of the Stutsman County Memorial Museum.)

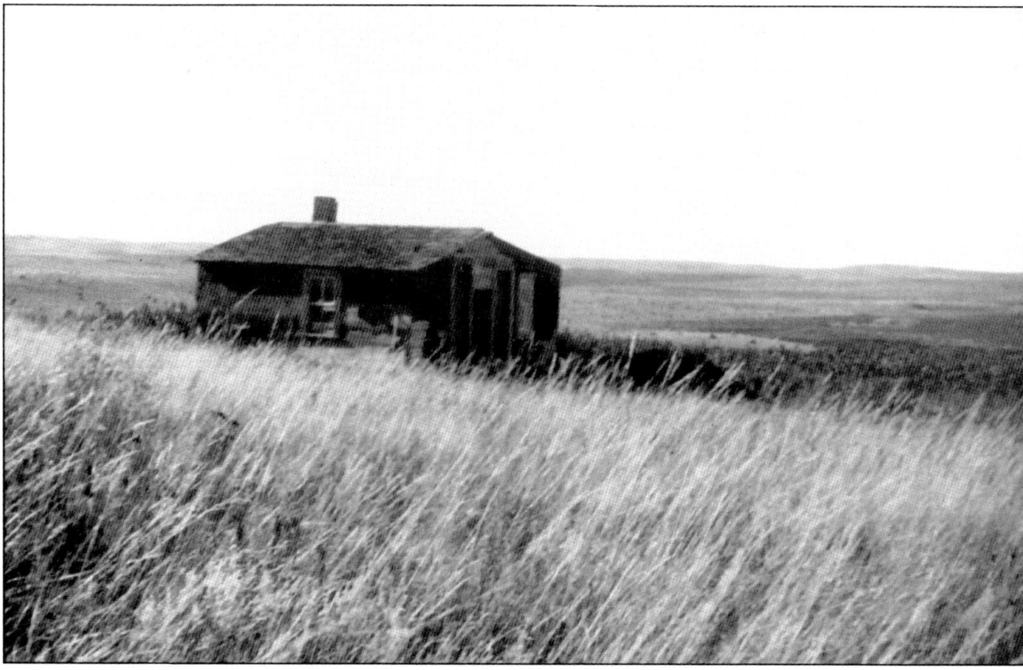

This shanty, set on the wide-open plains near Jamestown, epitomizes the diminutive size of the original shacks and sod huts early homesteaders lived in while proving up their claims. (Photograph courtesy of the Stutsman County Memorial Museum.)

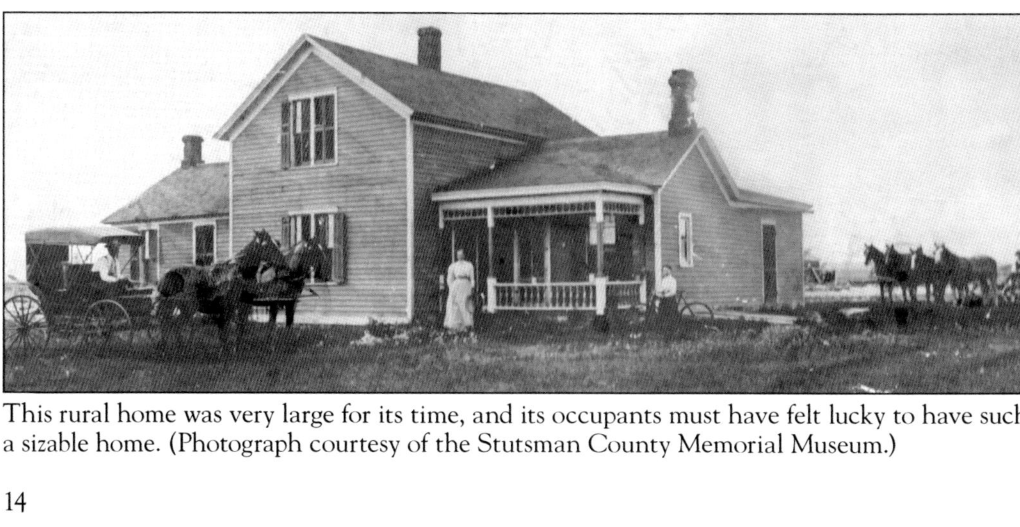

This rural home was very large for its time, and its occupants must have felt lucky to have such a sizable home. (Photograph courtesy of the Stutsman County Memorial Museum.)

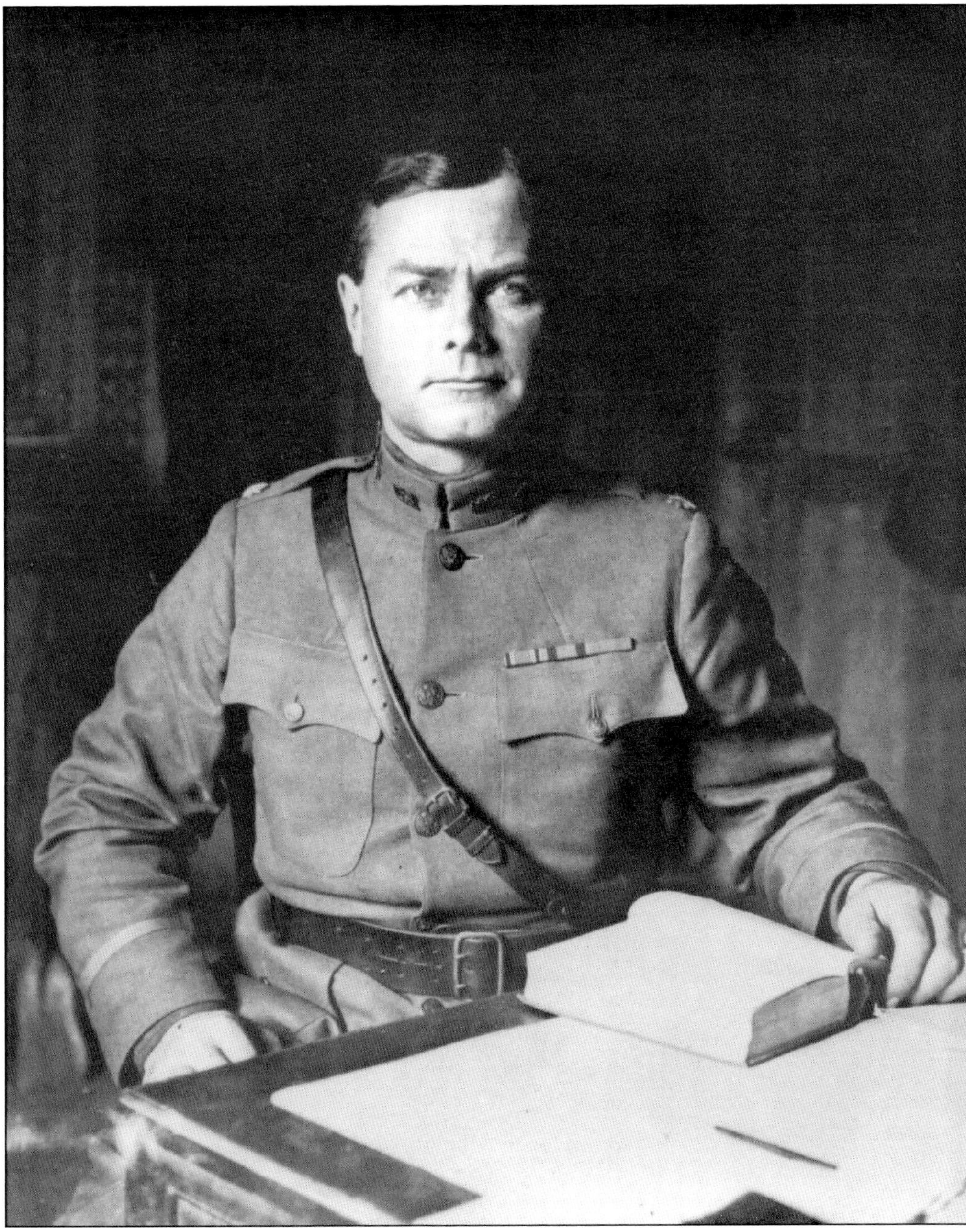

Notable Jamestown military man Dana Wright was born in Eaton Rapids, Michigan, in 1878. At the age of three, he came to the Dakota Territory. He served in the Philippines during the Spanish-American War and on the Mexican border during Pancho Villa's raids in and around Columbus, New Mexico, in 1916. Wright was also a battalion commander in World War I and served as Stutsman County sheriff for two years. (Photograph courtesy of the Stutsman County Memorial Museum.)

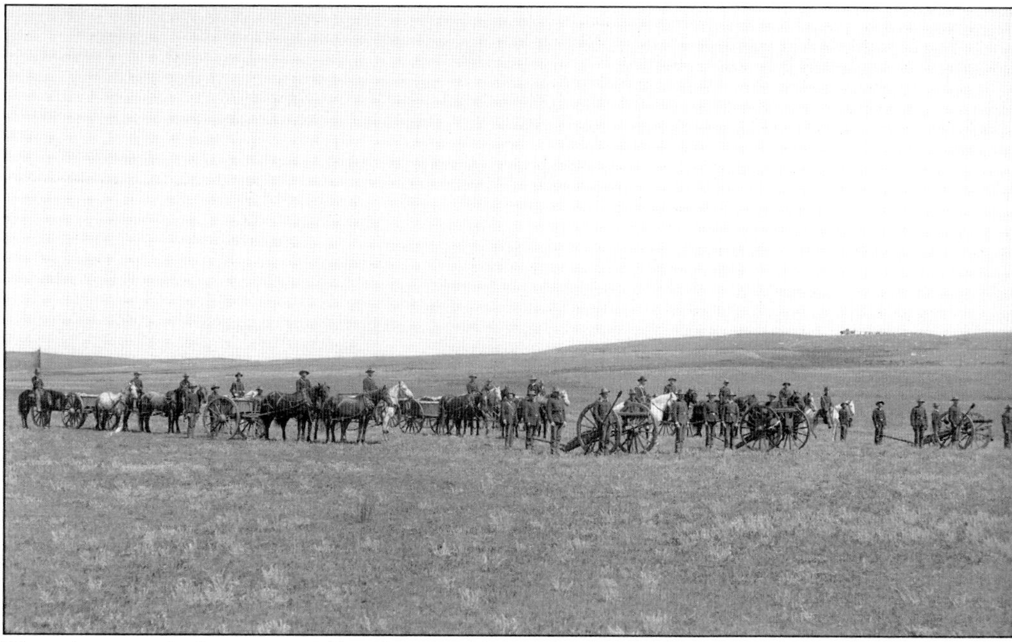

This photograph shows an artillery battery of two cannons and a carriage-mounted Gatling gun in drill at Fort Seward in 1899. The unit includes the limbers and caissons used to transport the guns and ammunition along with the horses used to move the unit. (Photograph courtesy of Lenard Cave.)

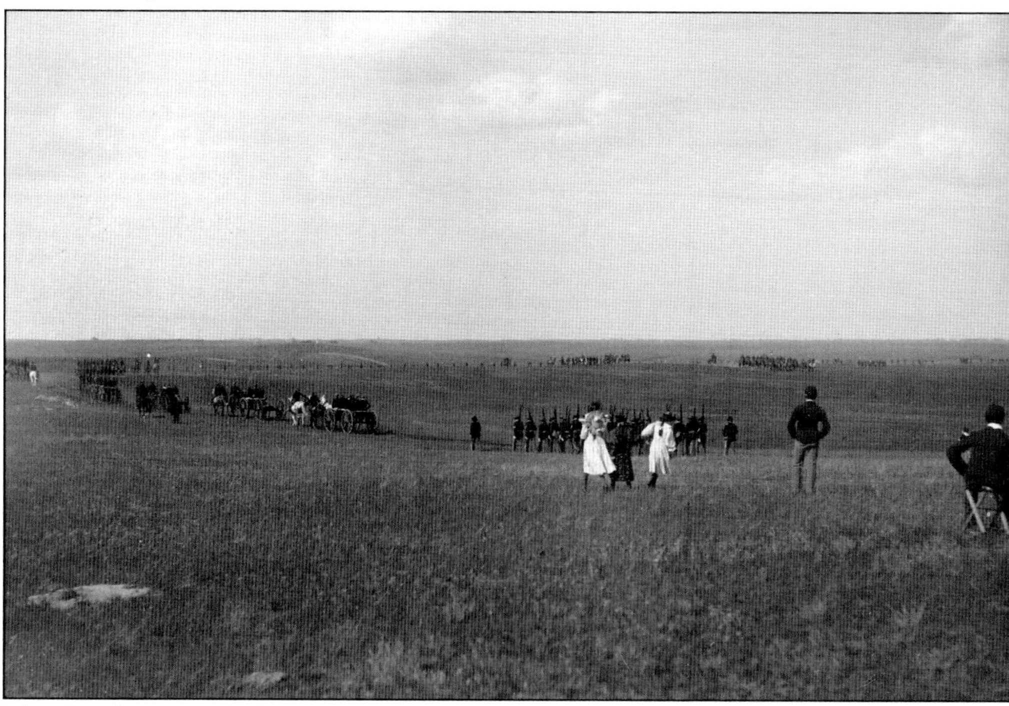

The October 1899 drill included a simulated skirmish with infantry, cavalry, and artillery maneuvering on the Fort Seward grounds. The event was observed by some of the soldiers as well as the children of the community. (Photograph courtesy of Lenard Cave.)

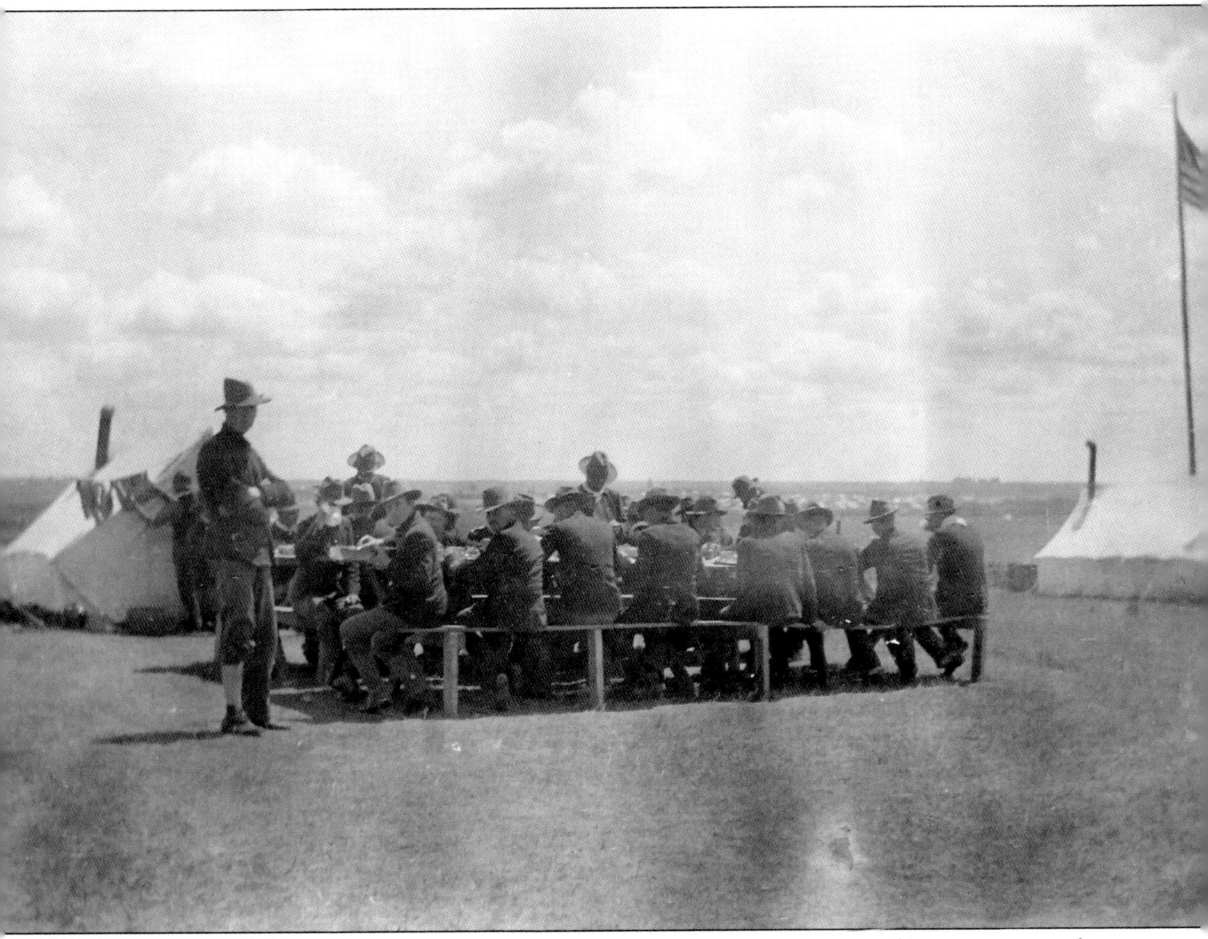

Soldiers were served lunch as part of the drills at Fort Seward. The town of Jamestown can be seen in the valley below the encampment, with the buildings of the North Dakota State Hospital visible on the far horizon. (Photograph courtesy of Lenard Cave.)

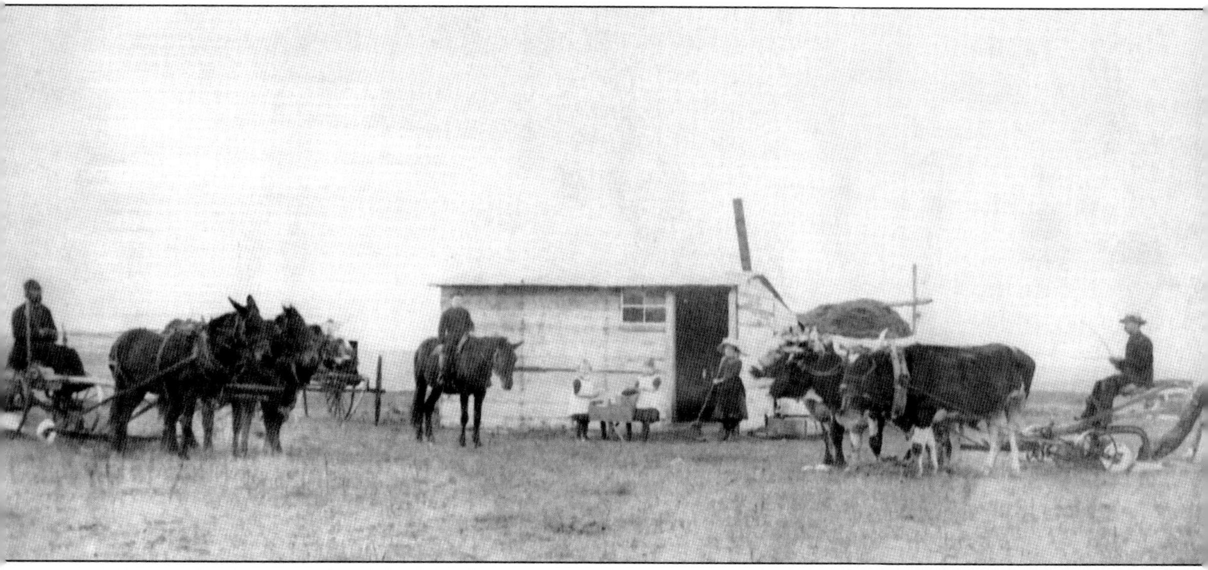

This early photograph of the Newberry estate shows a somewhat modest dwelling with teams of burros, oxen, and horses at the service of the men who brought European-style agriculture to the region. (Photograph courtesy of the Stutsman County Memorial Museum.)

Arthur W. and Caroline Kelley arrived in Jamestown from the east coast in 1872. Arthur was an early Jamestown merchant and the town's first postmaster, earning just $1 a year for the privilege. The Kelleys both died in 1908. (Photograph courtesy of the Stutsman County Memorial Museum.)

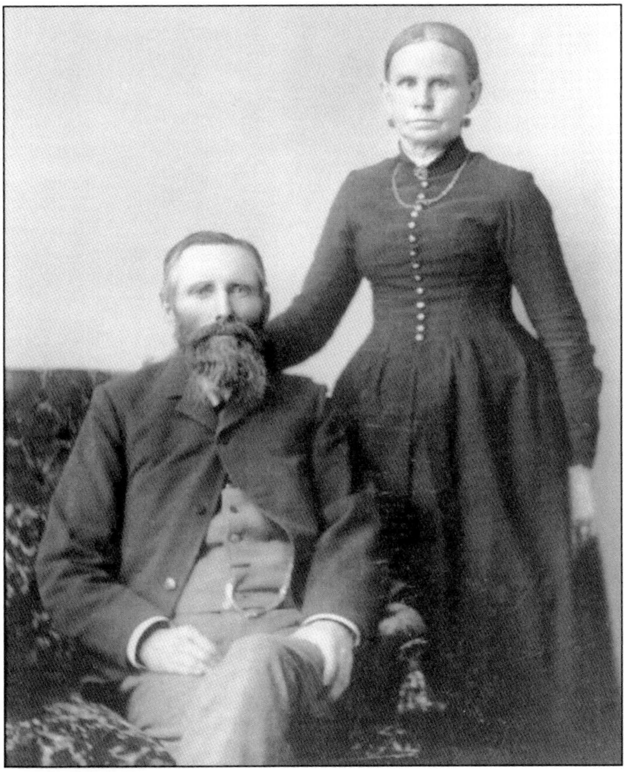

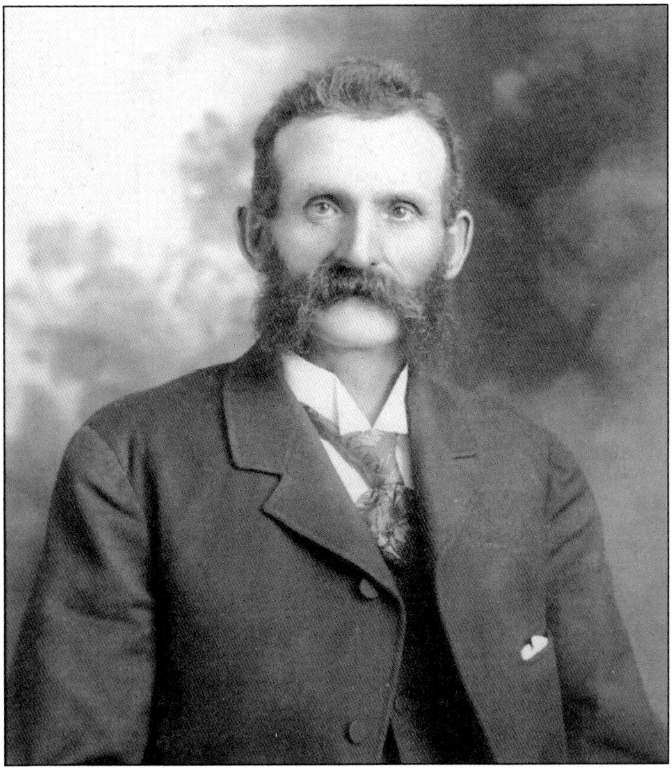

Jim Lees came to Jamestown in 1872 and is credited as the first homesteader in Homer Township, the original township of the city. He also served as a freighter on the Fort Totten to Fort Seward Trail. (Photograph courtesy of the Stutsman County Memorial Museum.)

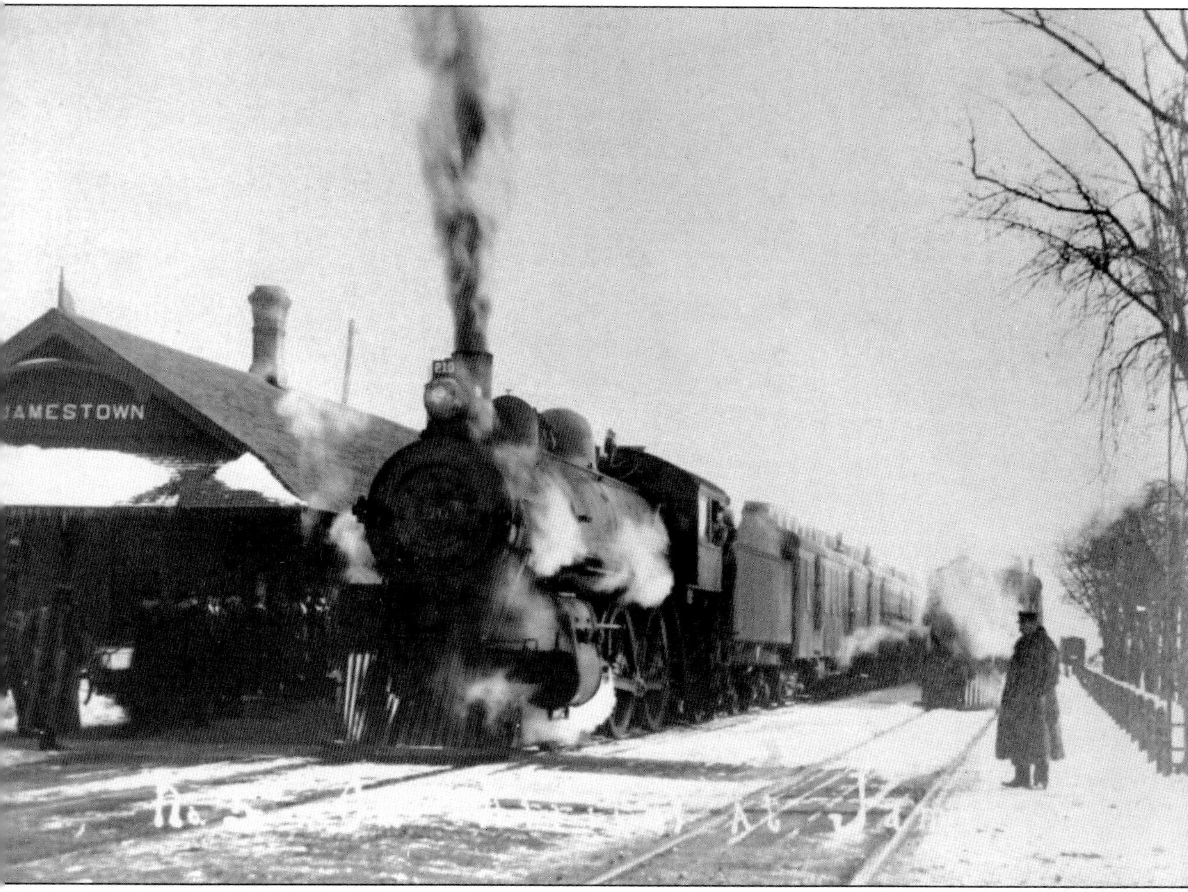

This popular image of early Jamestown is found on business walls all around town. It shows a train expelling steam and soot alongside the depot, which was built by the Northern Pacific Railroad. Even the deep cold of a North Dakota winter could not stop the rush of progress into this region of the country. (Photograph courtesy of the Stutsman County Memorial Museum.)

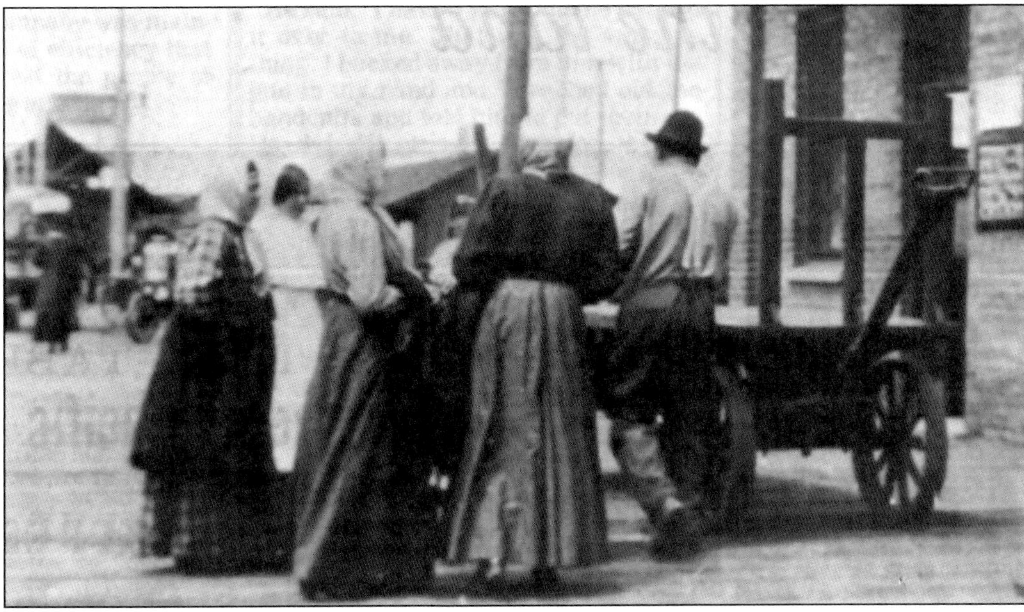

Immigrants gather near the railroad line in Jamestown early in the last century. The flush of immigrants from such lands as Germany, Sweden, Norway, Russia, and Poland helped to populate the area surrounding Jamestown and further advanced the agrarian culture. (Photograph courtesy of the Stutsman County Memorial Museum.)

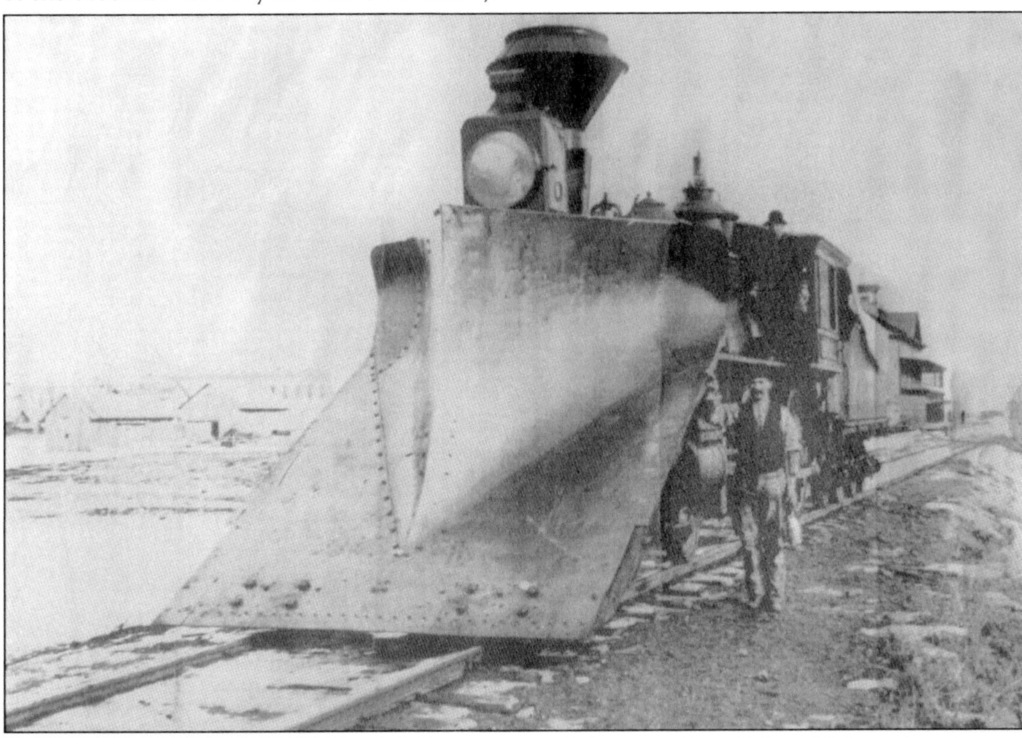

The Northern Pacific Railroad used different types of plows on the rail line. This wedge plow was likely used during the 1880s or 1890s for lighter snow accumulations. Rotary plows were used for heavier snow. (Photograph courtesy of Dave Robertson.)

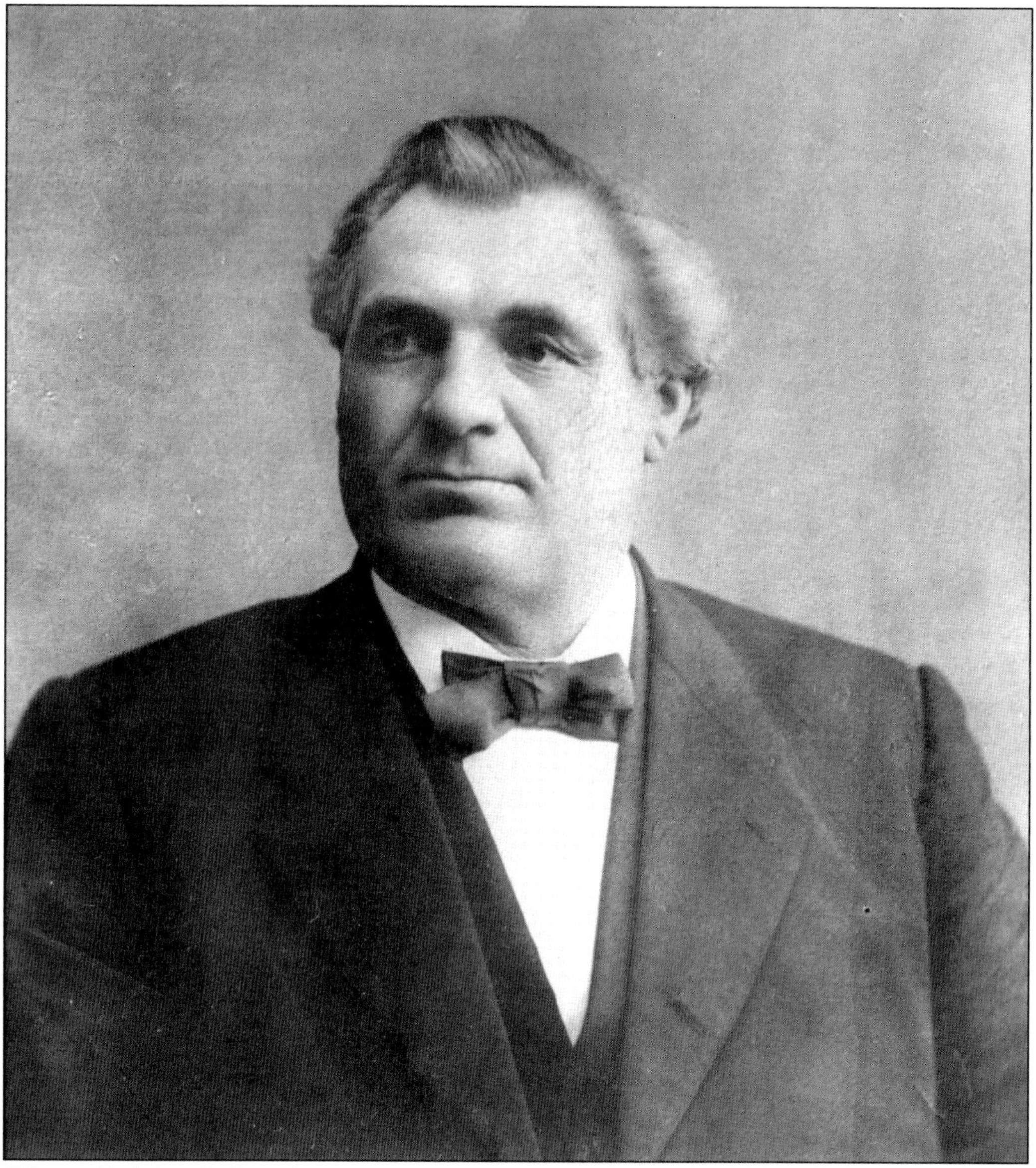

Often called the "Father of Jamestown," Anton Klaus was a truly dynamic entrepreneur. Born in Prussia in 1829, Klaus came to America at the age of 20 and settled in Green Bay, Wisconsin, where he amassed a fortune through the sale of lumber and shingles. By 1870, he was known as the Shingle King of the World. The Panic of 1873 wiped him out, however, and by 1878 he moved to Jamestown. There, Klaus reestablished himself, investing, selling land, and building a general store, hotels, a flour mill, homes, a skating rink, and a brick factory. He donated the land for the original county courthouse along with 15 acres that became known as Klaus Park. His Gladstone Hotel was a major centerpiece of the town. The much-beloved Klaus died of a heart attack in 1897. (Photograph courtesy of the Stutsman County Memorial Museum.)

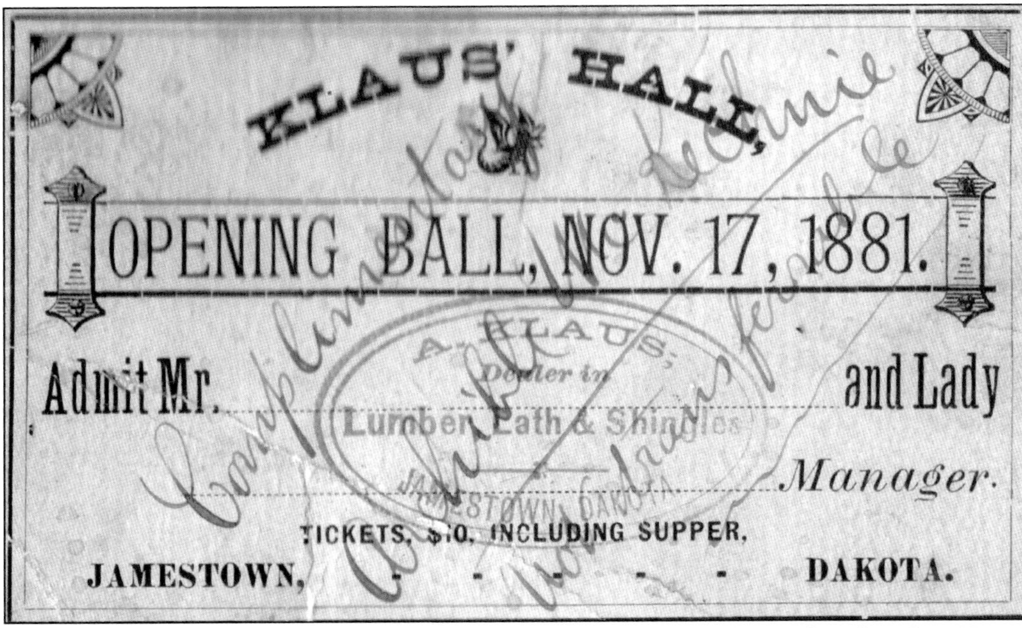
KLAUS' HALL,

OPENING BALL, NOV. 17, 1881.

Admit Mr. .... and Lady

A. KLAUS, Dealer in Lumber, Lath & Shingles, JAMESTOWN, DAKOTA.

.... Manager.

TICKETS, $10, INCLUDING SUPPER,

JAMESTOWN, - - - - - - DAKOTA.

This ticket for two announces an opening ball in Klaus Hall, likely located in the Klaus House. The ball included what was probably a festive supper, all for just $10. (Image courtesy of the Stutsman County Memorial Museum.)

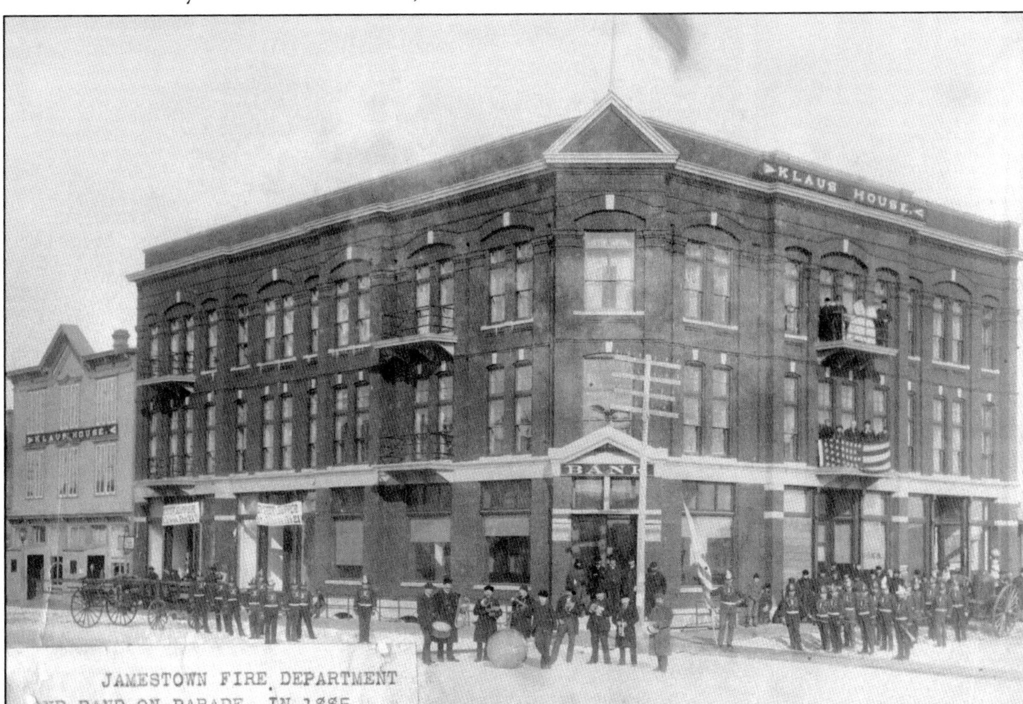

The Jamestown Fire Department, set up just outside the Klaus House, prepares for a parade in this 1885 photograph. The department played a major part in protecting and entertaining the community during the early days of Jamestown. (Photograph courtesy of the Stutsman County Memorial Museum.)

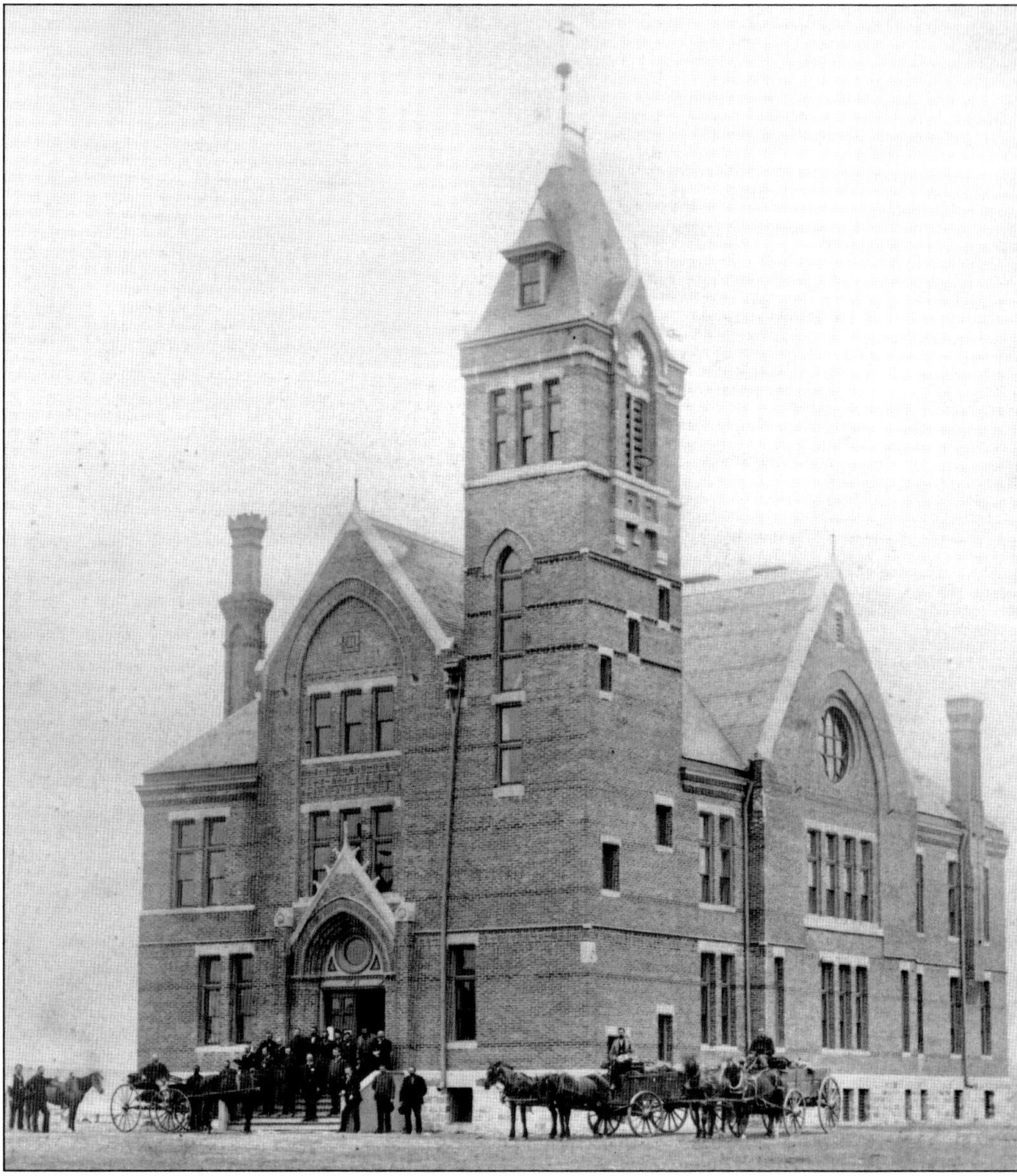

A handful of Jamestown's early residents and businessmen pose on the steps of the Stutsman County Courthouse in 1883, the year this handsome building was built. The courthouse served the residents of the county for nearly 100 years. In 1982, a new structure was constructed adjacent to the majestic original and has been serving residents ever since. (Photograph courtesy of the Stutsman County Memorial Museum.)

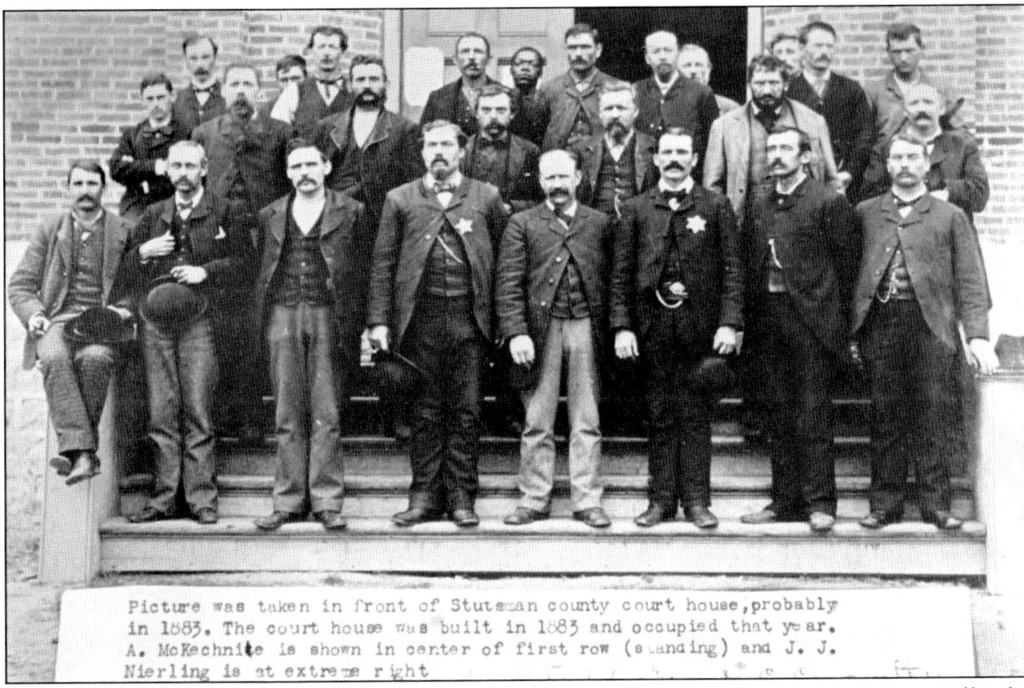

This 1883 photograph may be a companion to the one on the opposite page. Architecturally, the courthouse exemplifies Gothic Revival. It has been named a state historic site, is listed in the National Register of Historic Places, and is the oldest surviving courthouse in North Dakota. (Photograph courtesy of the Stutsman County Memorial Museum.)

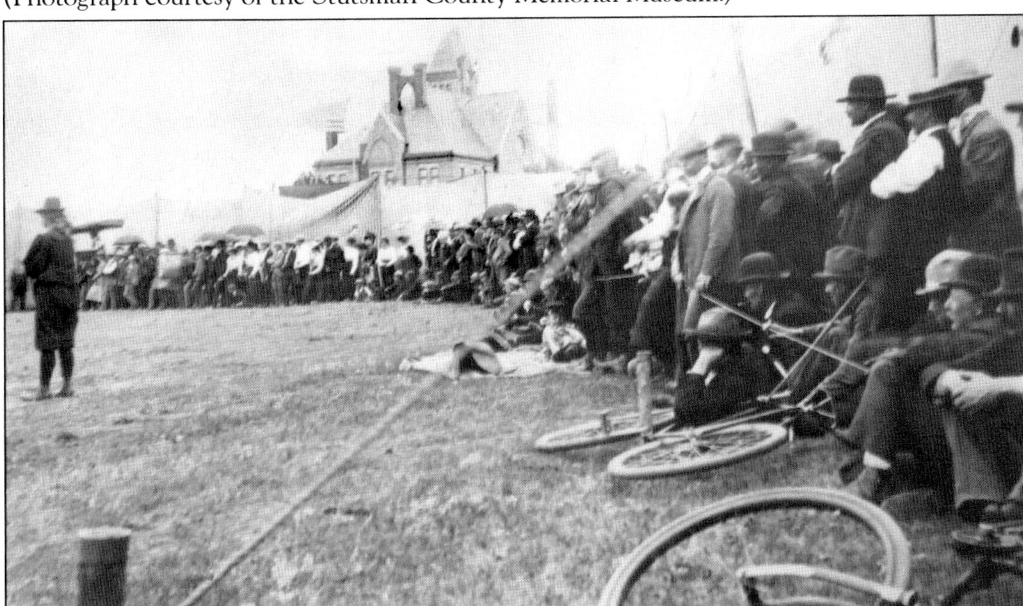

Fans encircle a ball field in Jamestown sometime prior to 1900. Ballgames drew enthusiasts from all walks of life, and the American passion for the game had grown immensely ever since the first competitive game on the Elysian Fields of Hoboken, New Jersey, in 1846. Note the Stutsman County Courthouse in the background. (Photograph courtesy of the Stutsman County Memorial Museum.)

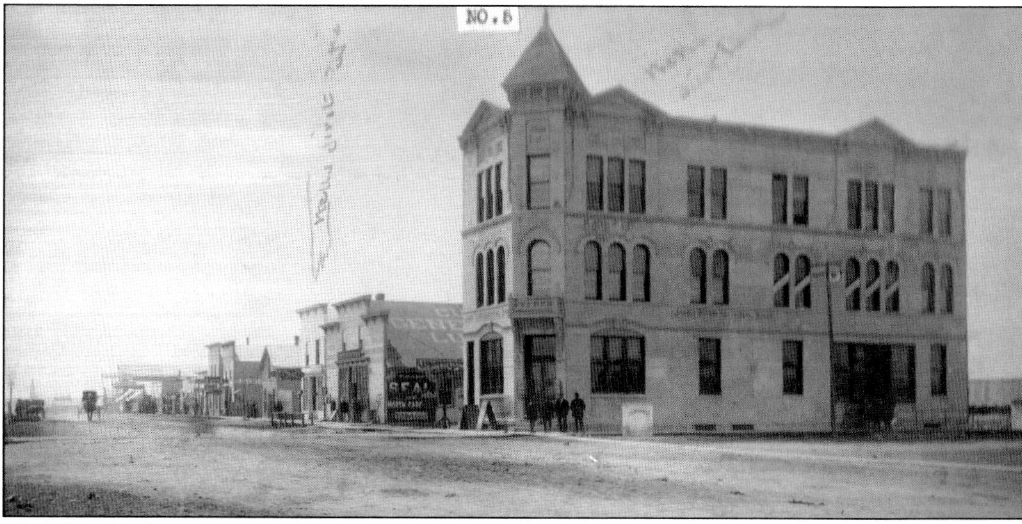

With bricks from Anton Klaus's brick factory, the buildings of Jamestown's downtown district were transformed from all-wood stores and structures to ones of brick and mortar. Note in this photograph the mix of both wood and brick structures. This building was the James River National Bank and is currently utilized by Babb's Coffee House. (Photograph courtesy of the Stutsman County Memorial Museum.)

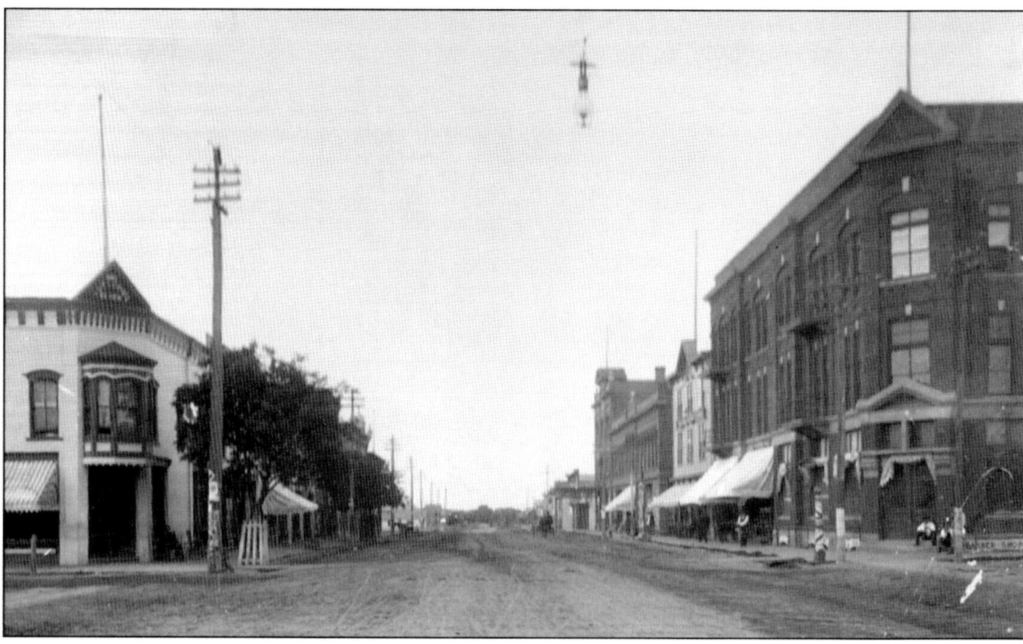

This early photograph, oriented to the north, shows the Capital Hotel on the left and the Gladstone Hotel on the right. Both hotels, located on First Avenue North, ultimately burned to the ground. (Photograph courtesy of the Stutsman County Memorial Museum.)

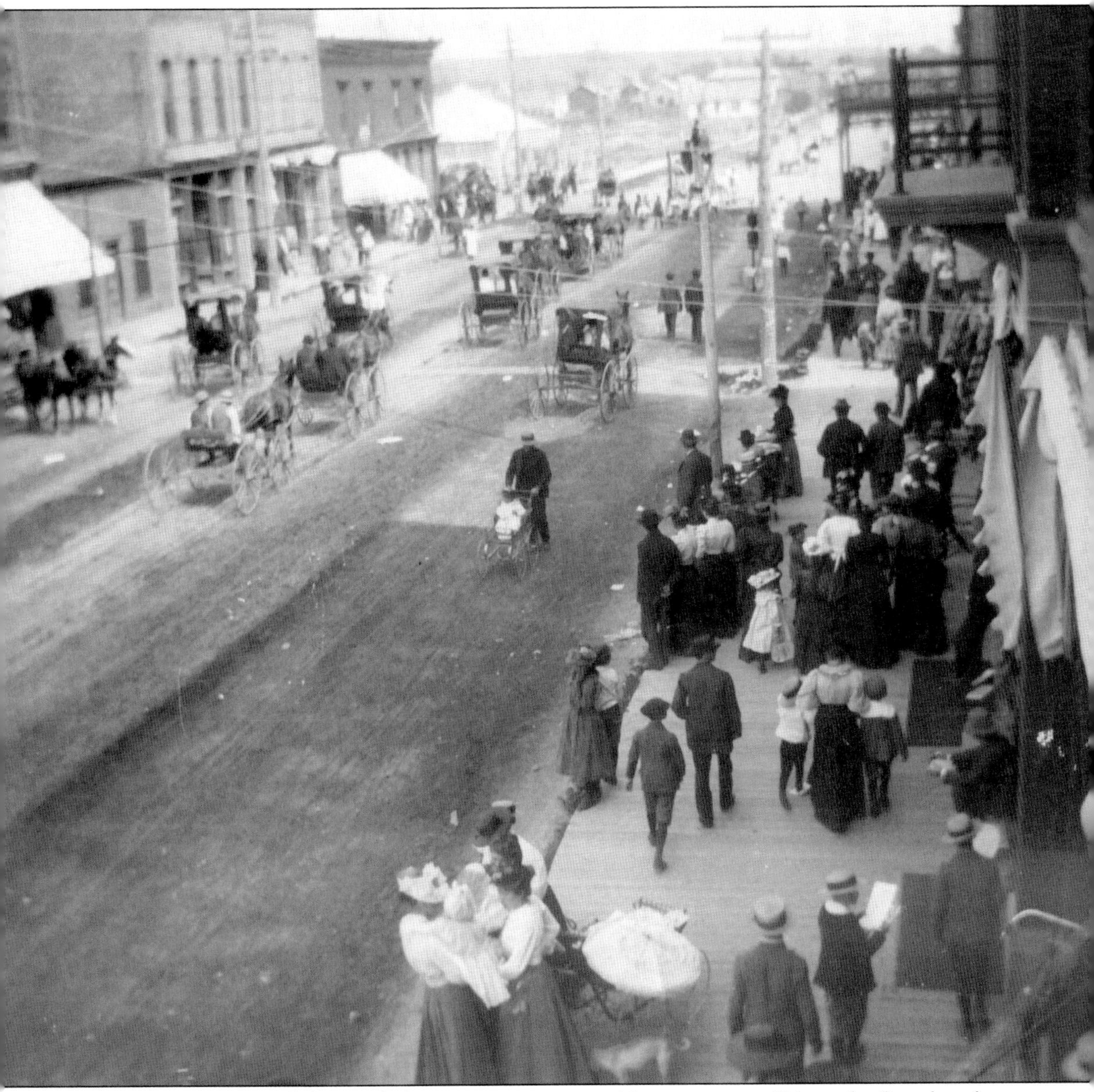

Where are the automobiles? Early Jamestown ran on real horsepower well into the first decade of the 20th century. (Photograph courtesy of the Stutsman County Memorial Museum.)

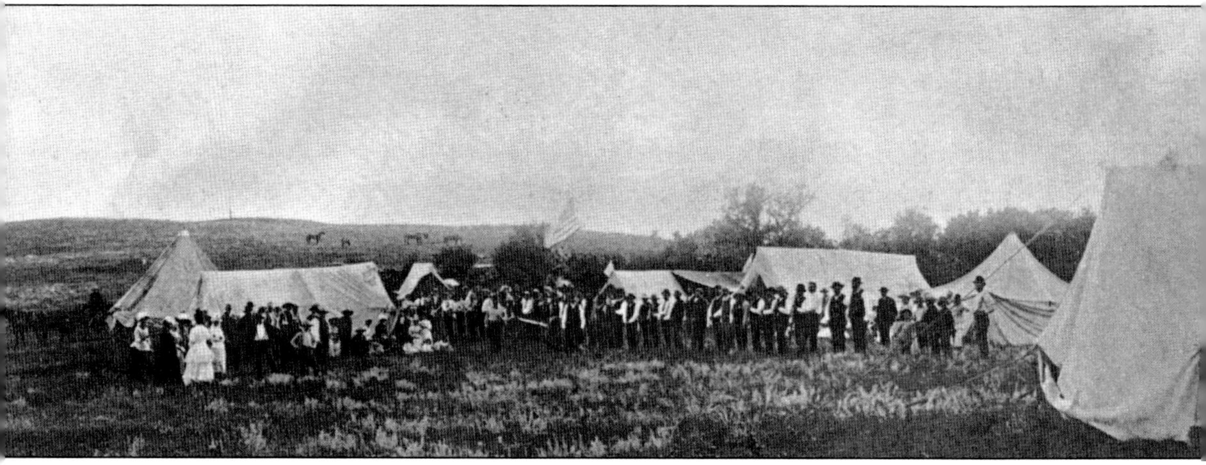

Civil War veterans and their families gather at Spiritwood Lake on July 4, 1880. This deep, naturally occurring lake has long been a recreational destination for county residents. Its name is tied to legend. According to one account, two young American Indians were in love. They both drowned in the lake, but their spirits continue to occupy the setting. (Photograph courtesy of the Stutsman County Memorial Museum.)

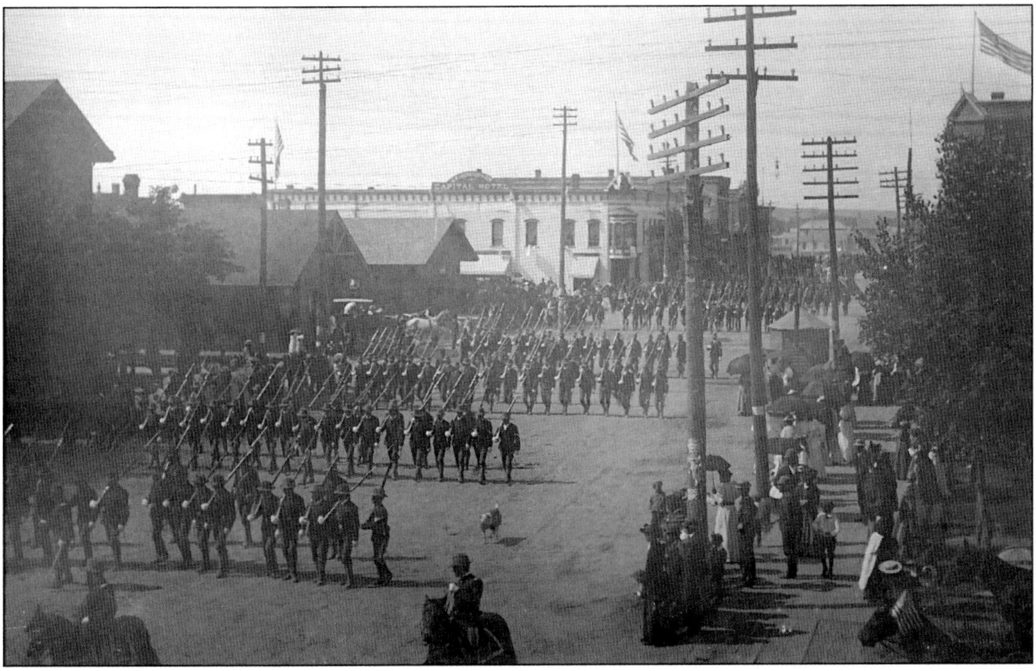

This northward-looking photograph was taken in 1899 from the location of the current Buffalo City Rotisserie Grill. While none of the people in the parade can be identified, it is known that the dog in the picture is Chino, a canine who traveled from the Philippines with the North Dakota National Guard and was noted by the *Jamestown Alert* for attacking several local dogs. (Photograph courtesy of Lenard Cave.)

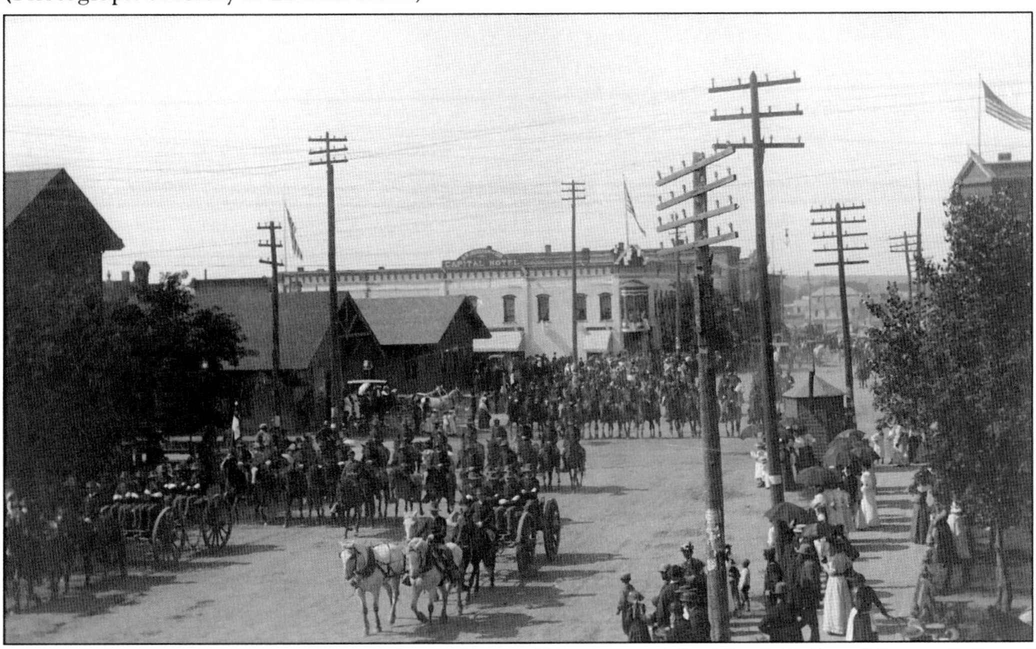

This photograph of the 1899 parade shows the artillery units of the North Dakota National Guard on display. Six men ride on the caissons drawn by a team of four horses traveling down what is now the principal street in Jamestown. (Photograph courtesy of Lenard Cave.)

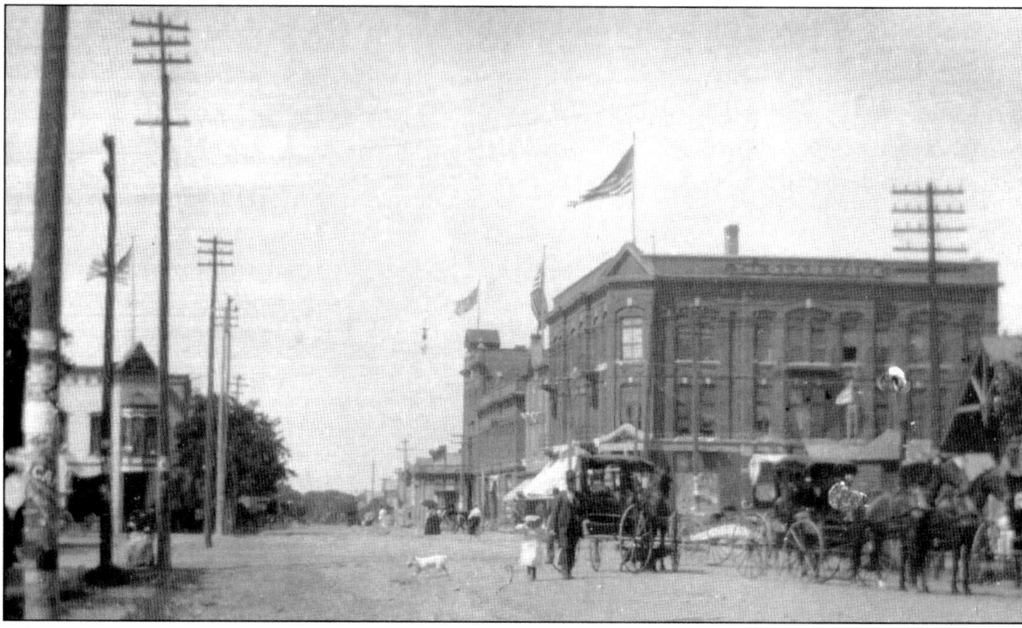

The Capital Hotel (left) and the Gladstone Hotel (right) offered some of the best lodging operations in Jamestown during their era. This photograph from the late 1800s shows a number of buggies on the street as local residents go about their business. (Photograph courtesy of the Stutsman County Memorial Museum.)

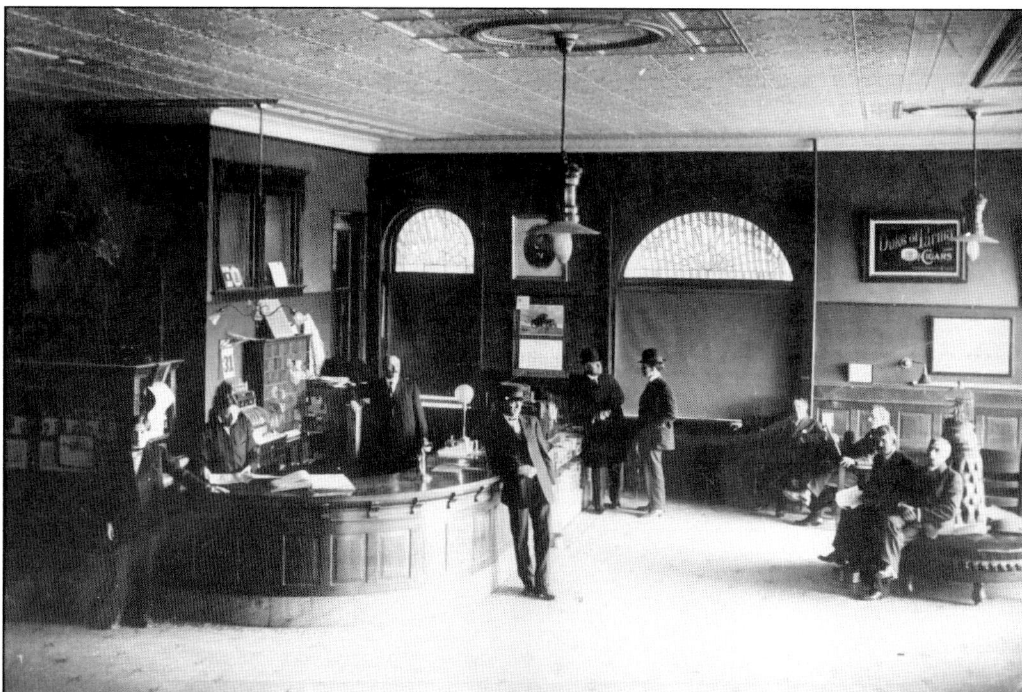

This photograph from the early 1900s shows the Gladstone Hotel lobby. The hotel offered the highest-quality lodging in Jamestown, and the lobby was also a gathering place for community leaders. (Photograph courtesy of Dave Robertson.)

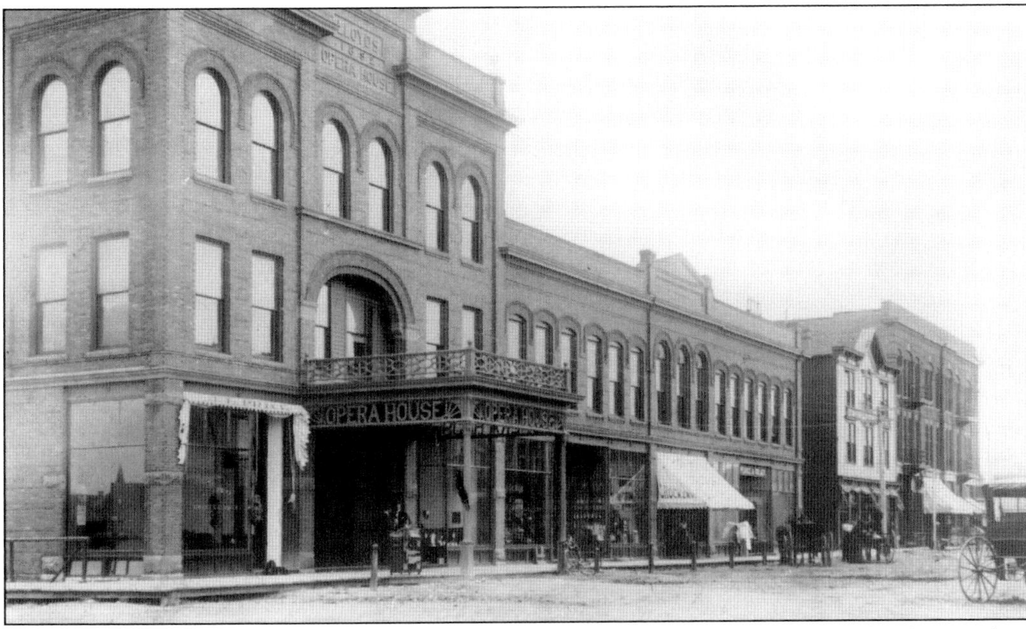

Lloyd's Opera House, built by William Lloyd, was dedicated February 19, 1893. The theater drew such luminaries as comedian W.C. Fields, actress Mary Pickford, composer John Phillip Sousa, and actor and composer George M. Cohan. The buildings to its right included Pearce & Orlady and the Gladstone Hotel. Note the store next door with a display of crockery that can be seen through the window. (Photograph courtesy of the Stutsman County Memorial Museum.)

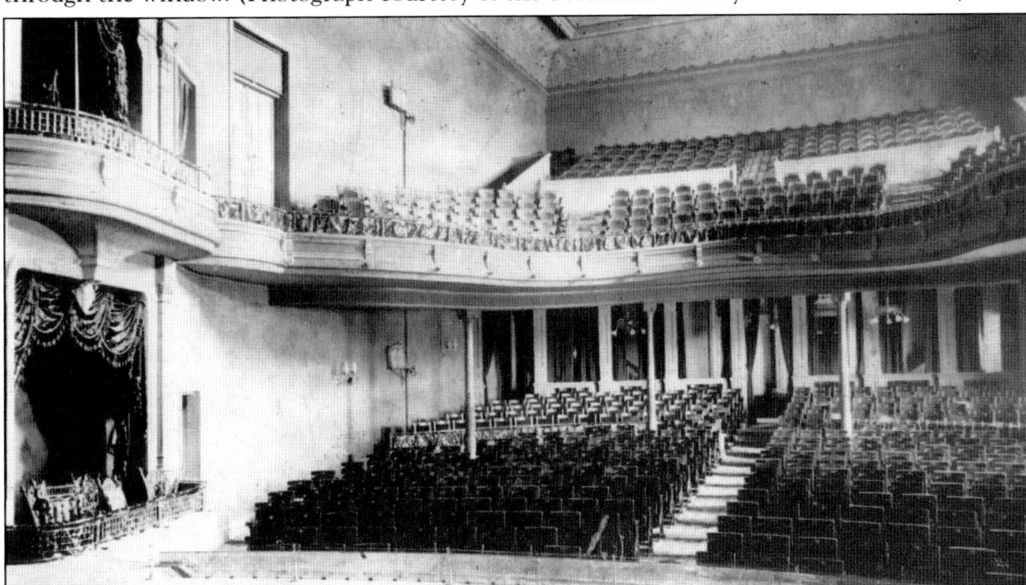

Lloyd's Opera House was the premier entertainment venue in Jamestown. Its interior setting was absolutely gorgeous, with huge curtains and draperies, hand-painted backdrops, two private boxes for theatergoers, and an orchestra pit, which was undoubtedly used over and over. The opera house eventually became the Grand Theater, but was sadly closed in 1975 and demolished as part of that decade's extremely controversial urban-renewal movement. (Photograph courtesy of the Stutsman County Memorial Museum.)

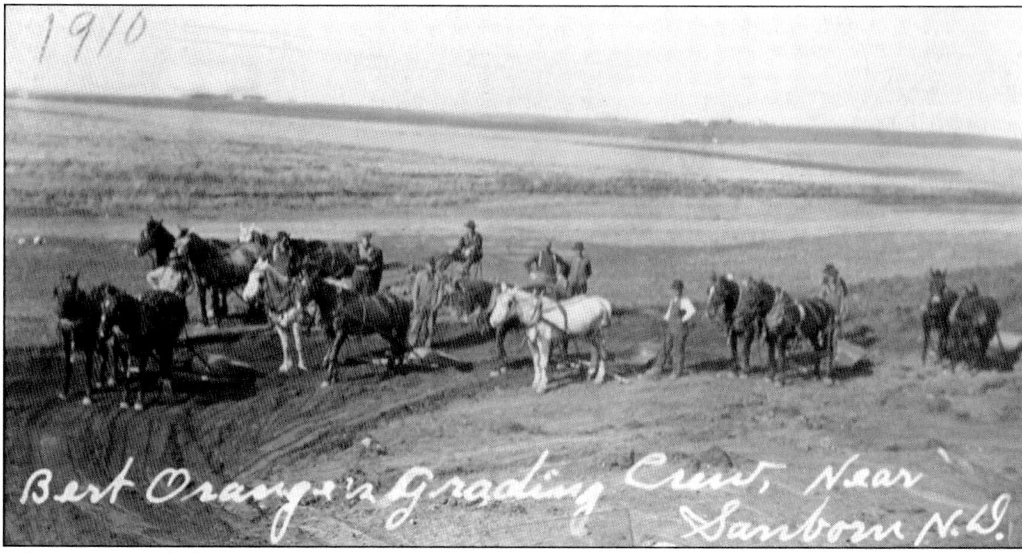

This photograph depicts a grading crew supervised by Bert Orange building a road near Sanborn in 1910. (Photograph courtesy of the Stutsman County Memorial Museum.)

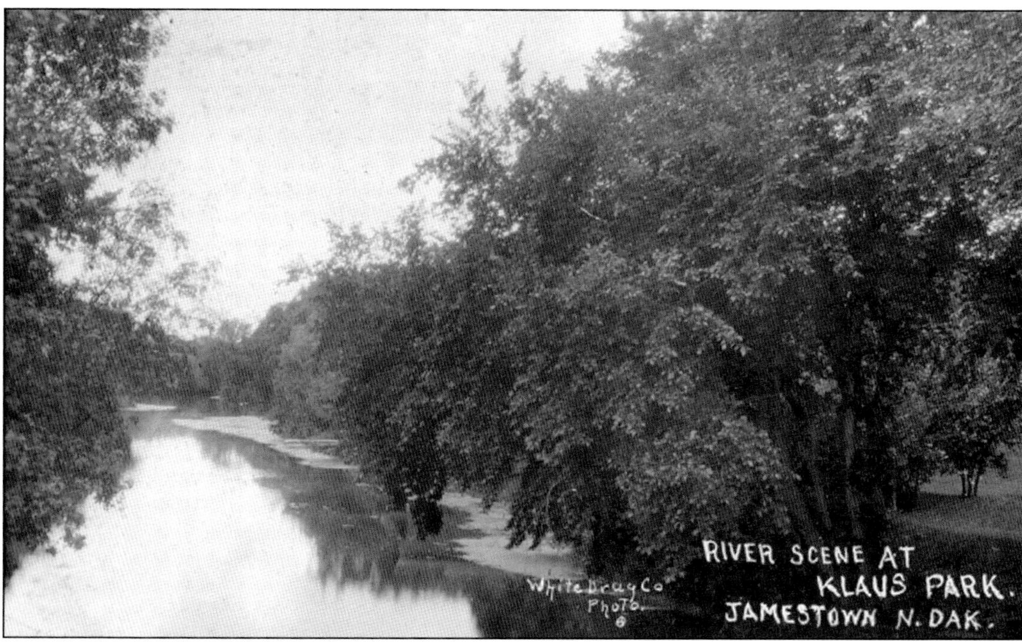

The natural artery of Jamestown is the James River, considered by some to be the longest river in the country that cannot be navigated by commercial boats. Anton Klaus and five associates tried unsuccessfully to set up commercial shipping on the river, and his James River Navigation Company lasted just one season. Apparently, the group of investors broke a rare and expensive bottle of wine over the bow of their steamer, the *Nettie Baldwin*, on May 4, 1880. (Photograph courtesy of the Stutsman County Memorial Museum.)

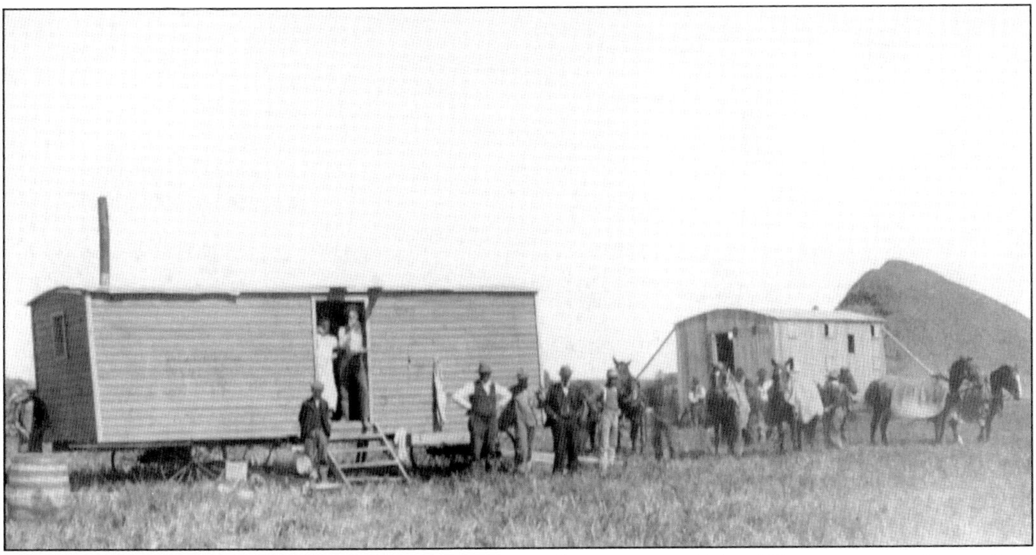

This early photograph shows how labor-intensive farming could be. The men stand outside a cook car, brought to the site during the threshing effort in the fall. (Photograph courtesy of the Stutsman County Memorial Museum.)

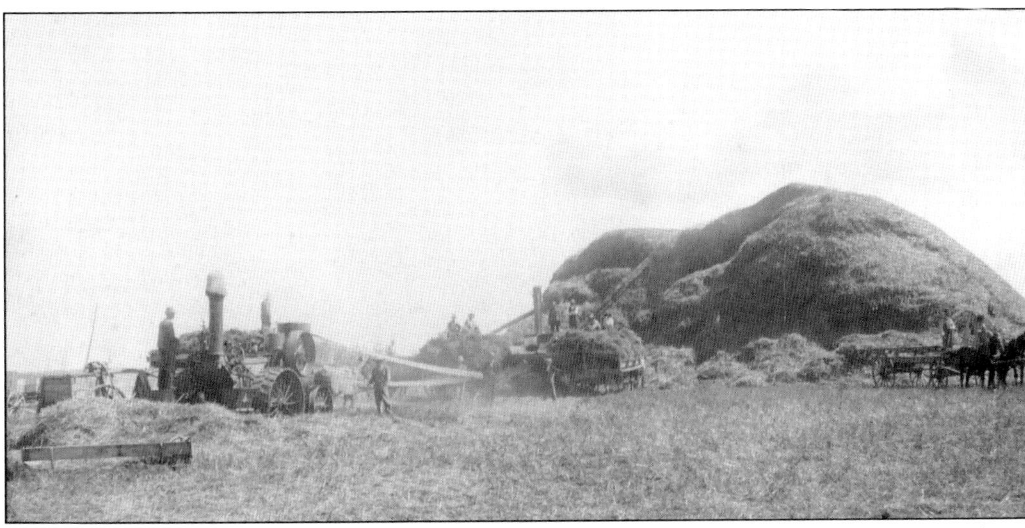

"Prairie gold" (the succulent grasses of the Plains) drew pioneers to the region from many places, including Europe and the steppes of Eurasia. Steam-powered machinery helped alter the native plains into croplands. Note the long belts used in the threshing operation. (Photograph courtesy of the Stutsman County Memorial Museum.)

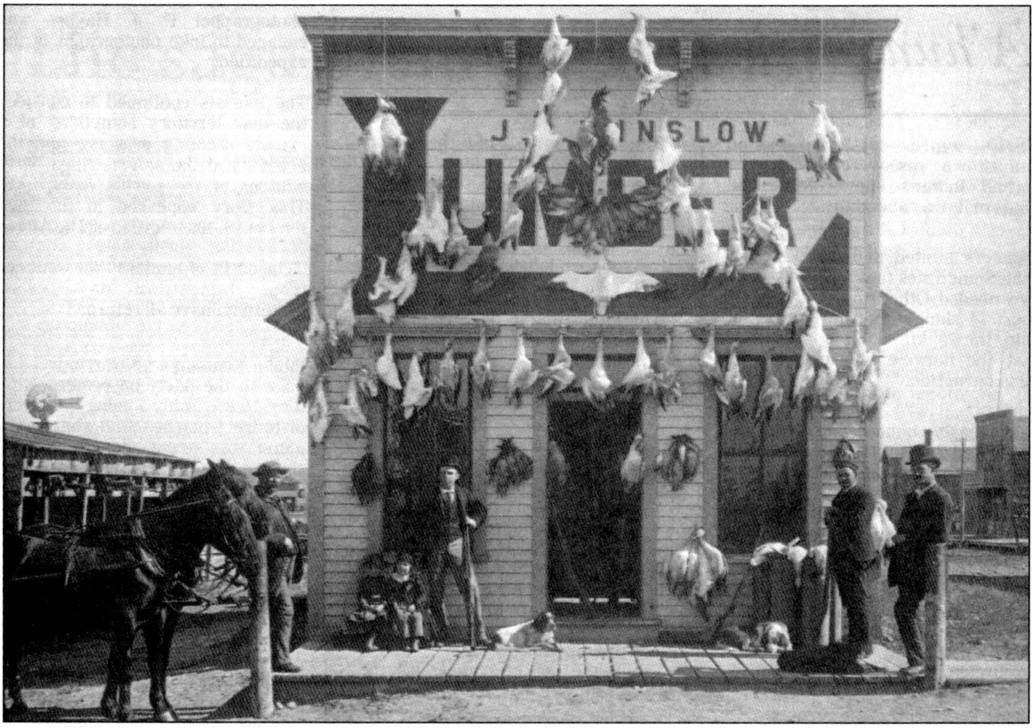

There is conflicting information about this image, which can be found in both the Stutsman County Memorial Museum and the State Historical Society's North Dakota Archives in Bismarck. It may date to the 1870s, and possibly shows *Jamestown Alert* editor W.R. Kellogg standing in front of his trophies: ducks, snow geese, and brant geese. According to one source, the photograph was taken near Jamestown, possibly in Cleveland or Windsor, by Charles Judd. The J.R. Winslow Lumber Building is in the background. (Photograph courtesy of the Stutsman County Memorial Museum.)

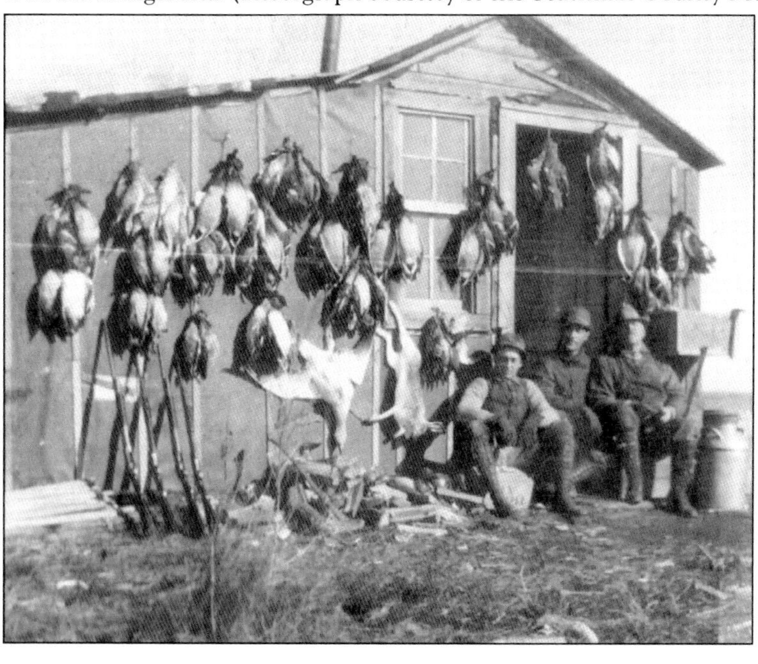

Here is another early photograph of a pretty respectable bounty of waterfowl. North Dakota has sometimes been called the "duck factory of the nation" because of the historically prodigious number of fowl produced on its potholes each spring. (Photograph courtesy of the Stutsman County Memorial Museum.)

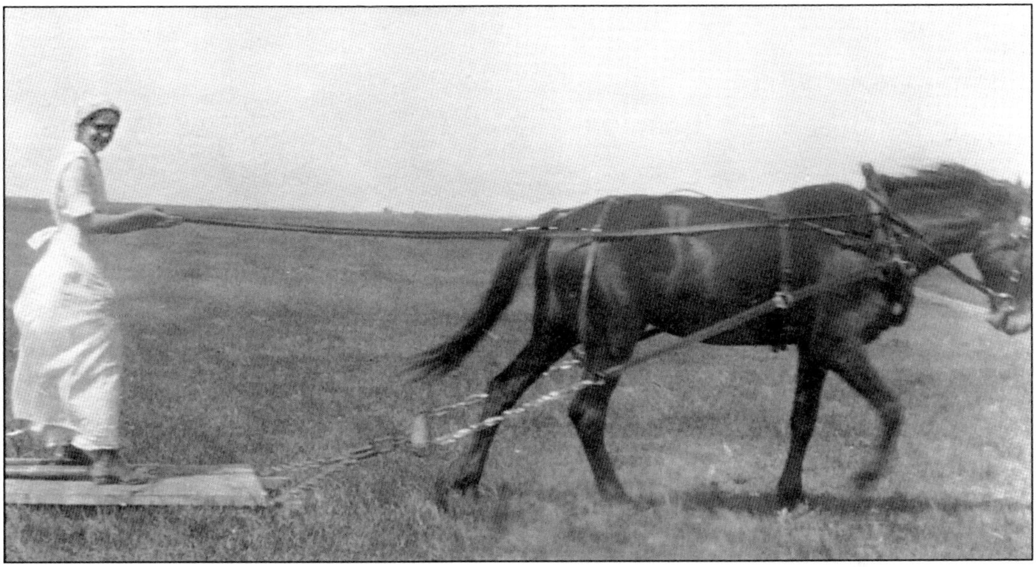

The original definition of horsepower is depicted in this early photograph. The woman appears to be enjoying herself, while the horse may be a little less than amused. (Photograph courtesy of the Stutsman County Memorial Museum.)

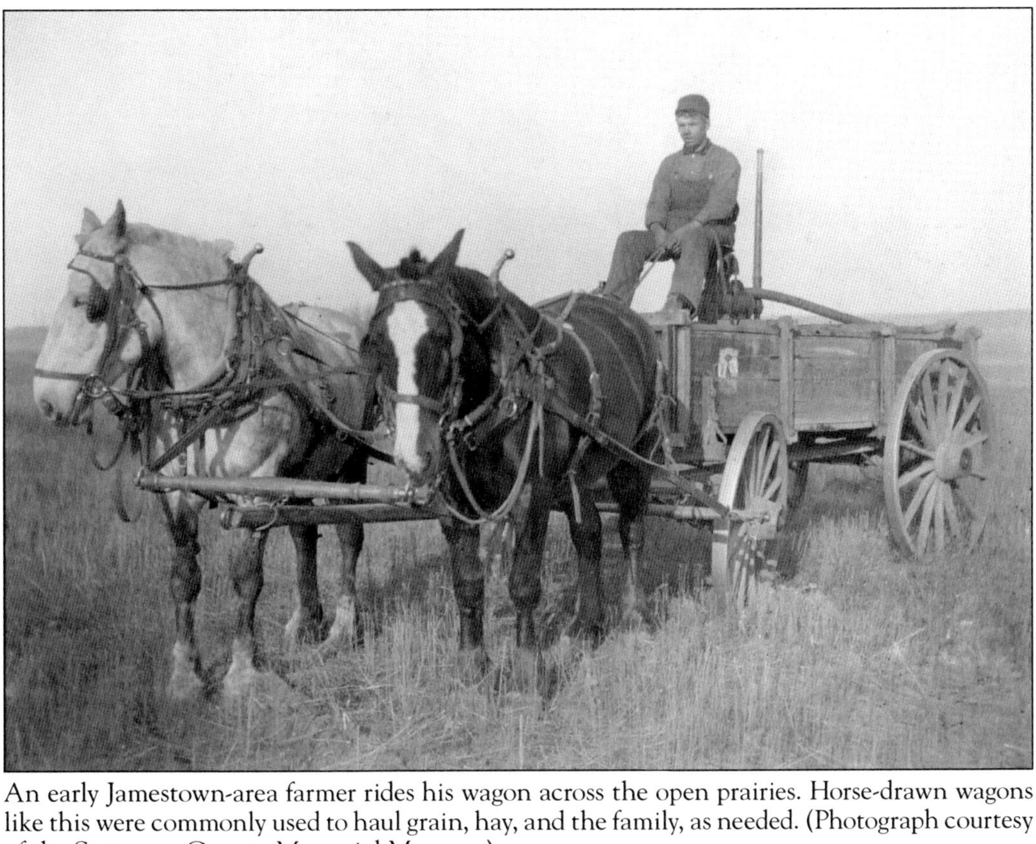

An early Jamestown-area farmer rides his wagon across the open prairies. Horse-drawn wagons like this were commonly used to haul grain, hay, and the family, as needed. (Photograph courtesy of the Stutsman County Memorial Museum.)

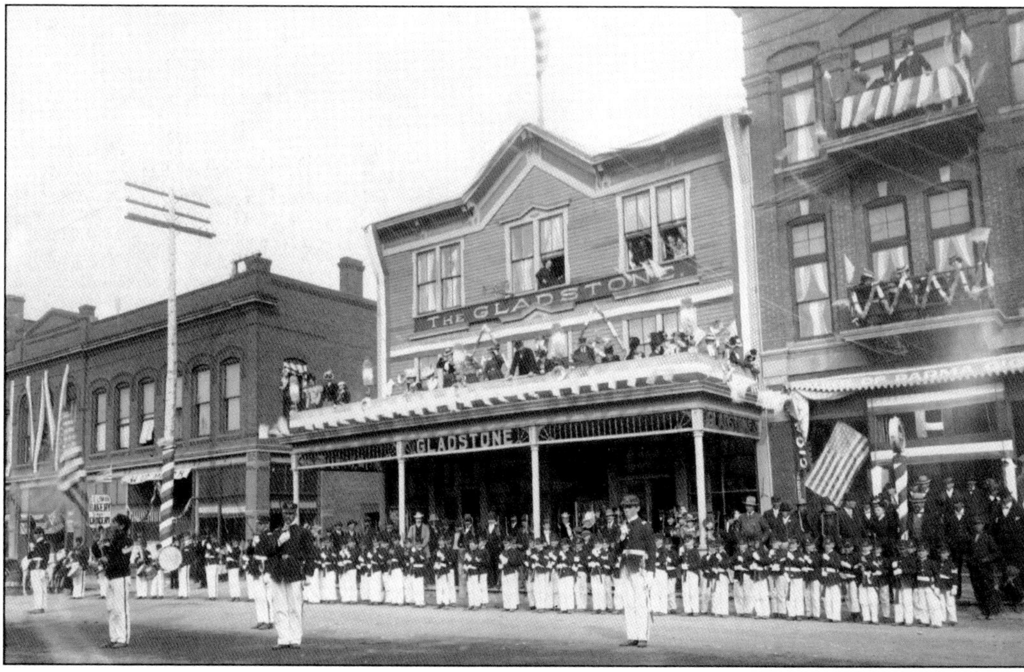

The Gladstone Hotel was another of Anton Klaus's early ventures, built adjacent to his Klaus House. This c. 1885 photograph shows a band entertaining the townsfolk with their lively brass and the vivid raising of the colors. (Photograph courtesy of the Stutsman County Memorial Museum.)

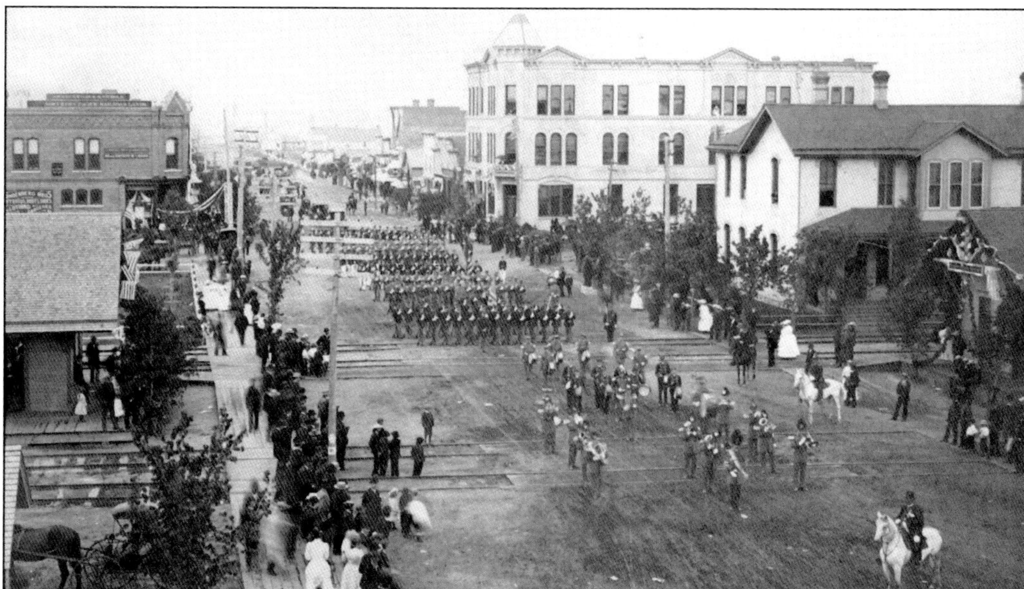

This photograph shows a long view of an early parade on Jamestown's main street. Note the boardwalks where parade viewers stand to view the procession. (Photograph courtesy of the Stutsman County Memorial Museum.)

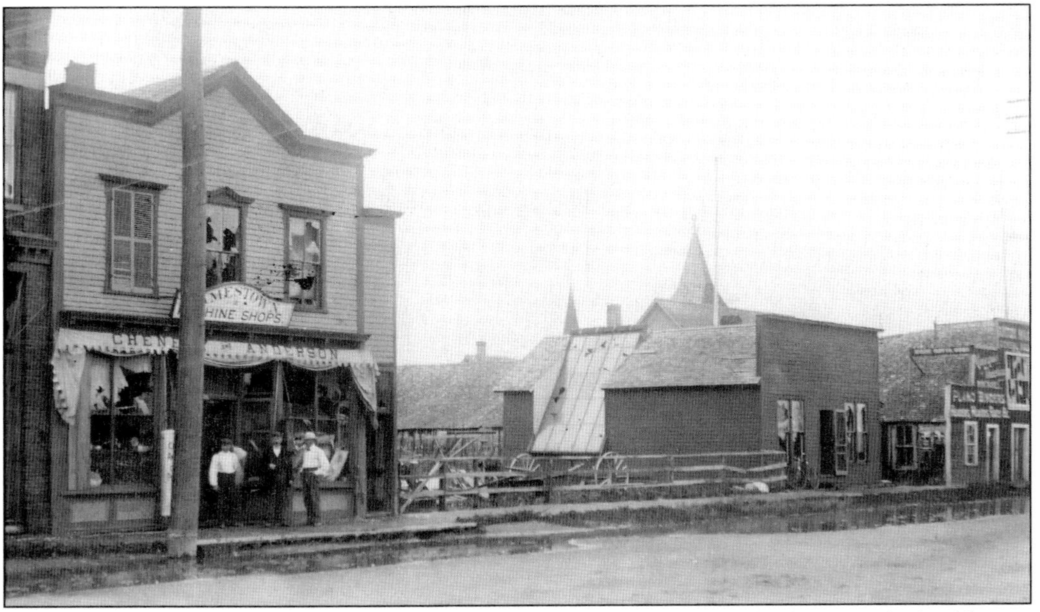

This photograph, taken around 1890, shows Jamestown possibly after a hailstorm. The building at the center was the town's photography studio and included a segment of glass roofing for lighting purposes. That segment, along with windows of neighboring buildings, appears to be broken, and the street appears to show some effects of flooding. (Photograph courtesy Bruce Berg.)

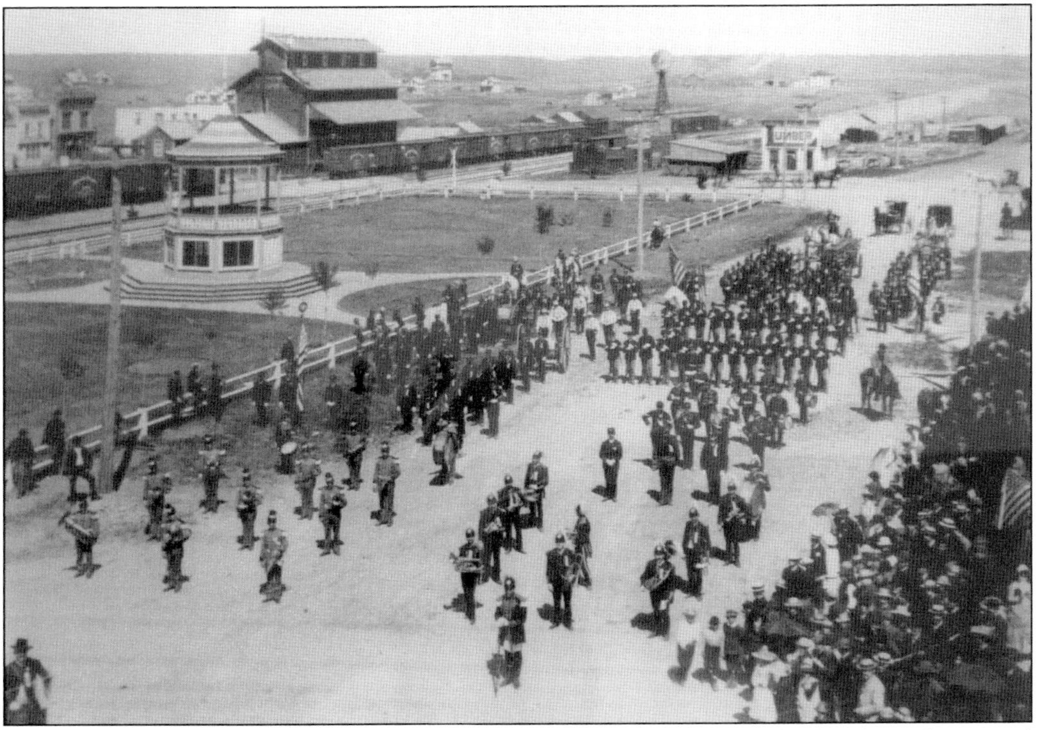

Here is yet another early Jamestown parade. This photograph was likely shot from the second or third floor of the James River National Bank building, with the parade moving from east to west. (Photograph courtesy of Dave Robertson.)

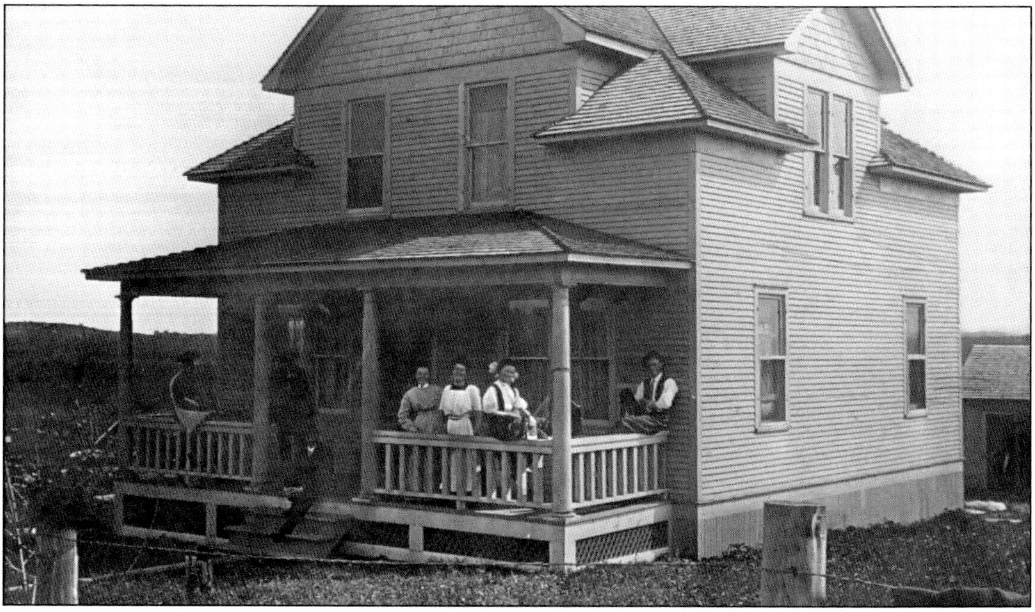

This is a good example of American Farmhouse–style architecture, which is really a blend of several other styles, including Greek Revival, Georgian, and Victorian, and is characterized by a practical approach to basic comfort and visually pleasing design. Its core elements include covered porches, white paint, and dormer windows. These strong homes were sturdy and meant to last, an important consideration for those living through the harsh seasons on the northern Great Plains. (Photograph courtesy of the Stutsman County Memorial Museum.)

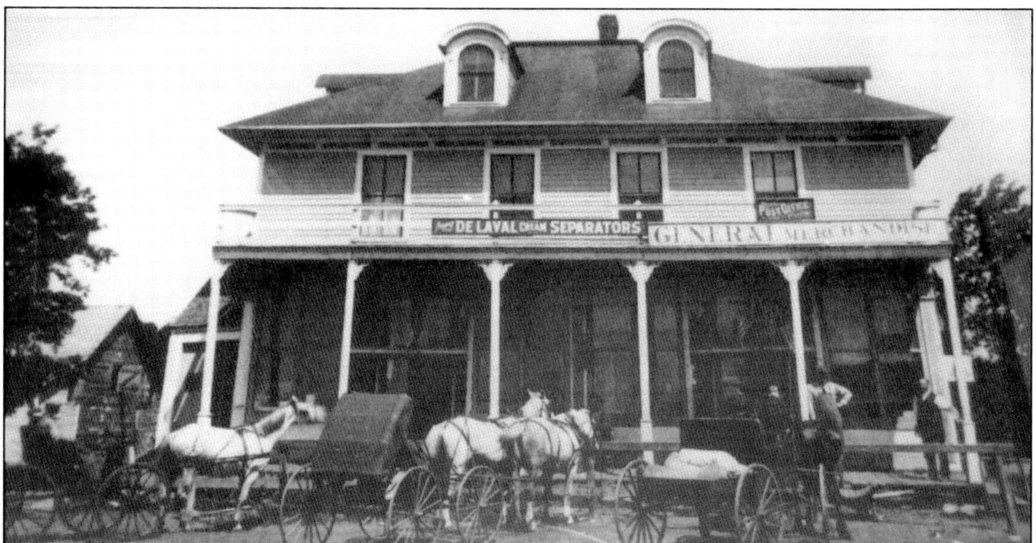

General stores, iconic of the Old West, were a staple in prairie towns all across the country during the frontier period. This store was located in Eldridge, just west of Jamestown. For decades, it served surrounding farm families, providing them with a wide selection of the products and equipment they needed to thrive on the plains. This particular store, which eventually closed, has since been restored and is now open for tours at Frontier Village on the south end of Jamestown. (Photograph courtesy of the Frontier Village Visitors Center.)

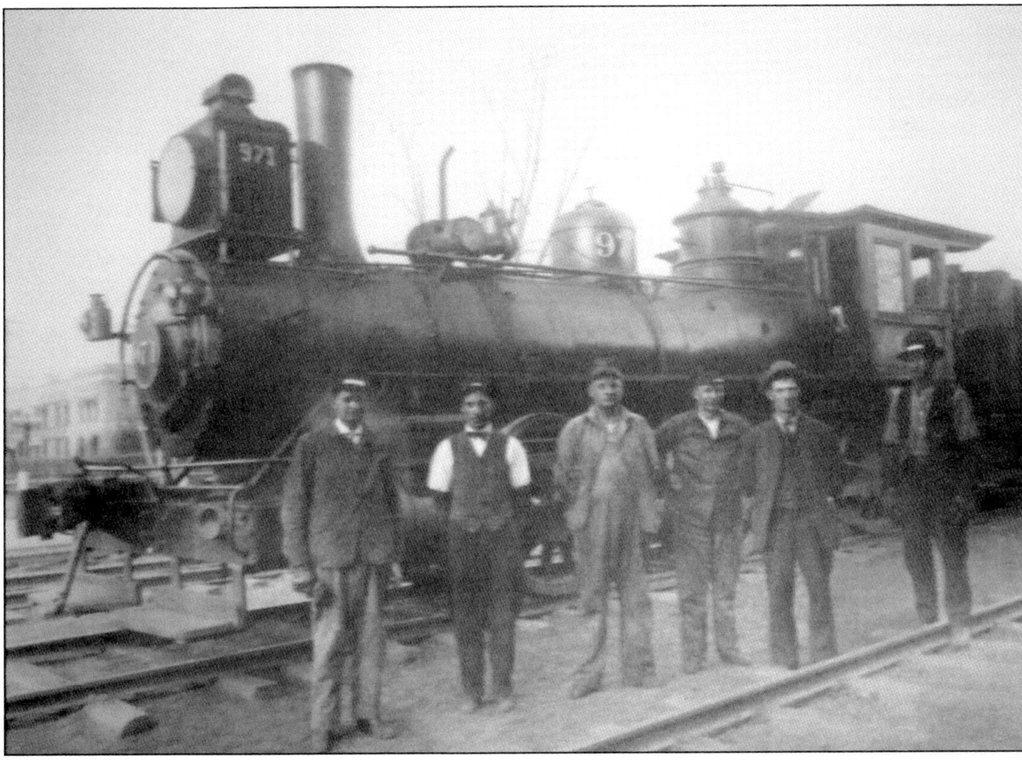

Pictured here is Northern Pacific steam locomotive No. 971. According to the Northern Pacific, this steam engine was built between 1881 and 1883 by a manufacturer identified as "Portland." There were 29 others built in its class, but none survive today. (Photograph courtesy of the Stutsman County Memorial Museum.)

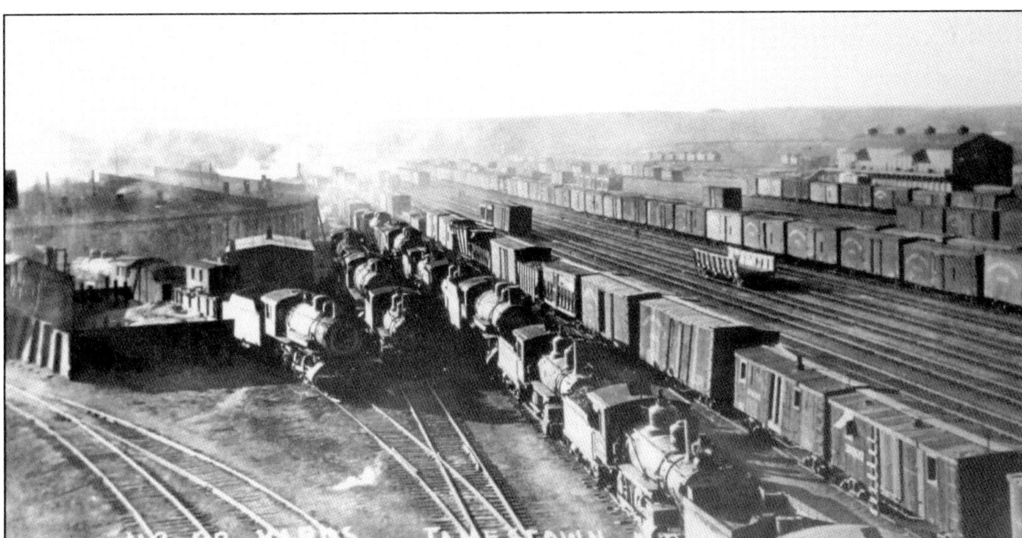

The Northern Pacific's railway yard is shown in this popular photograph of Jamestown. Note the string of steam locomotives at the center and the long lines of freight in the switching yard. (Photograph courtesy of the Stutsman County Memorial Museum.)

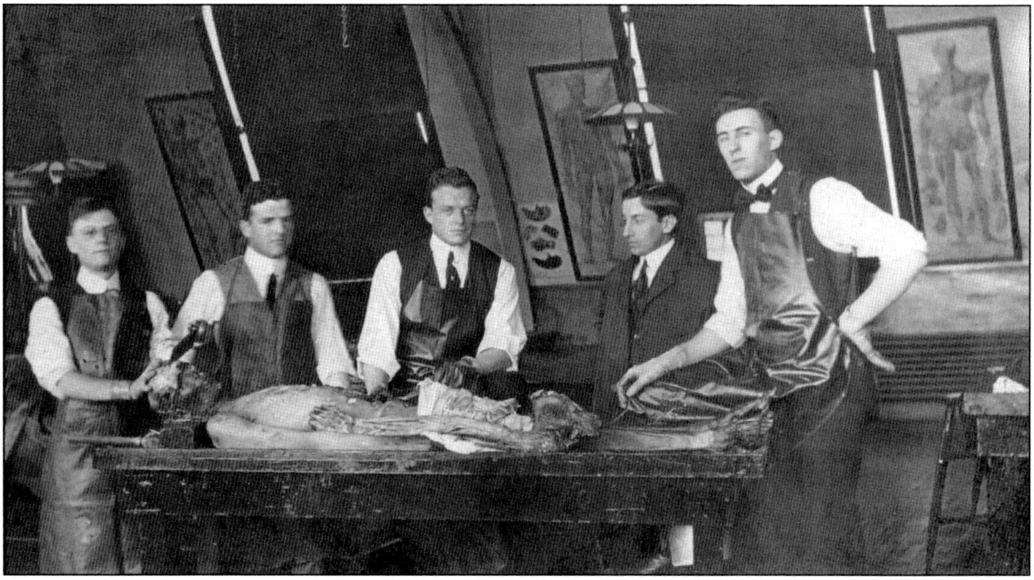

This undated photograph shows staff at the North Dakota State Hospital examining a cadaver. (Photograph courtesy of the Stutsman County Memorial Museum.)

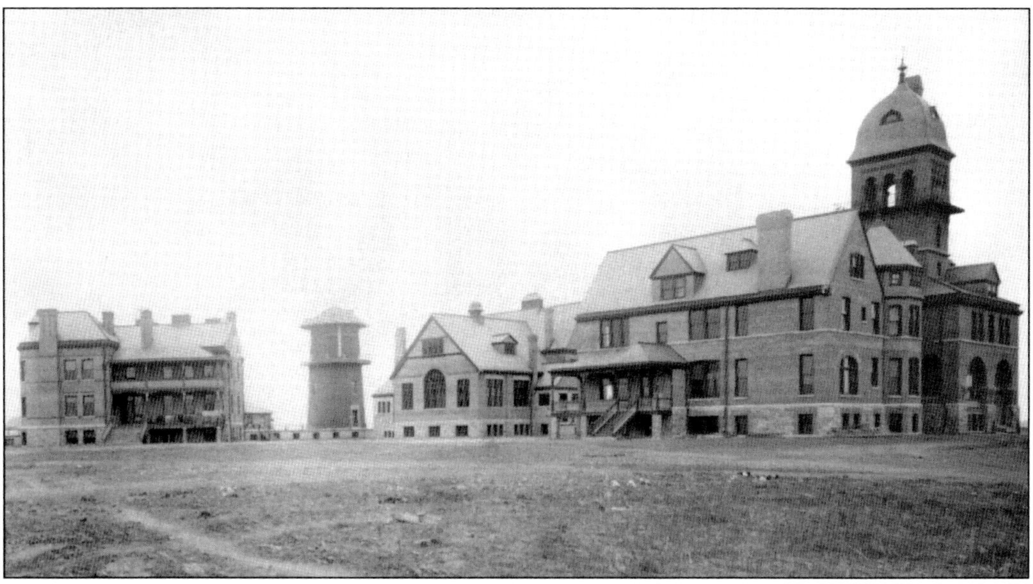

This 1885 photograph shows the State Hospital for the Insane, which was already a functioning facility with a campus and treatment center. The facility opened four years before North Dakota became a state and remains in Jamestown today, with many of its original structures still standing. (Photograph courtesy of the Stutsman County Memorial Museum.)

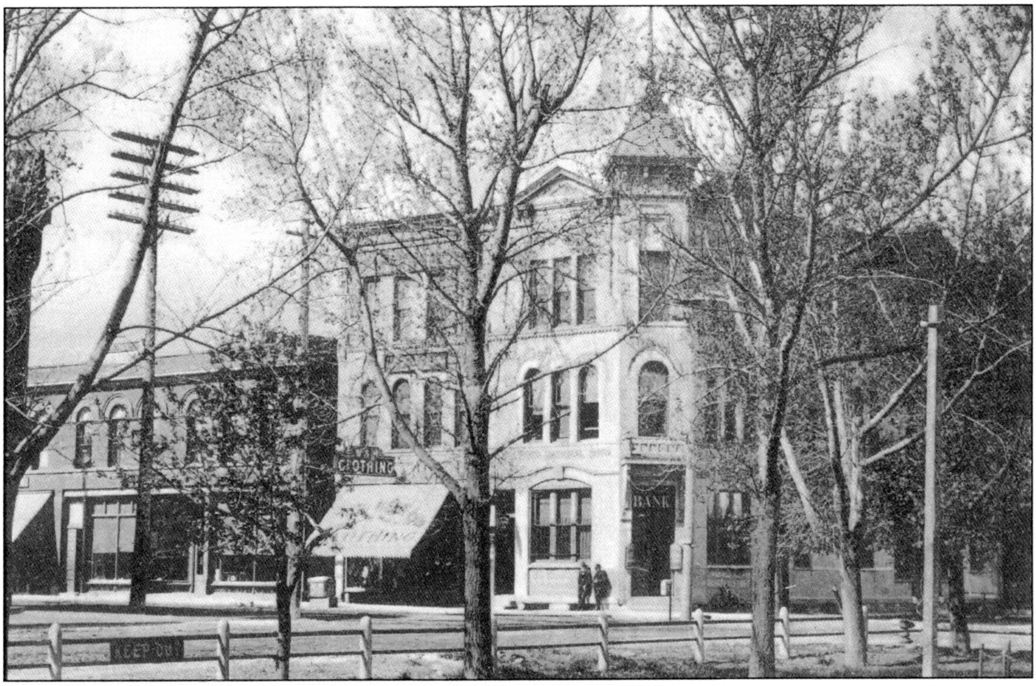

The James River National Bank was originally built in 1883 and continues to be a fixture in the community. The building is currently the home of Babb's Coffee House, with offices on the second floor. The third floor, visible in this picture, was demolished in the 1930s. (Photograph courtesy of Dave Robertson.)

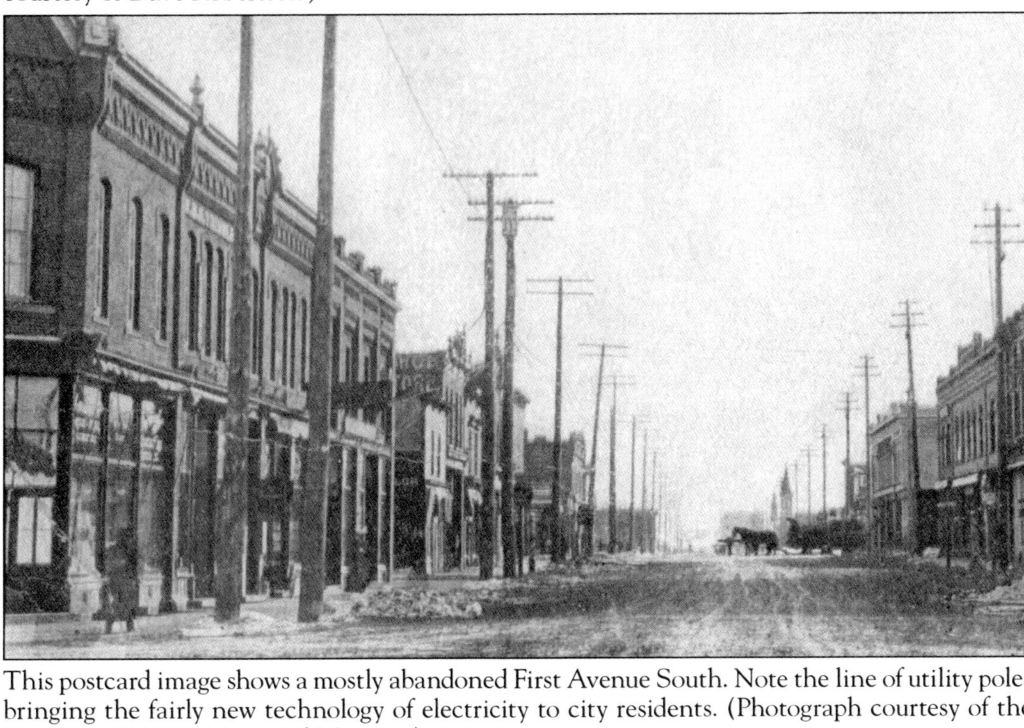

This postcard image shows a mostly abandoned First Avenue South. Note the line of utility poles bringing the fairly new technology of electricity to city residents. (Photograph courtesy of the Stutsman County Memorial Museum.)

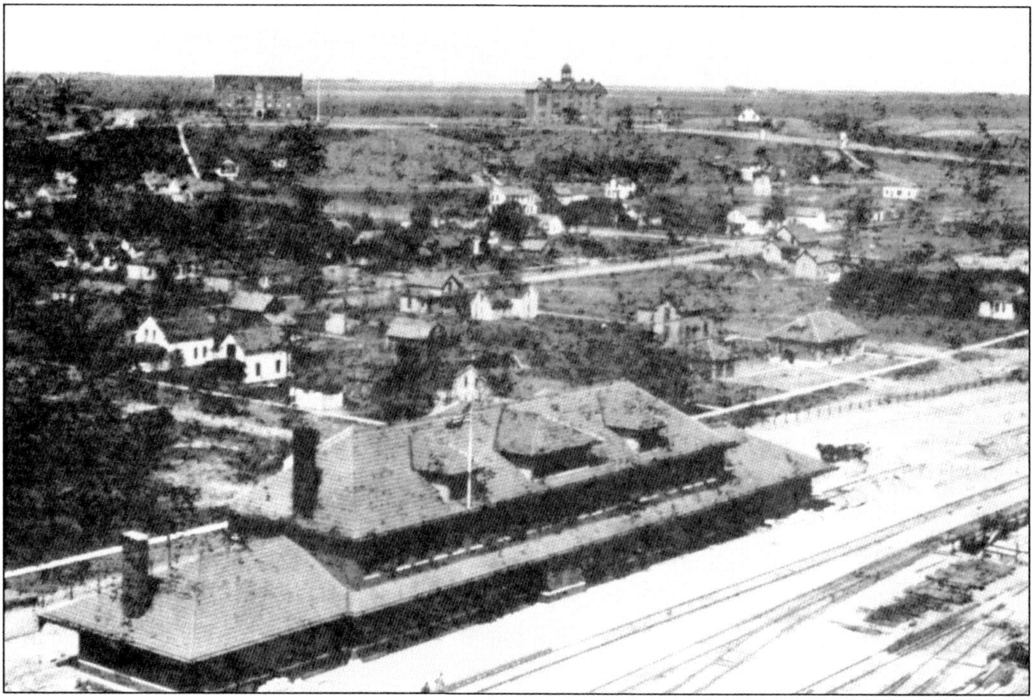

This northeastward-looking photograph, taken by Gilbert R. Horton, shows the new, nearly completed Northern Pacific Depot in 1916. Jamestown College can be seen on the bluff. (Photograph courtesy of the Stutsman County Memorial Museum.)

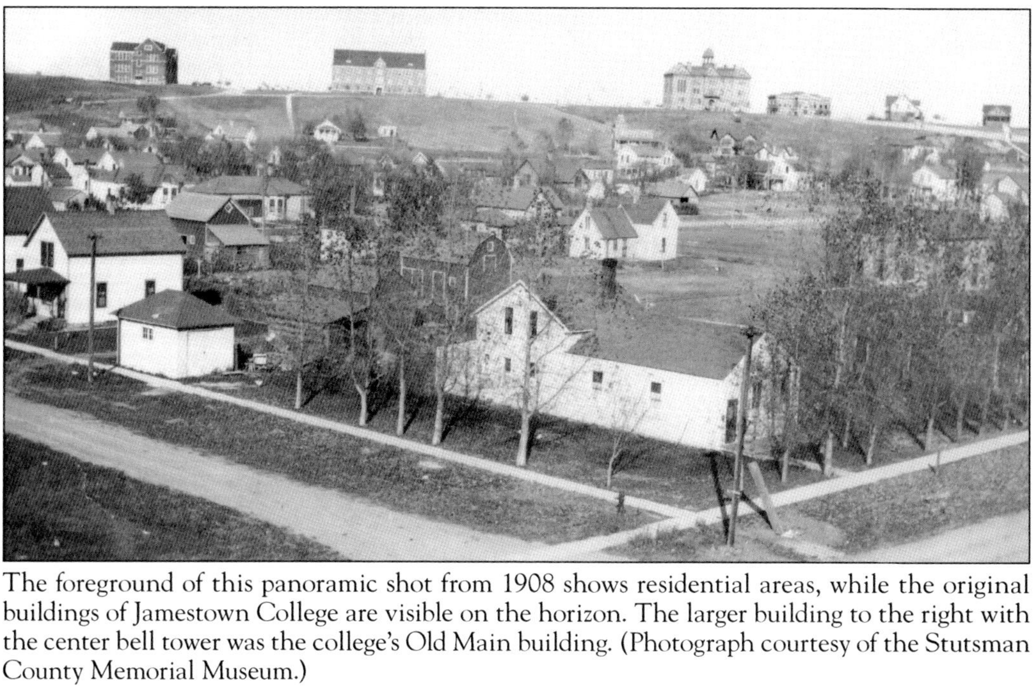

The foreground of this panoramic shot from 1908 shows residential areas, while the original buildings of Jamestown College are visible on the horizon. The larger building to the right with the center bell tower was the college's Old Main building. (Photograph courtesy of the Stutsman County Memorial Museum.)

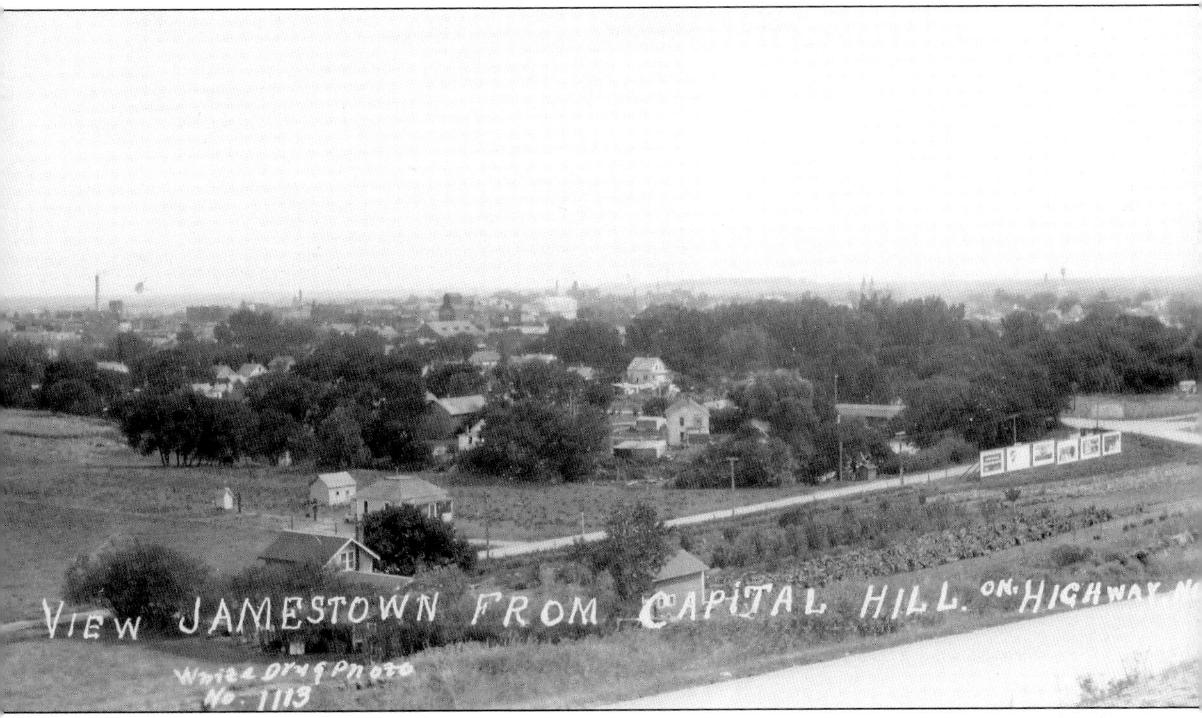

This 1950s-era photograph shows Jamestown as viewed from Capital Hill, to the north of the Fort Seward site. The area was named during an unsuccessful effort to bring the North Dakota state capital to Jamestown in the 1930s. (Photograph courtesy of the Jamestown Parks & Recreation Department.)

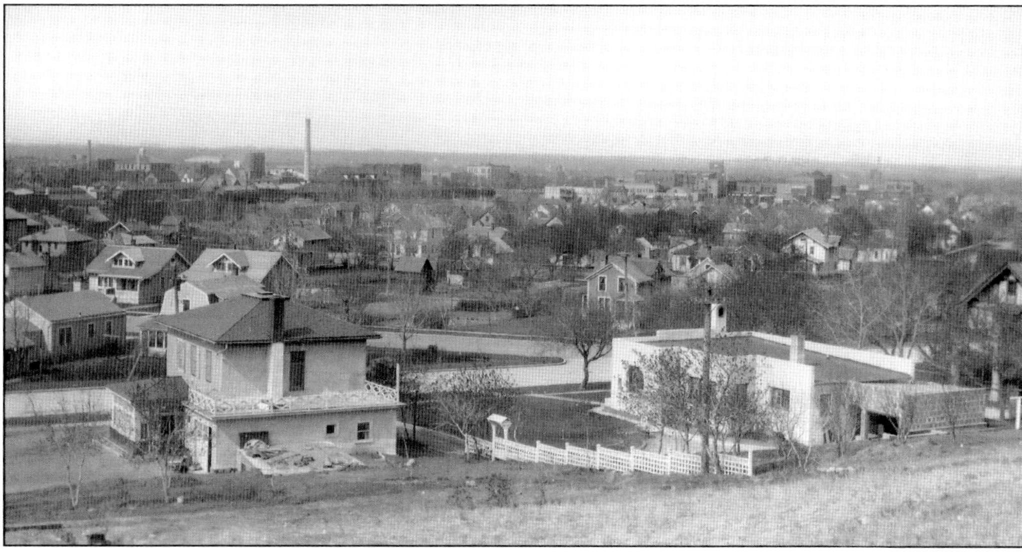

This photograph shows the view from Jamestown College toward downtown Jamestown in about 1950. The tall smokestack was at the Ottertail Co. power plant, located near the present city hall. (Photograph courtesy of the Jamestown Parks & Recreation Department.)

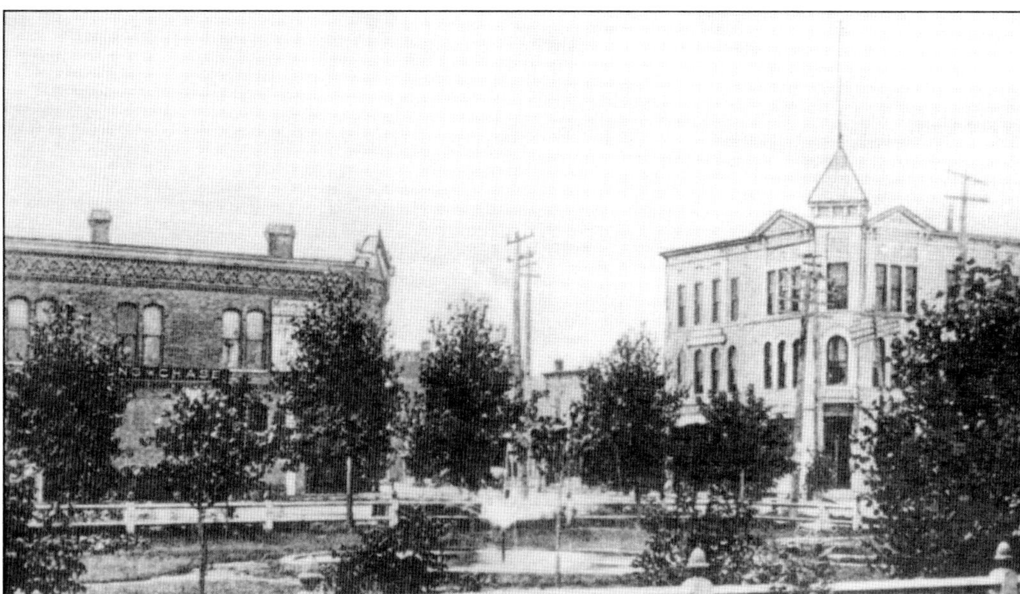

Pictured here is the old city park, situated along the Northern Pacific Railroad's main line that cuts through Jamestown from east to west. (Photograph courtesy of the Stutsman County Memorial Museum.)

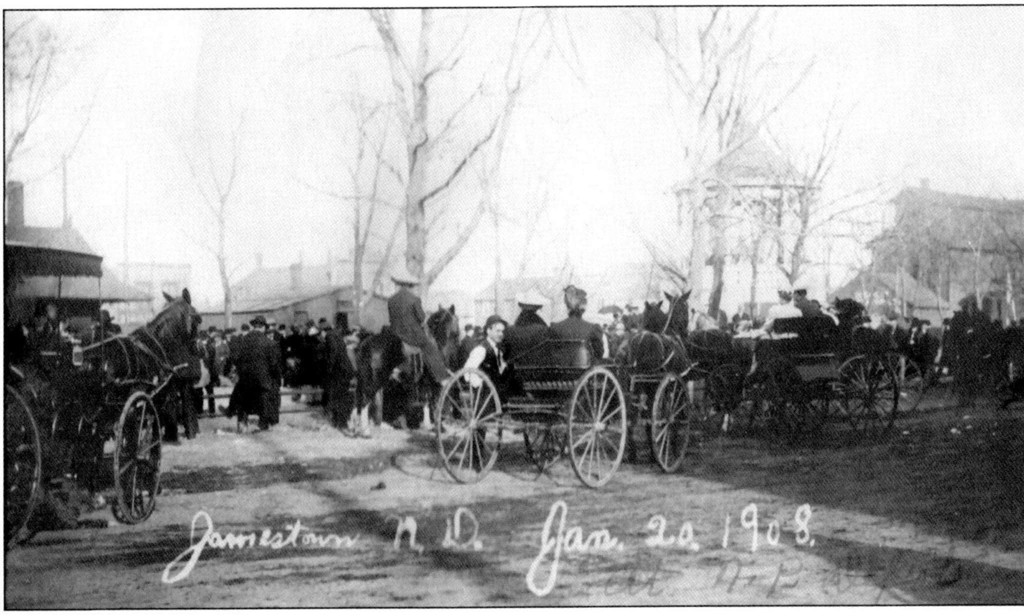

During its early years, Jamestown held regular winter festivals. This gathering in January 1908 occurred in the railroad parks of the downtown area and was attended by men and women on foot, on horseback, and in buggies. (Photograph courtesy of the Stutsman County Memorial Museum.)

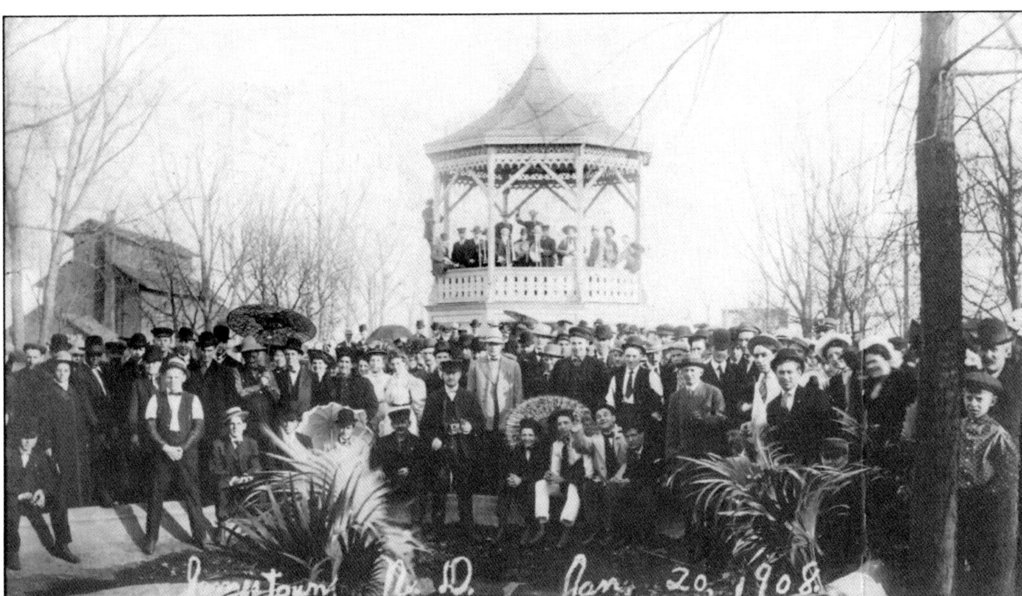

The 1908 winter festival was held in shirtsleeve weather. The gazebo in the background, built in 1883, had hosted dignitaries such as Pres. Ulysses S. Grant. The area in front of the crowd pictured here was normally a reflecting pool that would have been drained during the winter. (Photograph courtesy of Dave Robertson.)

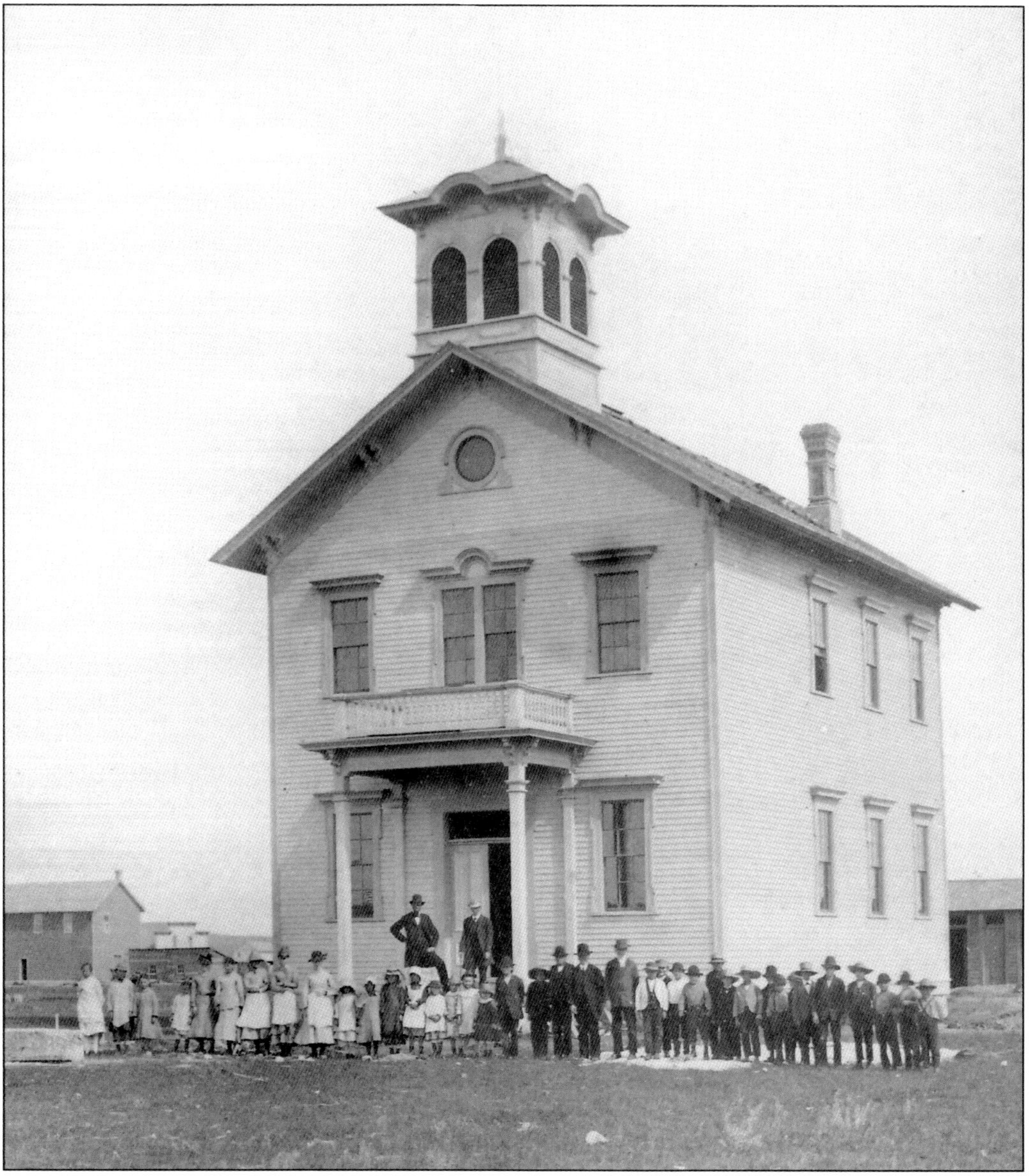

This photograph by Jay Haynes, taken around 1880, shows the first public school in Jamestown. The image was likely marketed to immigrants and prospective homesteaders and shows little scholars and teachers. (Photograph courtesy Lenard Cave.)

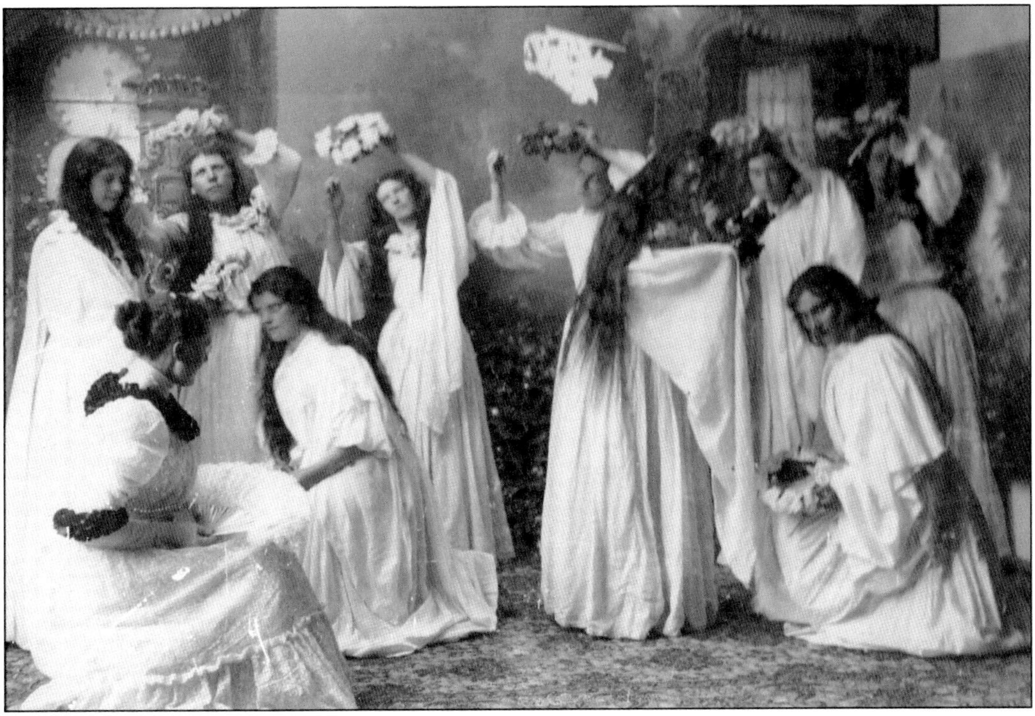

These beautiful young women appear to be rehearsing for a theater production. The photograph dates to before 1900. (Photograph courtesy of the Stutsman County Memorial Museum.)

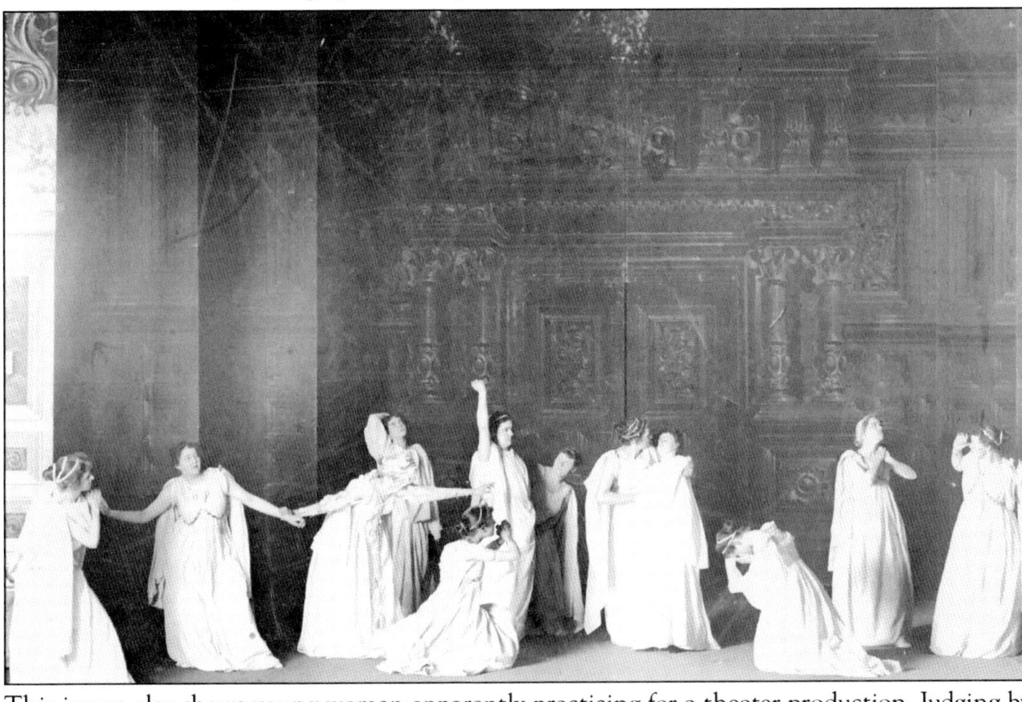

This image also shows young women apparently practicing for a theater production. Judging by the backdrop, they may be in Lloyd's Opera House. (Photograph courtesy of the Stutsman County Memorial Museum.)

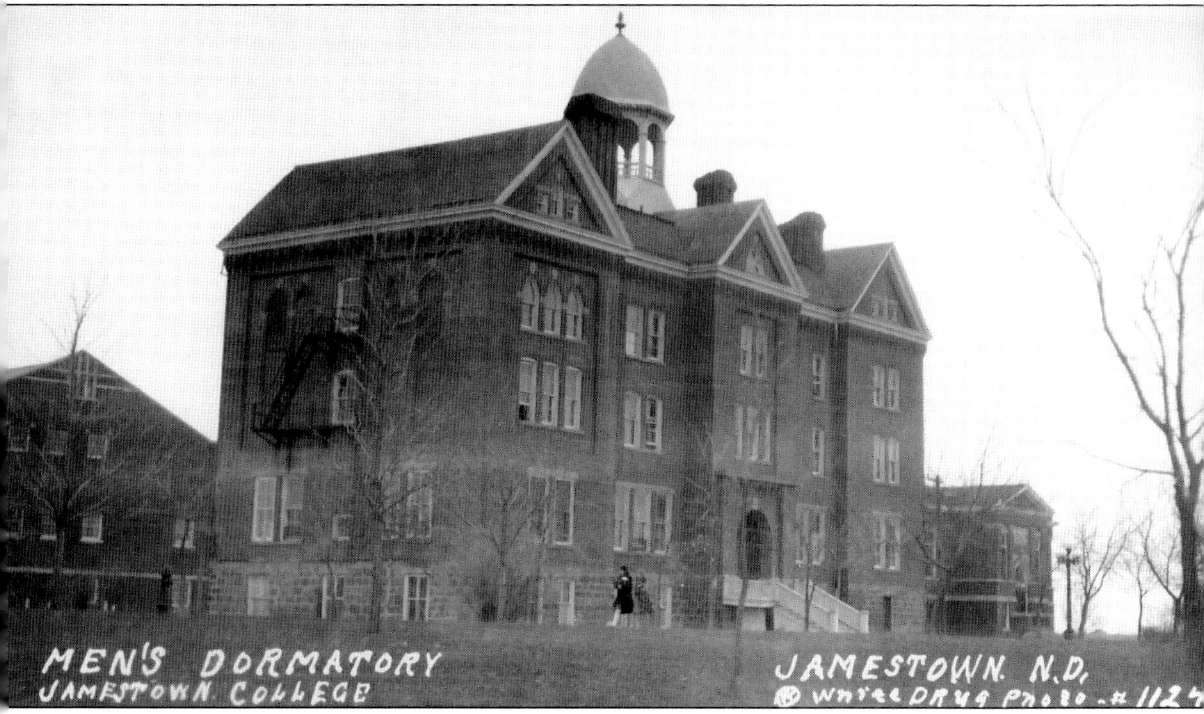

Seen here is Jamestown College's men's dormitory around the 1940s. The technician who processed the picture misspelled "dormitory" when he noted it on the image. The building was destroyed by fire. (Photograph courtesy of the Jamestown Parks & Recreation Department.)

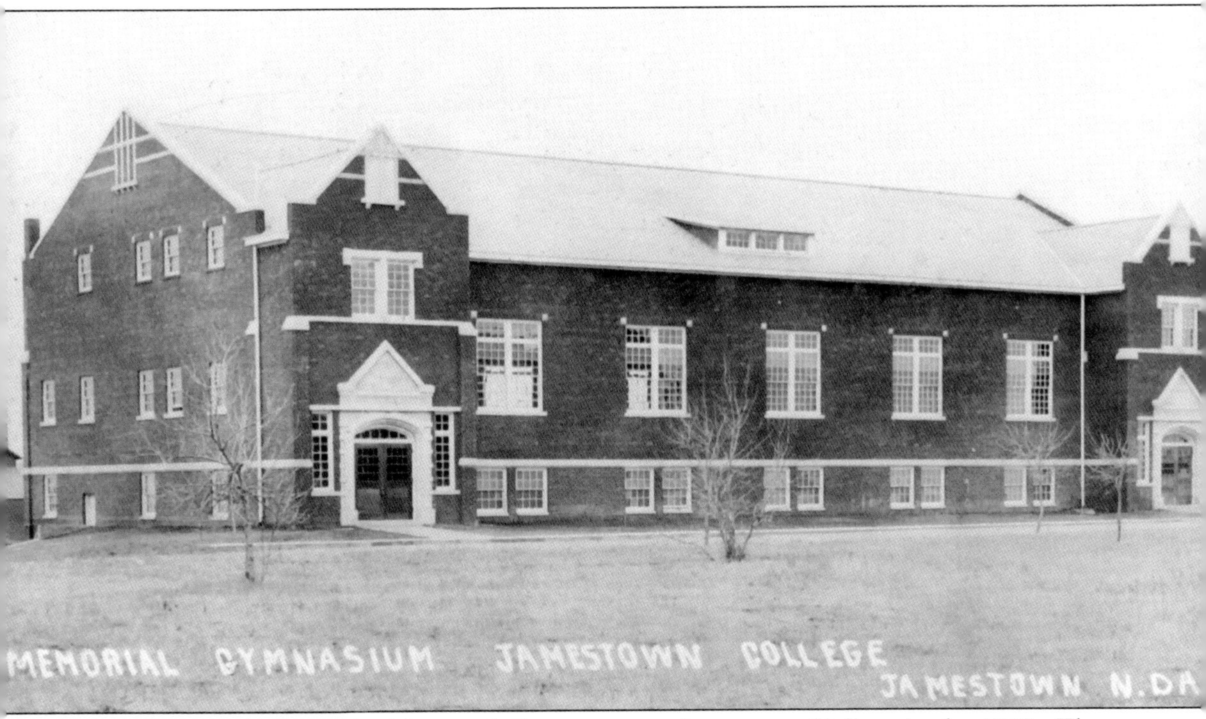

This photograph shows the Memorial Gymnasium at Jamestown College in the 1940s. The building, now named the Hansen Center, is still utilized by the college for practice and games. (Photograph courtesy of the Jamestown Parks & Recreation Department.)

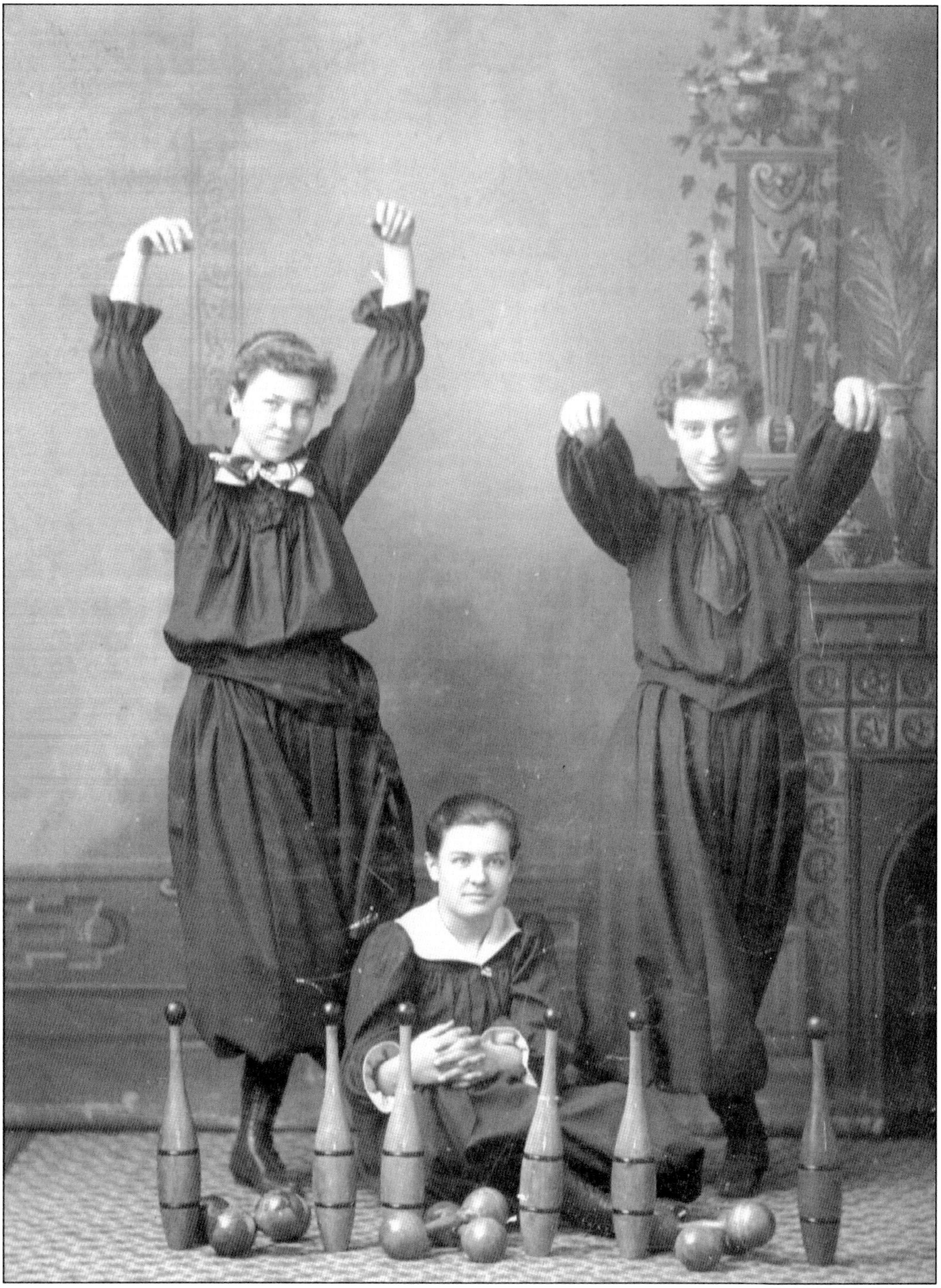

Three young ladies pose in a rather affected way, displaying pins and weights likely used for the purposes of exercise. Depending on their weight and size, the pins (known as Indian clubs) could be used for exercise or juggling to promote coordination. (Photograph courtesy of the Stutsman County Memorial Museum.)

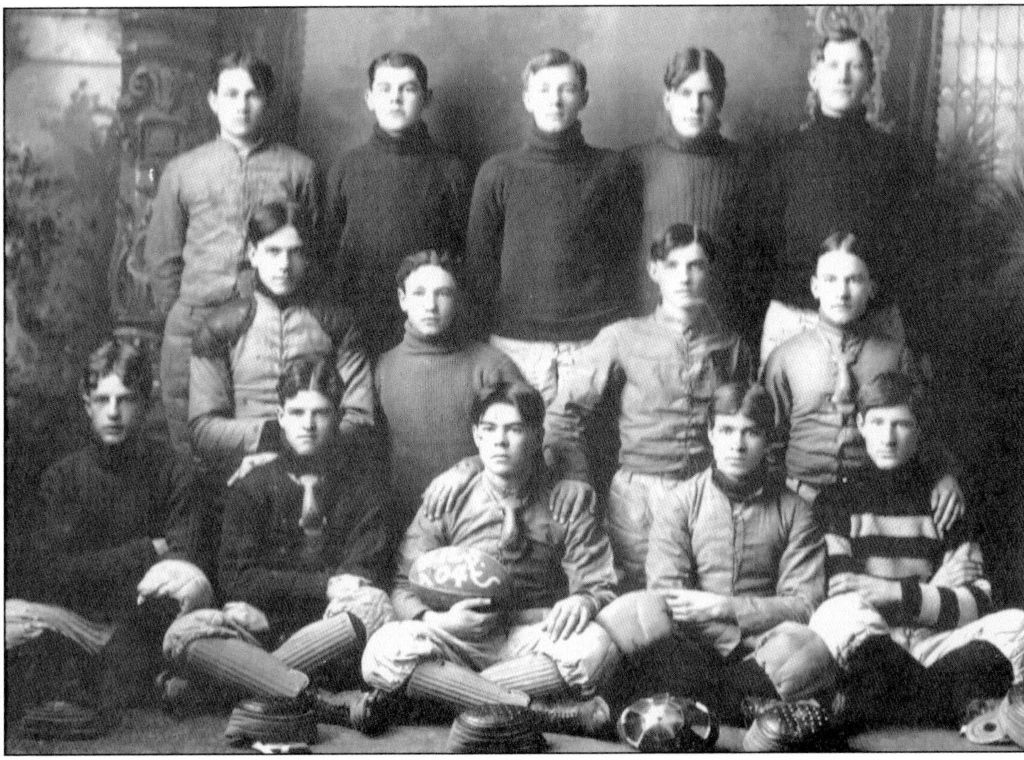

Jamestown High School's football team poses for posterity in 1904. Note the leather helmets on the floor in front and the shoulder pads that seem to be a part of the uniform of the player on the far left of the second row. (Photograph courtesy of the Stutsman County Memorial Museum.)

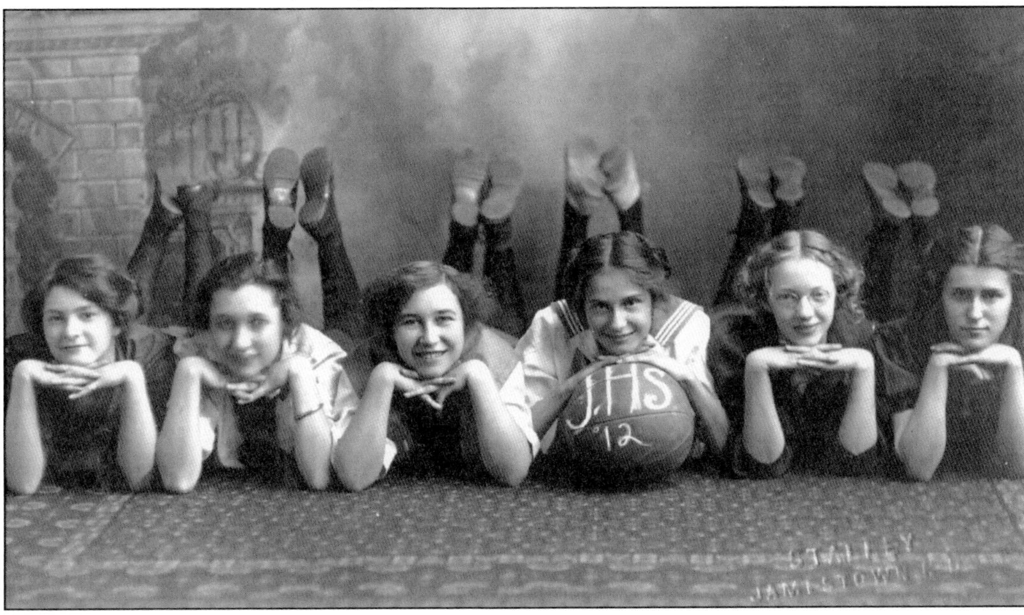

Girls formed sports teams too. This 1912 Jamestown High School basketball team poses in front of the same backdrop used in many of the high school–sports pictures of that era. (Photograph courtesy of the Stutsman County Memorial Museum.)

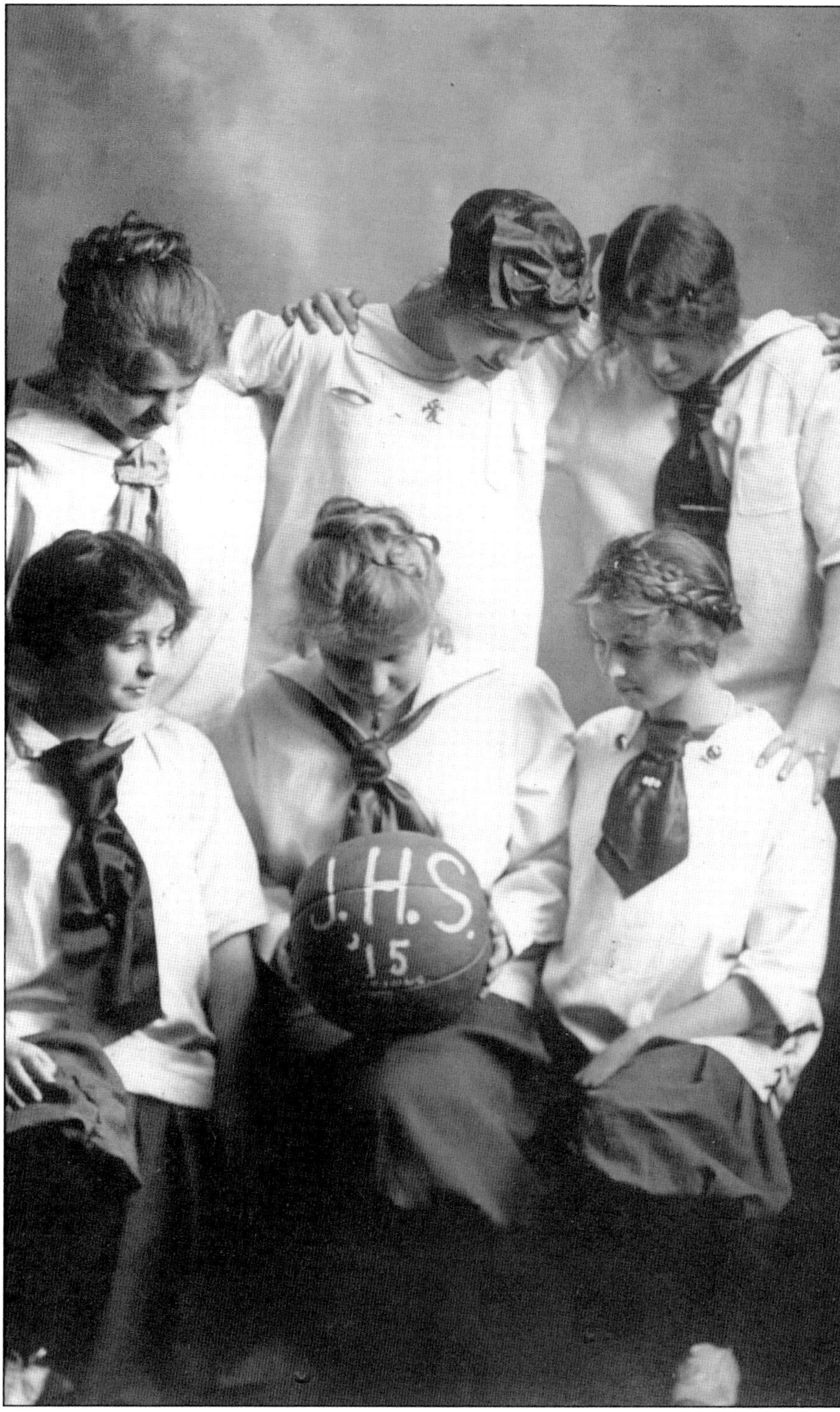

Another year's Jamestown High School girls' basketball team is pictured here. These fashionable girls undoubtedly played a decent game of "buckets." (Photograph courtesy of the Stutsman County Memorial Museum.)

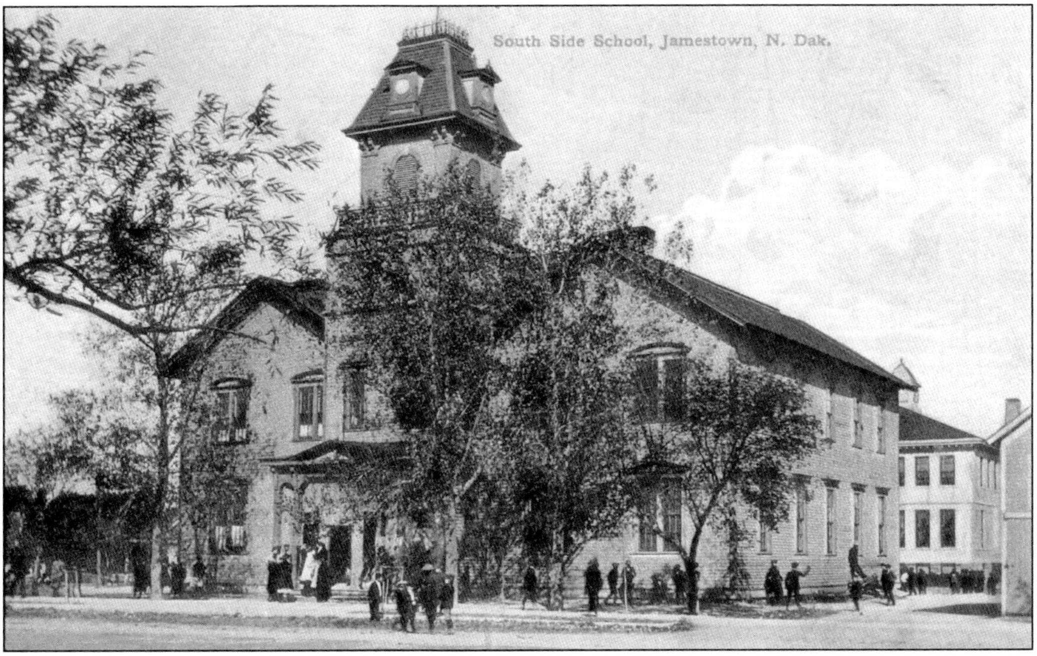

This postcard depicts Jamestown's original high school. The building burned in about 1929, leading to construction of the facilities currently serving as Jamestown Middle School. (Photograph courtesy of Dave Robertson.)

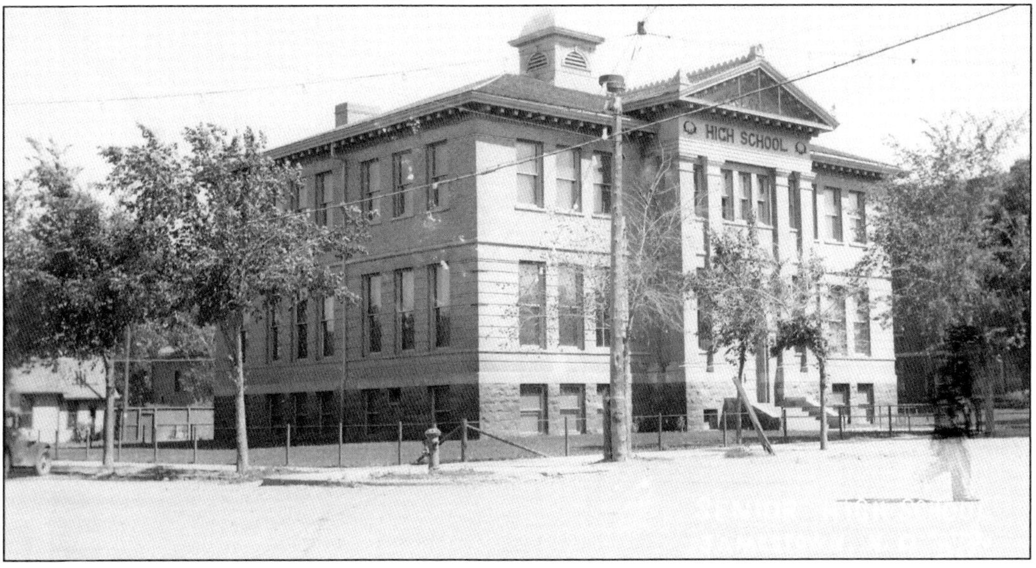

In 1879, when the city's population was 200, Jamestown boasted 19 public school students and a single teacher. By 1884, the population had risen to around 4,000, and Jamestown's school system had 487 students with 10 teachers. The city was booming. This photograph from the 1930s or 1940s depicts the most modern of the city's school buildings during that era. (Photograph courtesy of the Stutsman County Memorial Museum.)

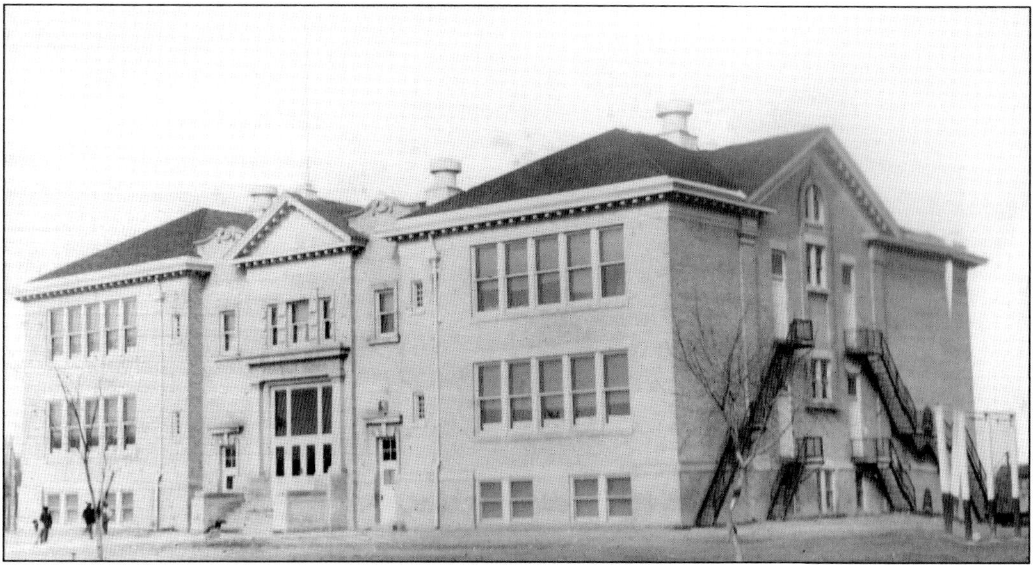

Franklin School was originally built as an elementary school in Jamestown. When the building was retired from its educational use, it was repurposed as the headquarters of Cable Services Inc. and now includes office space and a television studio. (Photograph courtesy of the Stutsman County Memorial Museum.)

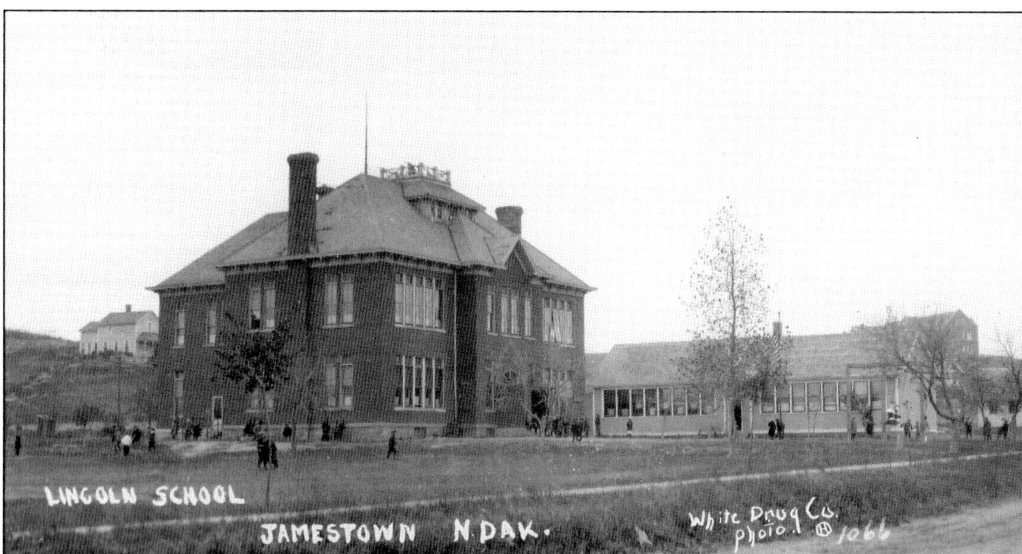

This photograph shows the original Lincoln School from the 1920s. This facility was located on the same grounds as the current Lincoln Elementary School, near the base of Hospital Hill. Note the children at play. (Photograph courtesy of the Jamestown Parks & Recreation Department.)

Displayed here is the beautiful American Gothic–style architecture of St. James Basilica Roman Catholic Church in Jamestown. Construction of the church was completed in 1914. Designed as a minor basilica in 1989, the church is 140 feet long, 50 feet wide, and 42 feet high, and it can seat 750 people. (Photograph courtesy of the Stutsman County Memorial Museum.)

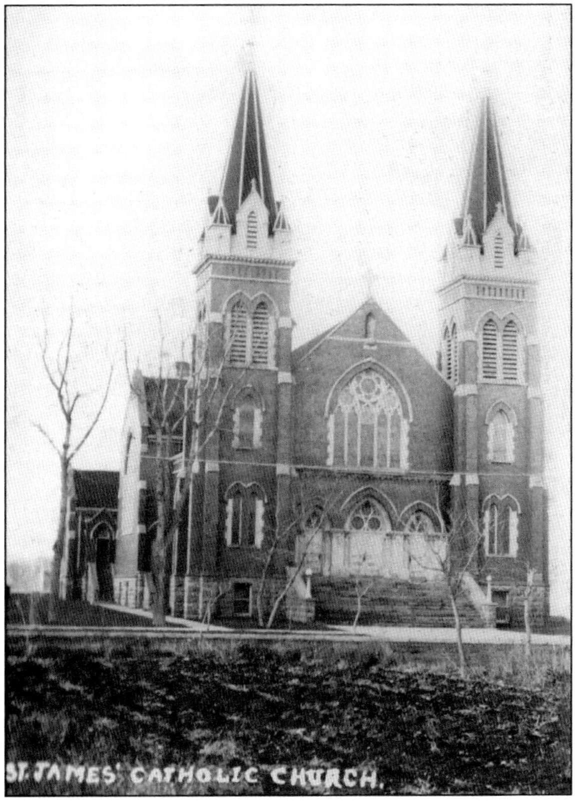

The first Presbyterian services in Jamestown were held in 1878 by an itinerant minister. The current church building was constructed in 1914 and continues to serve the congregation today. (Photograph courtesy of the Stutsman County Memorial Museum.)

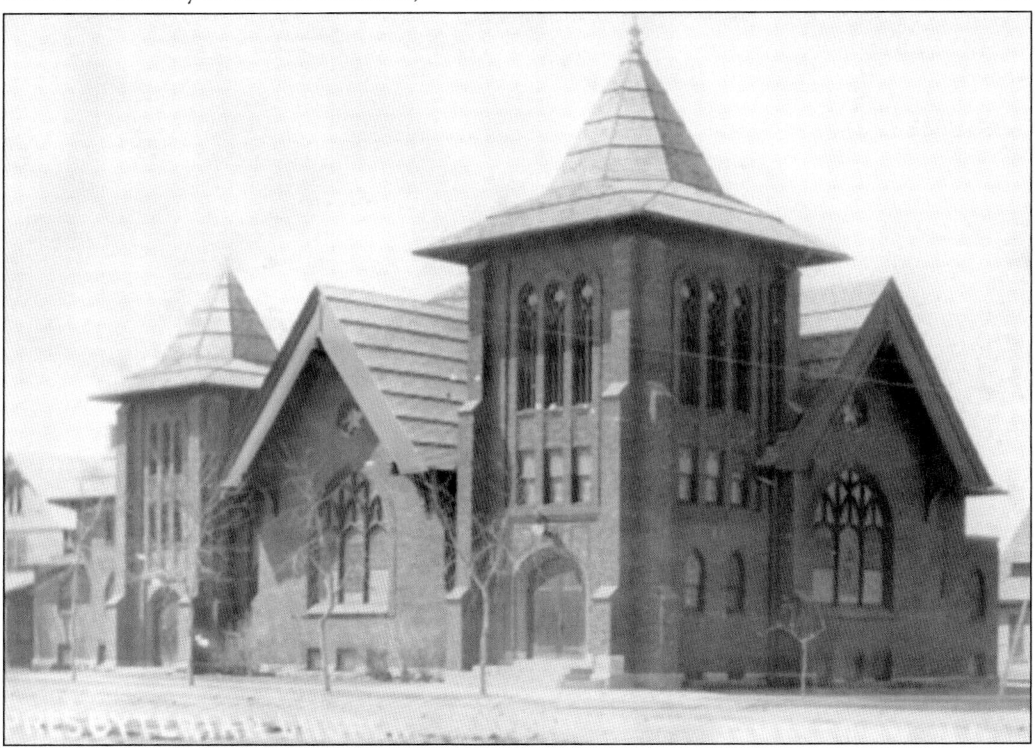

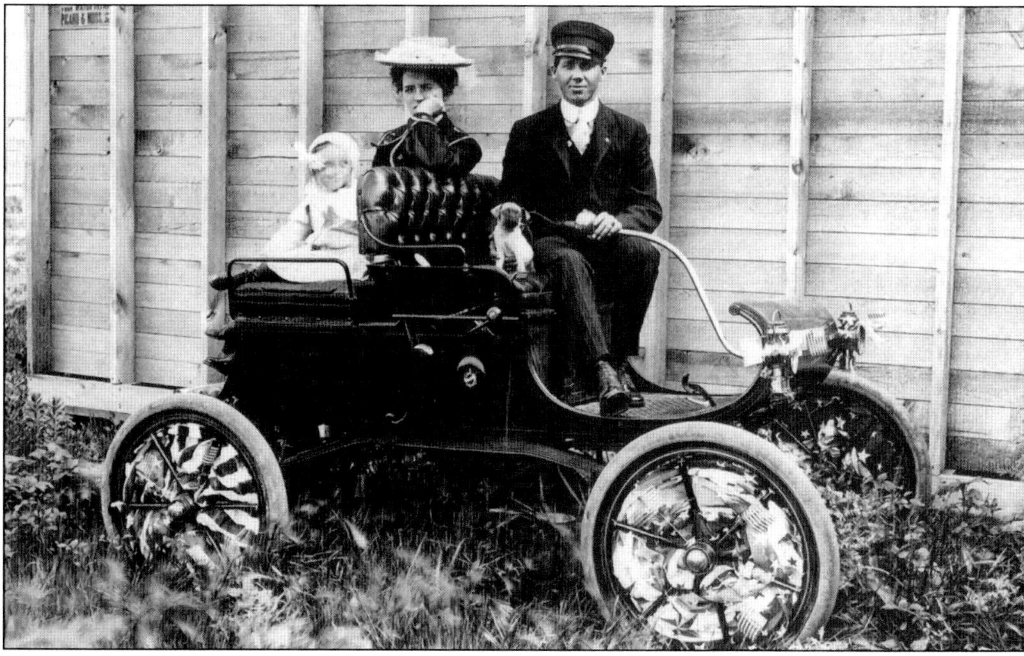

According to notes written on the back of this c. 1903 photograph, this may be Jamestown's first automobile. Although slightly illegible, the writing identifies two of the three people as Jennie and Florence Logan and the dog as Frisky. Motorized travel marked the end of one era—the Frontier West—and the beginning of another—America's Century. (Photograph courtesy of the Stutsman County Memorial Museum.)

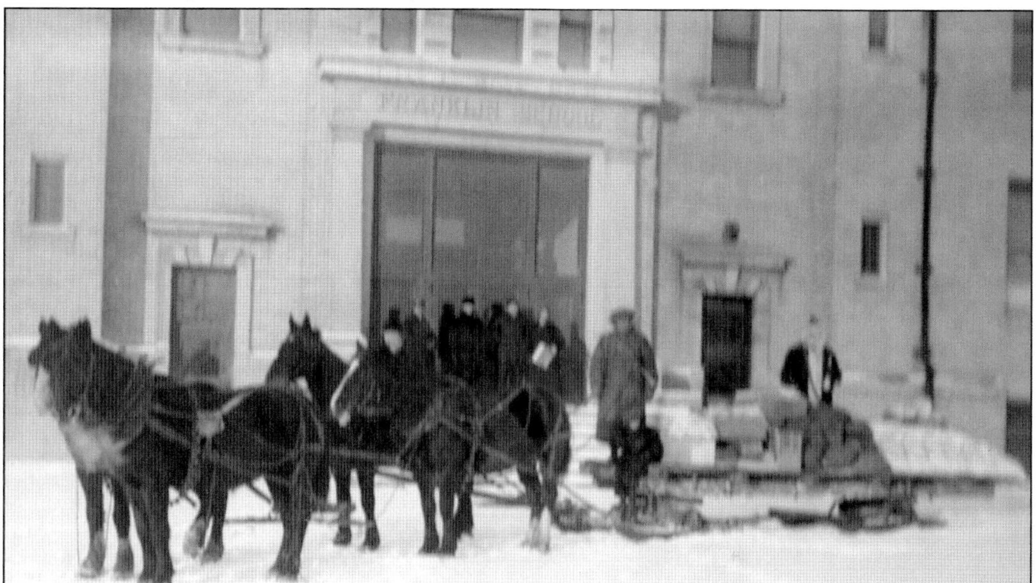

A team of horses pulling a sleigh stacked with Christmas packages stands idle in front of Franklin Elementary School in this photograph from 1916. The presents may have been part of a cooperative community Christmas program for disadvantaged children. (Photograph courtesy of the Stutsman County Memorial Museum.)

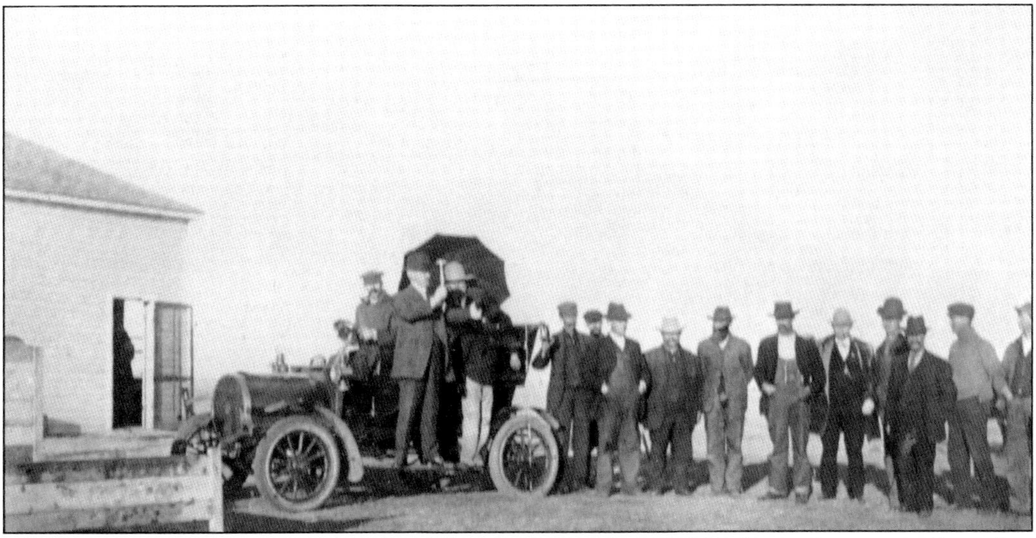

This photograph from 1909 shows locals lined up next to a 1907 Richmond air-cooled horseless buggy. The automobile would quickly change life, both on the farm and in the city. In the early days of motor vehicles, simply being around a car was an event worth commemorating with a picture. (Photograph courtesy of the Stutsman County Memorial Museum.)

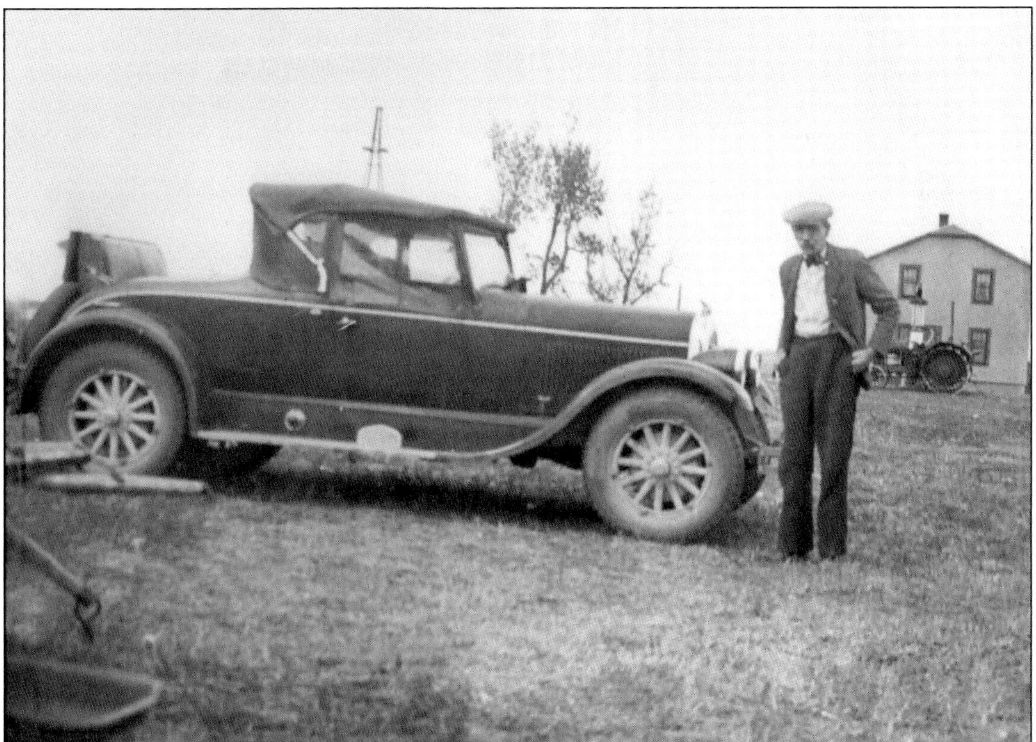

This undated photograph shows an elderly man standing proudly next to his automobile. By the second decade of the 20th century, car culture had arrived in the region. Note the steel-wheeled tractor in the background. (Photograph courtesy of the Stutsman County Memorial Museum.)

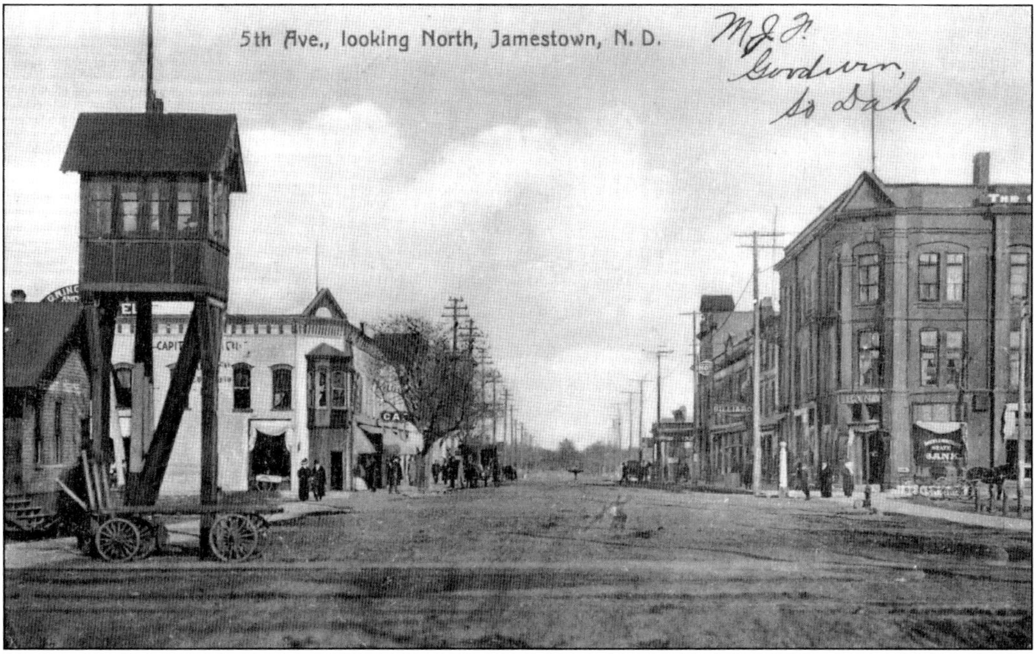

This postcard image from 1908 looks to the north from the Northern Pacific's mainline railroad tracks that pass through town. Note that Fifth Avenue (now known as First Avenue) is hard-packed dirt at this time. (Photograph courtesy of the Stutsman County Memorial Museum.)

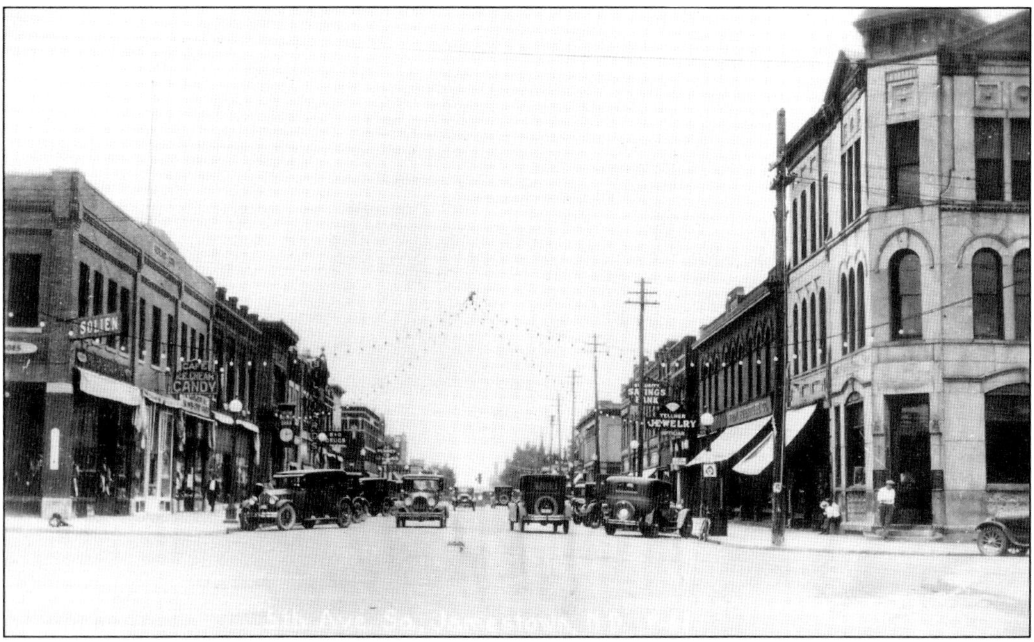

This 1920 photograph looks south from the same position as the view above. Today, Fifth Avenue is known as First Avenue. Apparently, traffic has always been flush. (Photograph courtesy of Dave Robertson.)

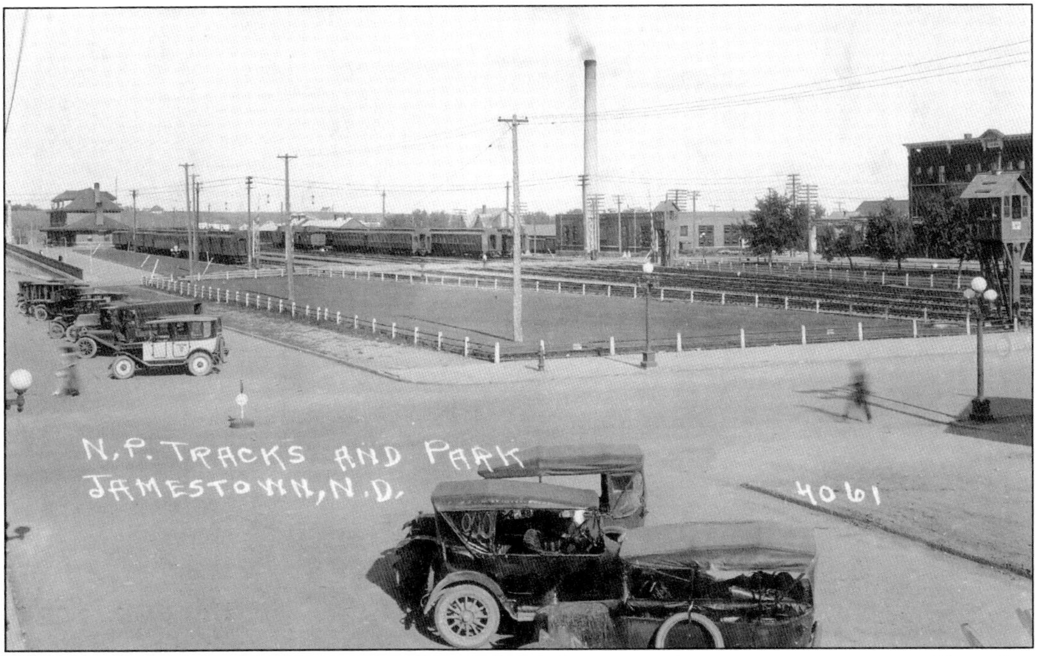

The areas to the north and south of the tracks in downtown Jamestown were originally parks. This 1923 picture, looking to the southeast, shows the space between the depot and what is now First Avenue. (Photograph courtesy of Dave Robertson.)

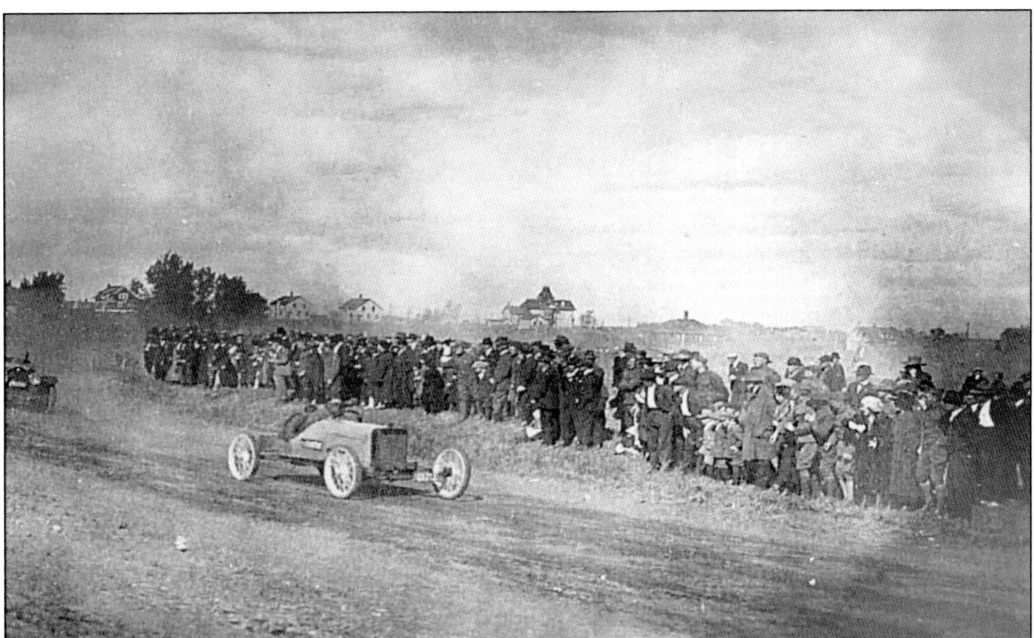

In 1919, at least, automobile racing was a homecoming activity at Jamestown College. Football has been the standard homecoming activity since the 1930s, and the tradition continues today with the Jimmies, the college's team. (Photograph courtesy of Kent Horton.)

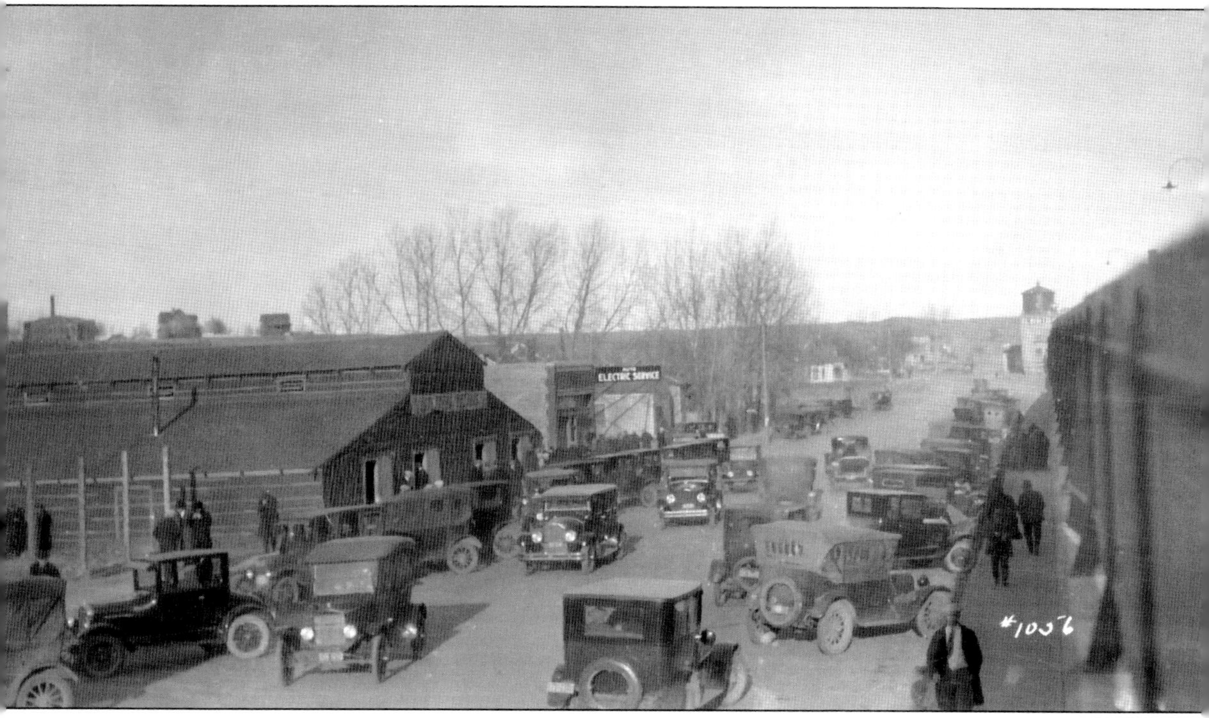

This c. 1920s photograph shows early cars moving through one of the streets along the tracks in Jamestown. Jamestown College buildings can be seen on the hill above. (Photograph courtesy of Kent Horton.)

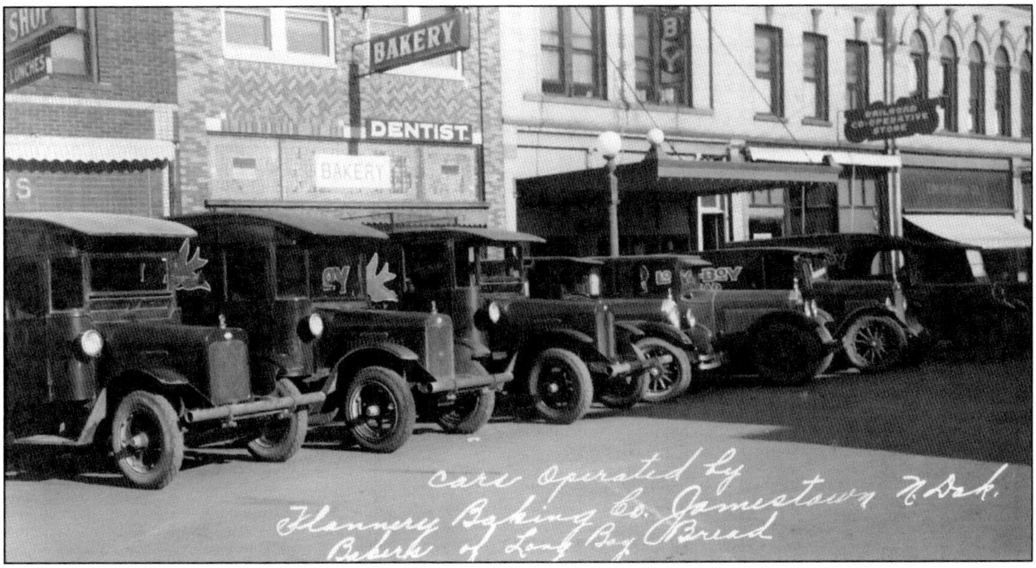

Company vehicles operated by Flannery Baking Company—makers of Long Boy Bread—line the street outside the bakery. The fleet of trucks delivered baked goods within the community. (Photograph courtesy of Bruce Berg.)

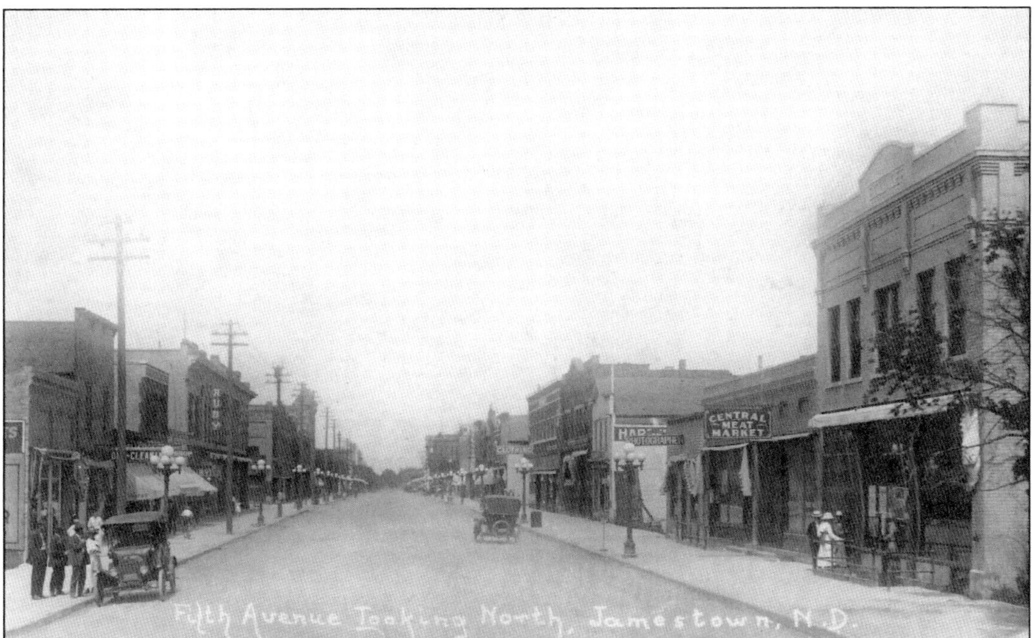

This photograph from 1923 shows Fifth Avenue (now First Avenue) looking to the north from the mainline railroad tracks. This street was, for many decades, the main artery for business in Jamestown. Shopping malls on the south side of the city now present major competition for downtown businesspeople. (Photograph courtesy of Dave Robertson.)

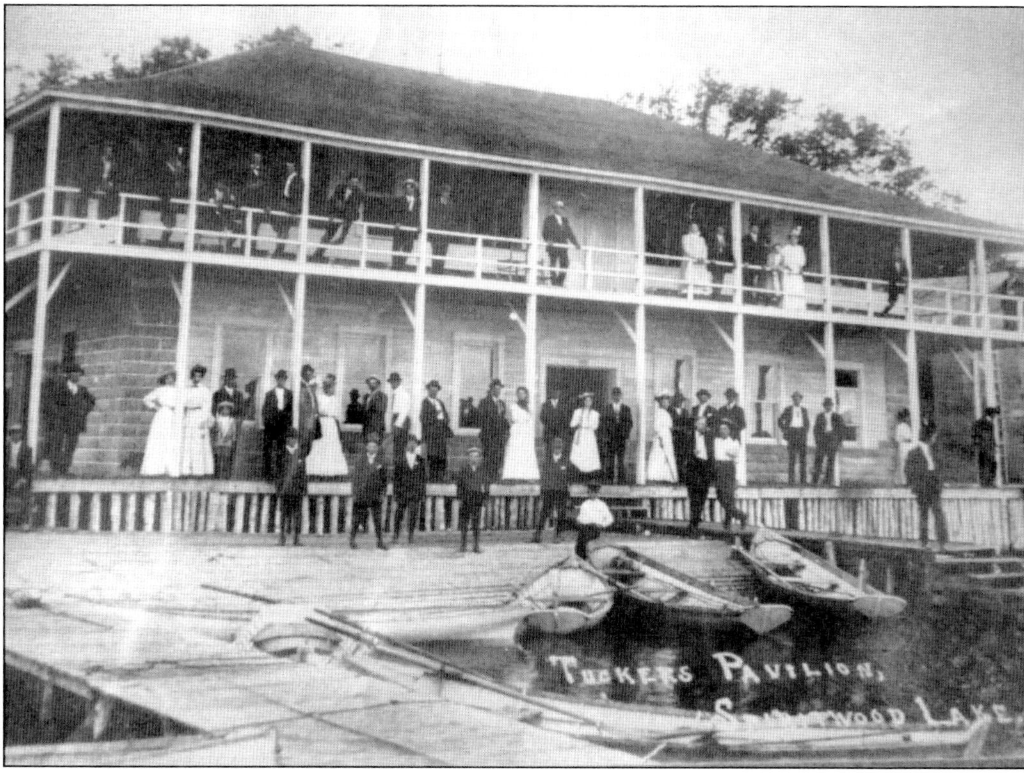

These ladies and gents pose in their Sunday best at Tucker's Pavilion on Spiritwood Lake. (Photograph courtesy of the Stutsman County Memorial Museum.)

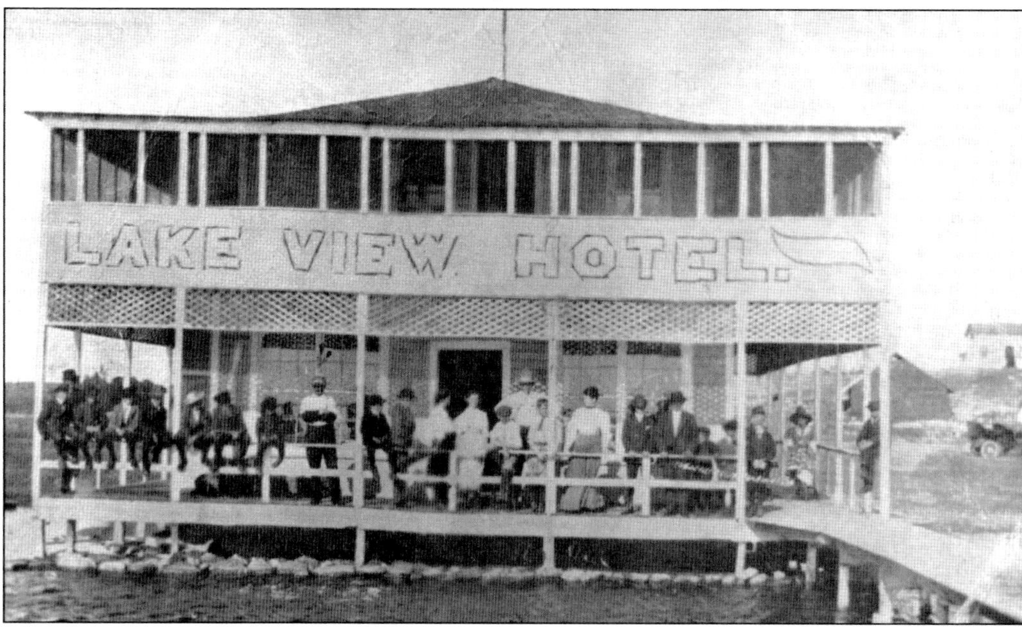

Lake View Hotel, on the east side of Spiritwood Lake, was a headquarters for Jamestown residents looking for summer recreation. It burned down in the 1930s. (Photograph courtesy of Dave Robertson.)

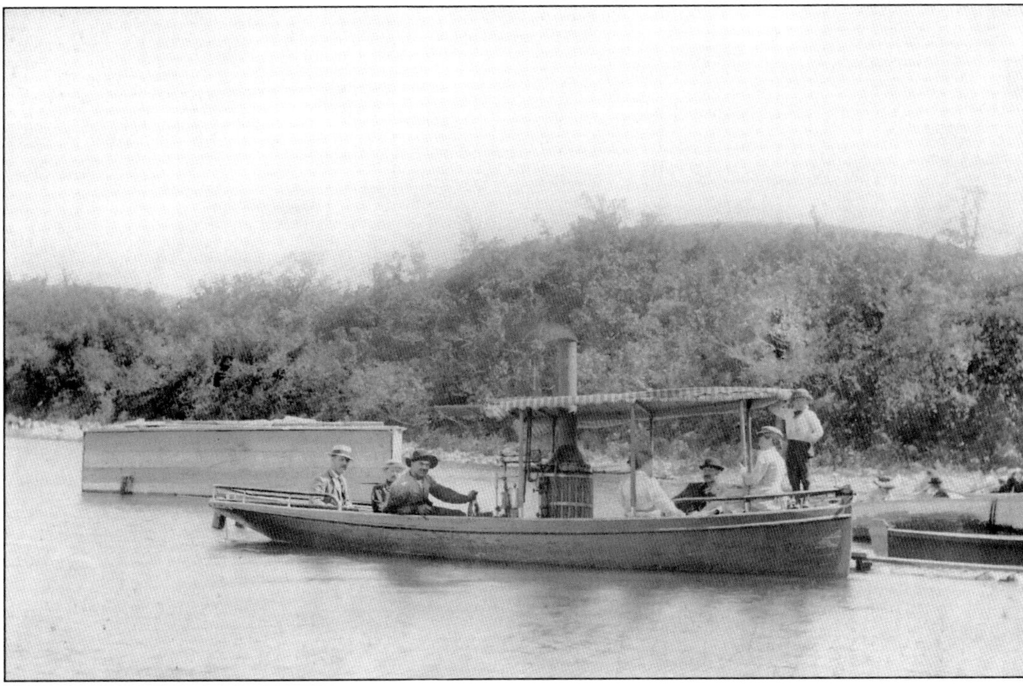

This 1892 photograph by C.L. Judd shows an excursion steamboat on Spiritwood Lake. The boat, possibly named the *Maid of the Mist*, provided summer excursions around the lake. (Photograph courtesy of Dave Robertson.)

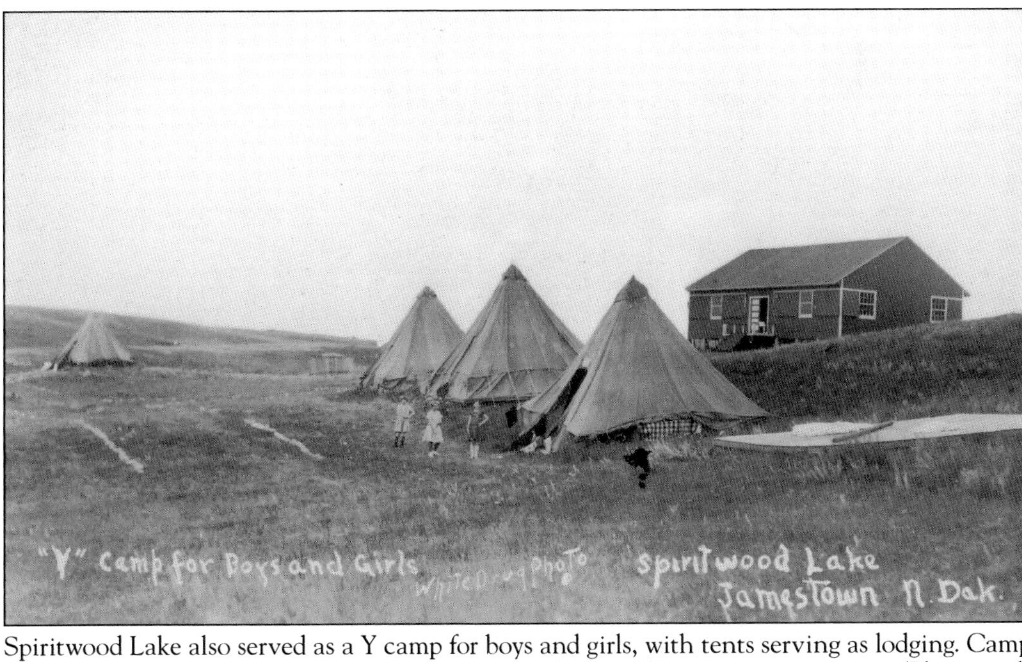

Spiritwood Lake also served as a Y camp for boys and girls, with tents serving as lodging. Camp Rokiwan at the lake continues the tradition of providing youth camping experiences. (Photograph courtesy of Dave Robertson.)

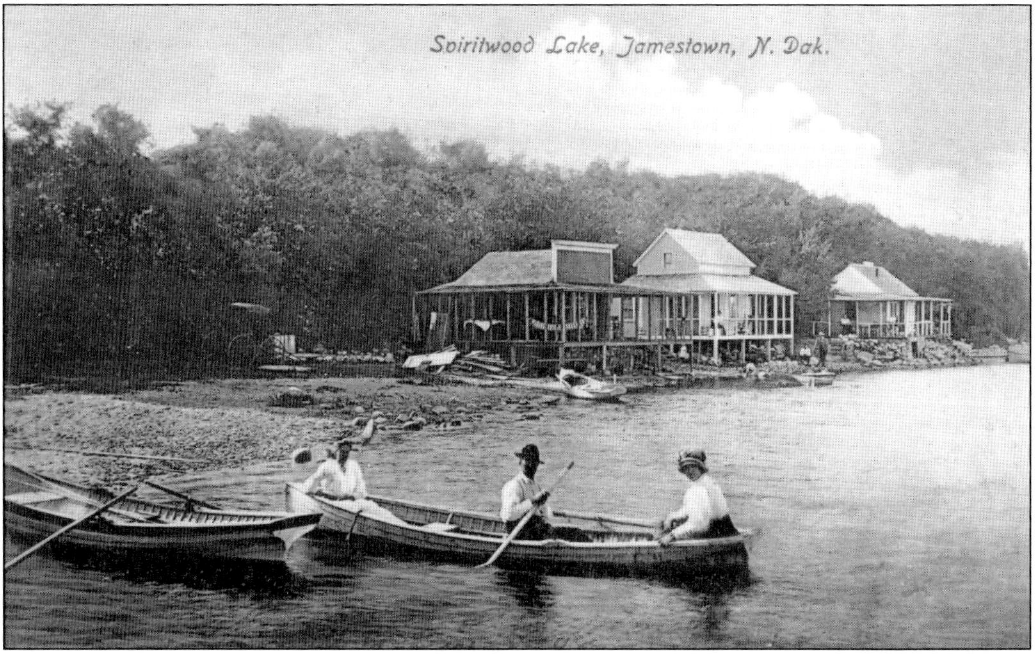

This photograph, possibly from the 1920s, shows some of the early cabins around Spiritwood Lake and depicts recreational boats powered by oars or paddles rather than outboard engines. (Photograph courtesy of Dave Robertson.)

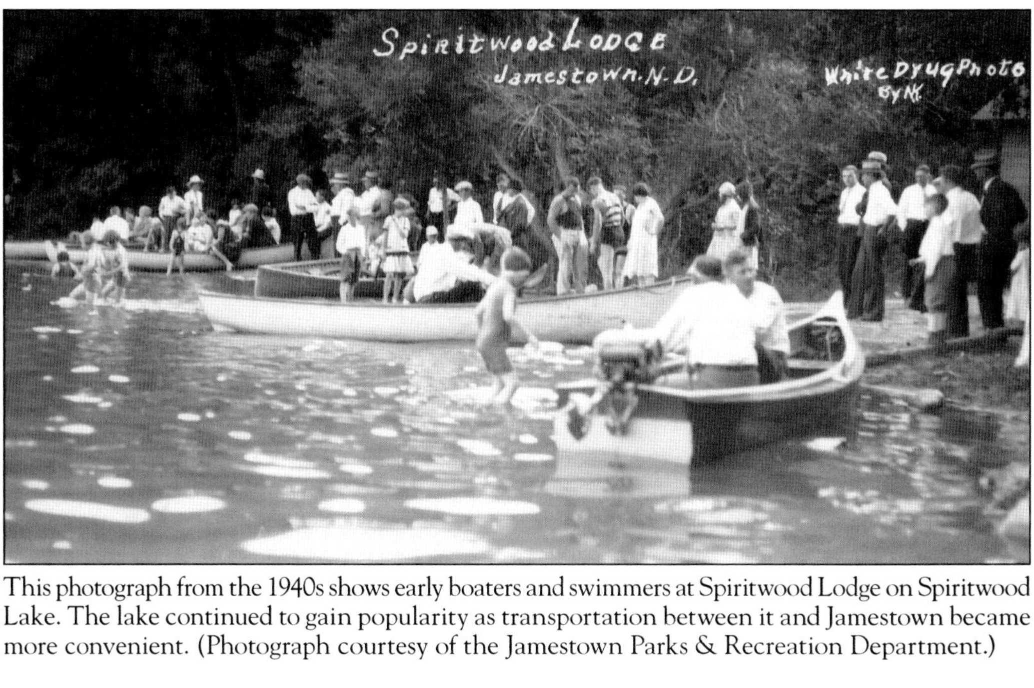

This photograph from the 1940s shows early boaters and swimmers at Spiritwood Lodge on Spiritwood Lake. The lake continued to gain popularity as transportation between it and Jamestown became more convenient. (Photograph courtesy of the Jamestown Parks & Recreation Department.)

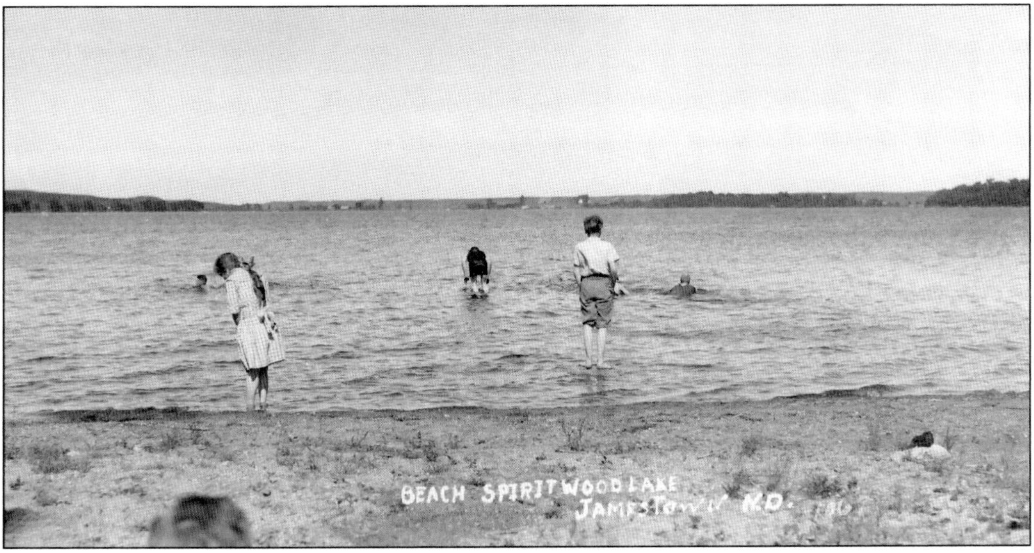

This photograph, possibly from the 1930s, shows some of the beach attire residents wore when enjoying an excursion to Spiritwood Lake. Sandy Beach at Spiritwood Lake remains popular, although beach attire has changed drastically. (Photograph courtesy of the Jamestown Parks & Recreation Department.)

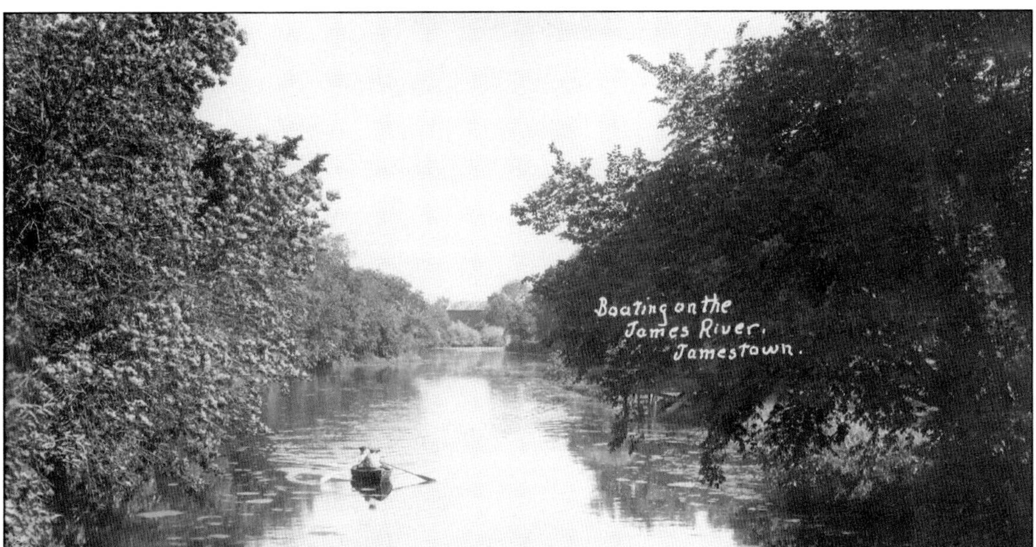

A rowboat cuts the surface of the James River in this early photograph. Before the construction of the Jamestown Dam in the 1960s and the Pipestem Dam in the 1970s, the level of the river would have varied greatly through the summer. Here, the water level and the leafy brush and trees indicate that it was probably springtime. (Photograph courtesy of Dave Robertson.)

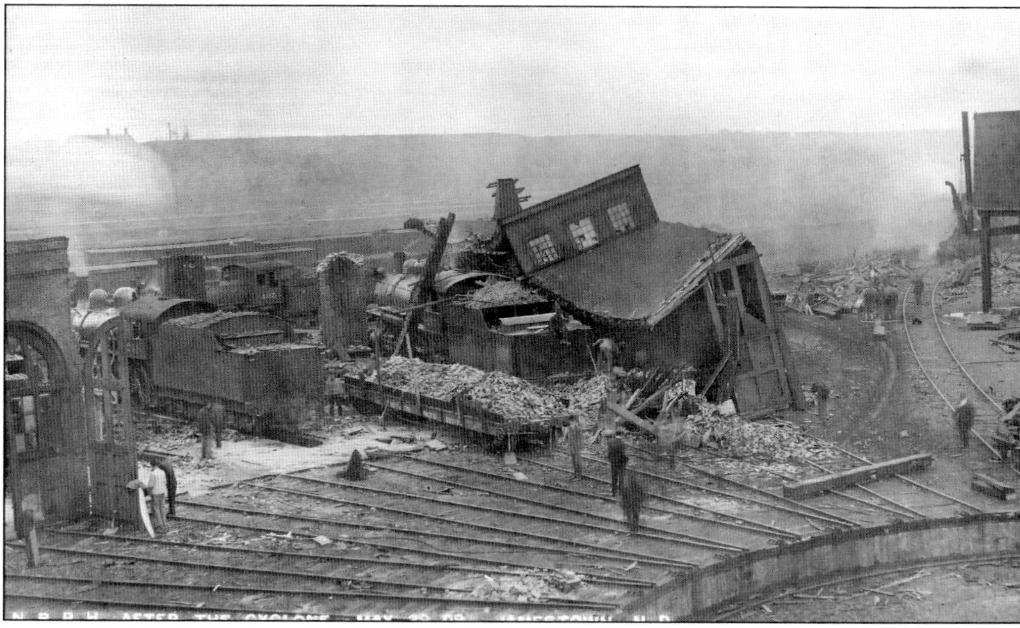

In May 1909, a tornado destroyed much of the Northern Pacific Railroad roundhouse and damaged several locomotives and cars. Here, crews appear to be surveying the damage. These engines were probably in the work sheds at the time of the storm. (Photograph courtesy of Lenard Cave.)

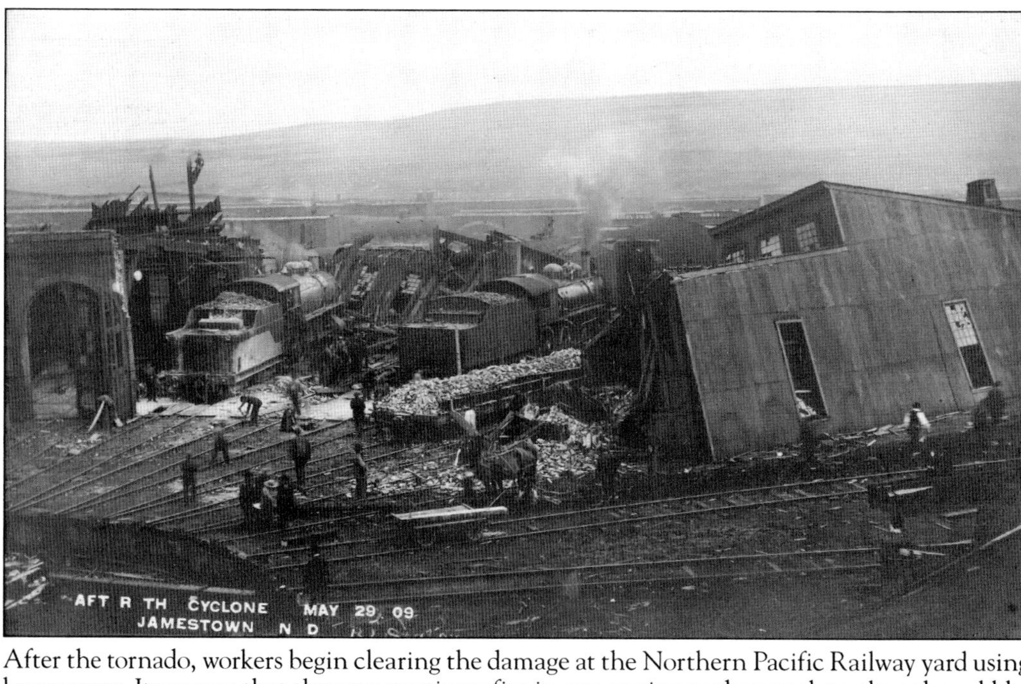

After the tornado, workers begin clearing the damage at the Northern Pacific Railway yard using horsepower. It appears that they are starting a fire in one engine as they work to clear the rubble. (Photograph courtesy of Lenard Cave.)

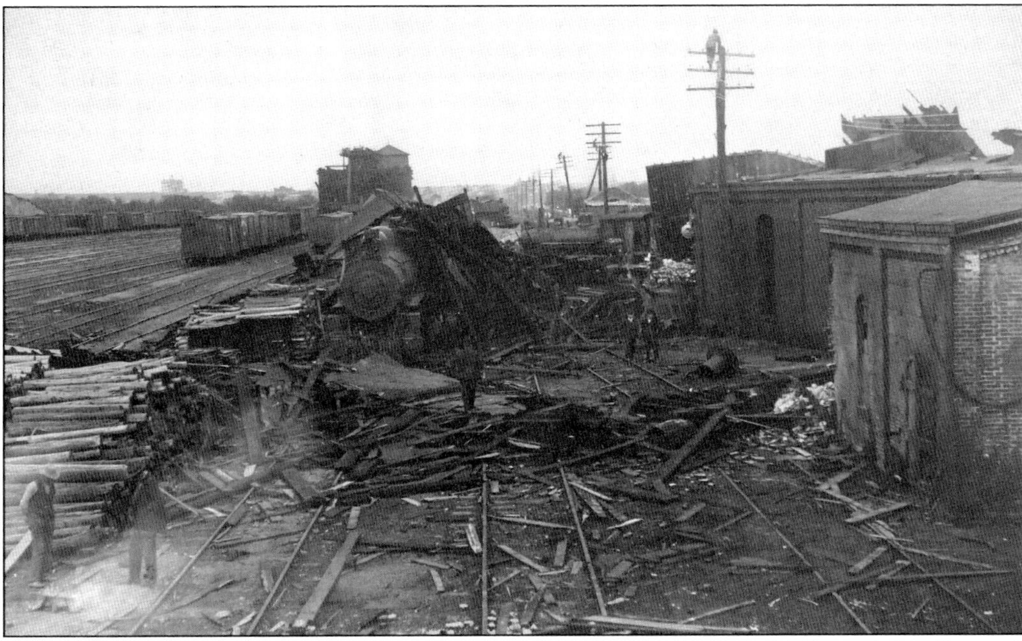

Crews repair the telegraph lines above the roundhouse after the May 1909 tornado. The early buildings of Jamestown College can be seen on the horizon above the rail yard. (Photograph courtesy of Lenard Cave.)

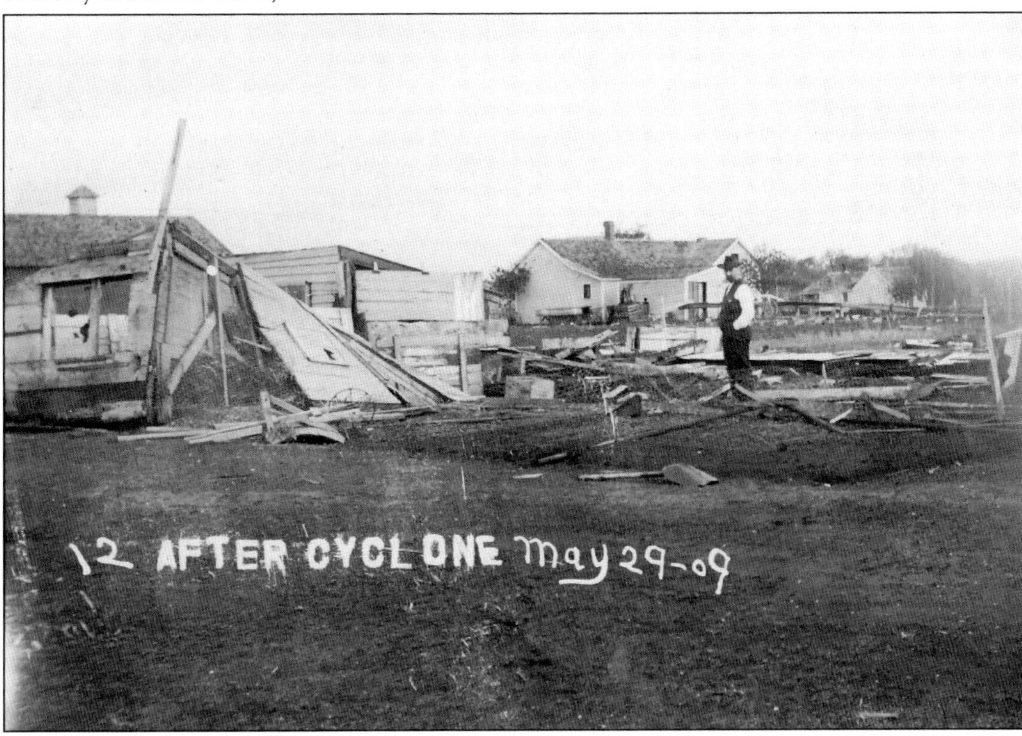

The tornado also affected the residential areas of Jamestown. Here, a local resident surveys the damage to a chicken yard, with poultry fencing visible amid the debris. (Photograph courtesy Lenard Cave.)

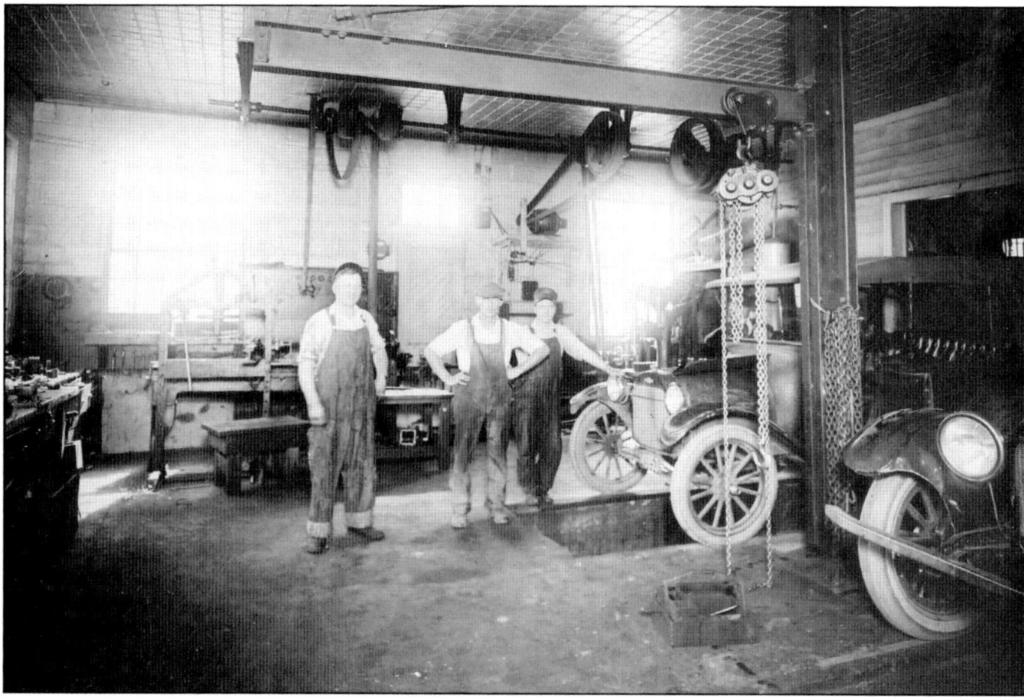

Pictured here is the shop of H.W. Lyons Buick in downtown Jamestown. Lyons Buick was one of the first in the area to offer automobile sales and service. (Photograph courtesy of Dave Robertson.)

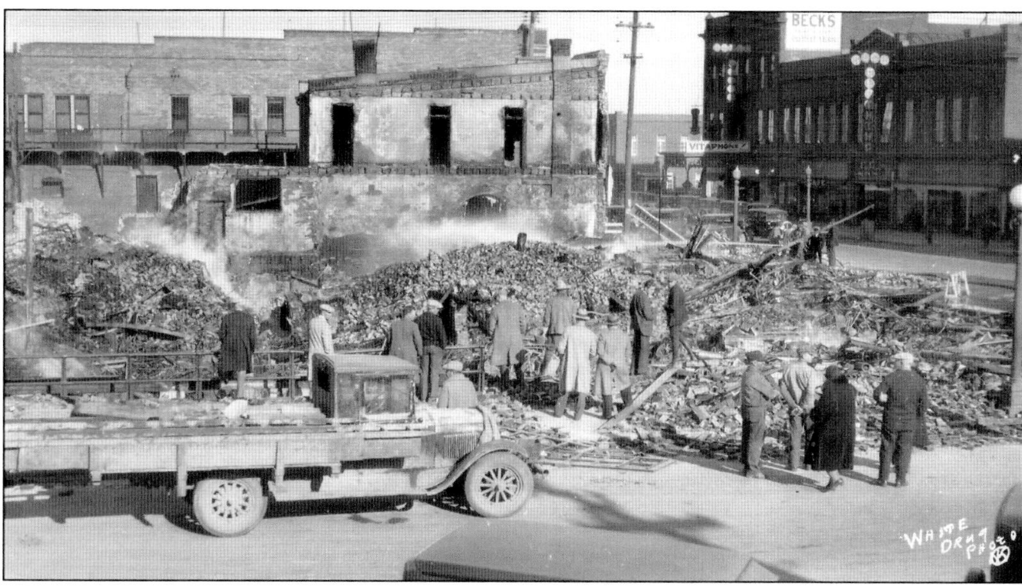

Fire was an all-too-common problem in Jamestown. This photograph shows a work crew clearing the rubble of the Capital Hotel after a 1930s blaze. The area was rebuilt and served for years as the home of Lil's Restaurant. (Photograph courtesy of the Jamestown Parks & Recreation Department.)

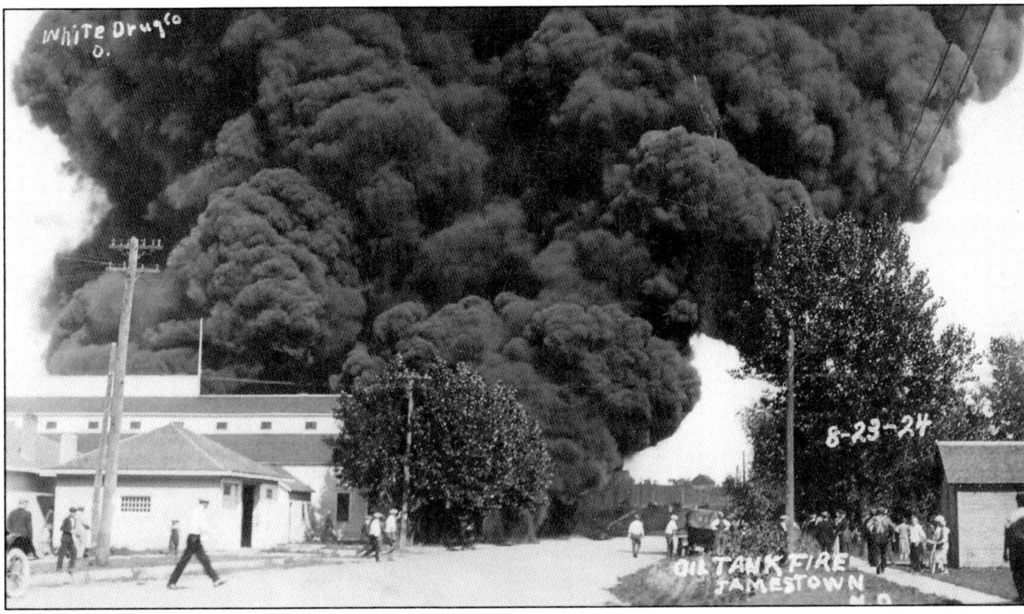

A 1924 fire at an oil tank on the east edge of Jamestown produced a very dark cloud, although there were no injuries. Even with what had to be foul-smelling smoke, the fire seemed to draw many onlookers. (Photograph courtesy of Dave Robertson.)

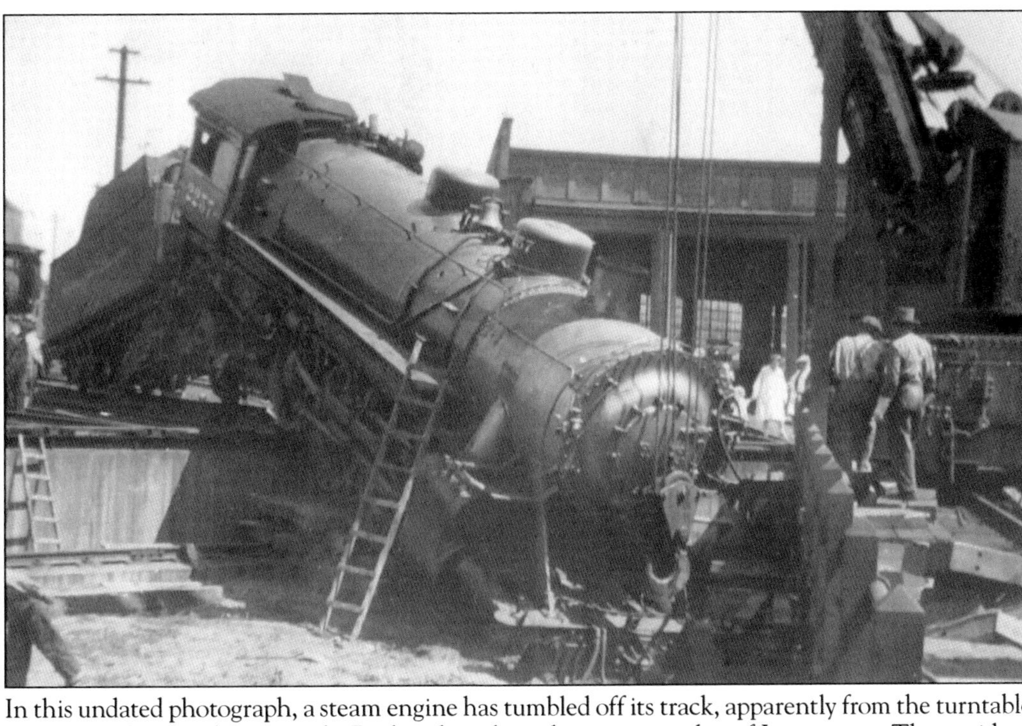

In this undated photograph, a steam engine has tumbled off its track, apparently from the turntable located at the Northern Pacific Railroad yard on the western edge of Jamestown. The accident likely occurred when the turntable was not properly placed as the train approached. (Photograph courtesy of the Stutsman County Memorial Museum.)

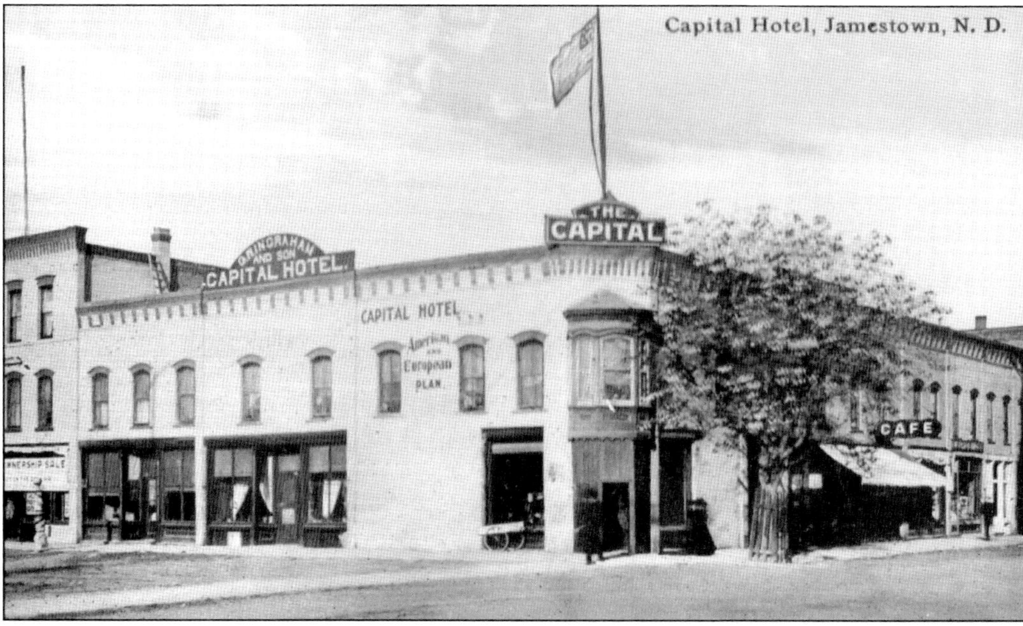

This photograph shows the Capital Hotel before fire destroyed it in the 1930s. The fire was one of several that changed the shape of downtown Jamestown over the years. The hotel's name probably originated during one of Jamestown's efforts to become the state capital. (Photograph courtesy of Dave Robertson.)

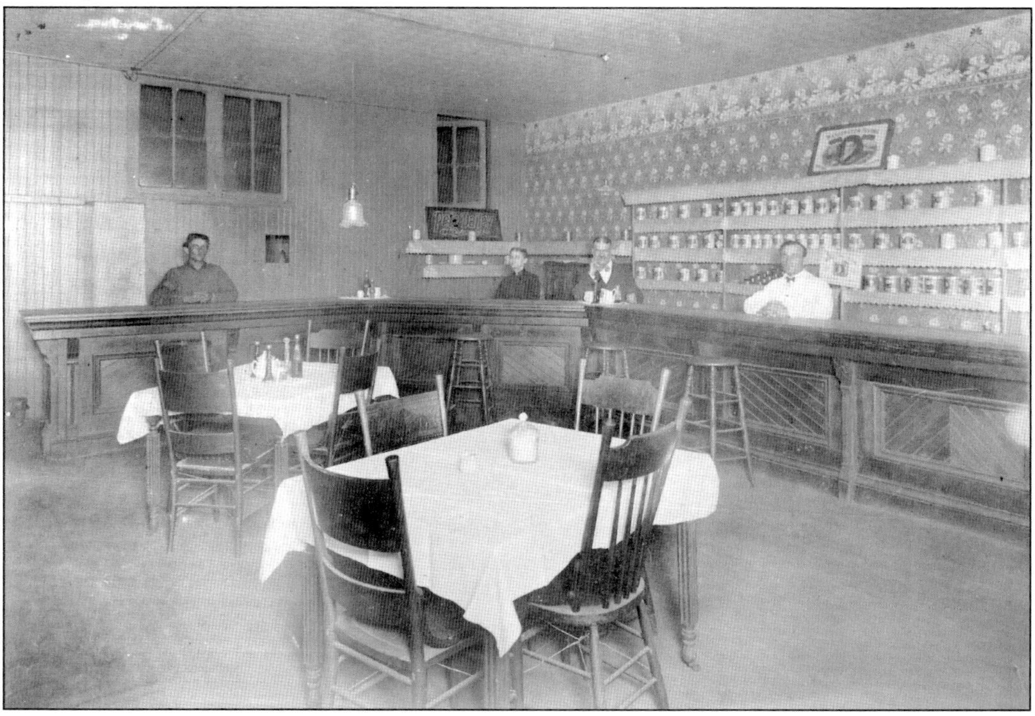

The restaurant at the Capital Hotel appears to function as both a bar and restaurant in this photograph from the 1880s. Prohibition went into effect in 1889 when North Dakota became a state. Most of the hotels offered meals as well as lodging. (Photograph courtesy of Lenard Cave.)

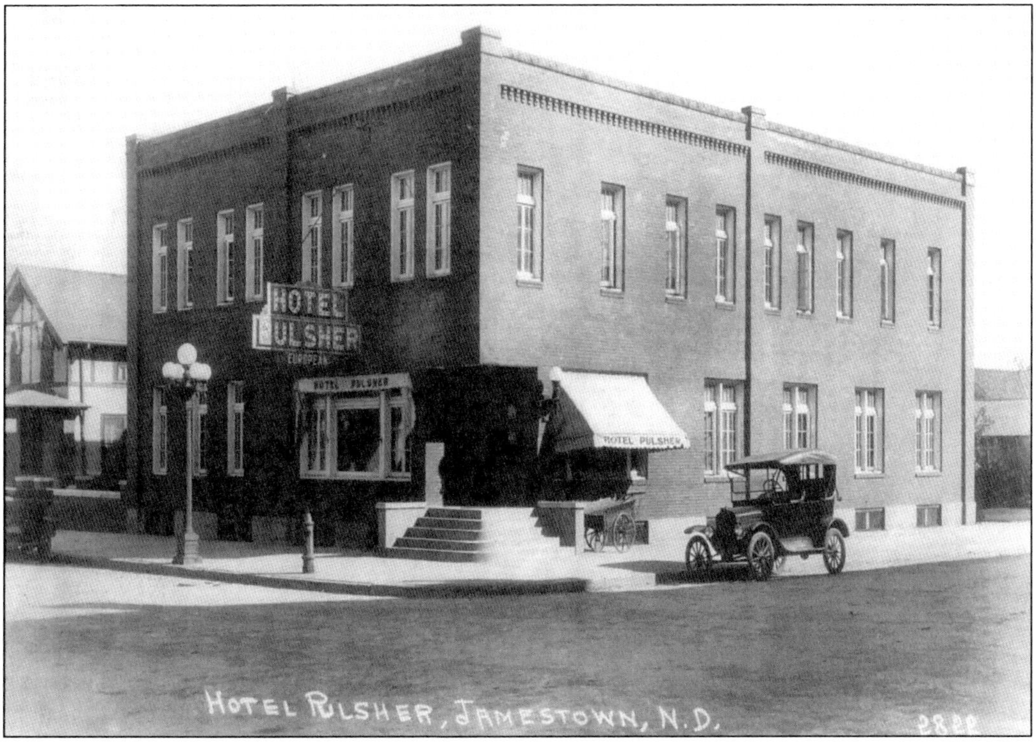

The Hotel Pulsher was just east of the Elks building. Though located within a block of the Gladstone and Capital Hotels, it offered more budget-friendly lodging. (Photograph courtesy of Dave Robertson.)

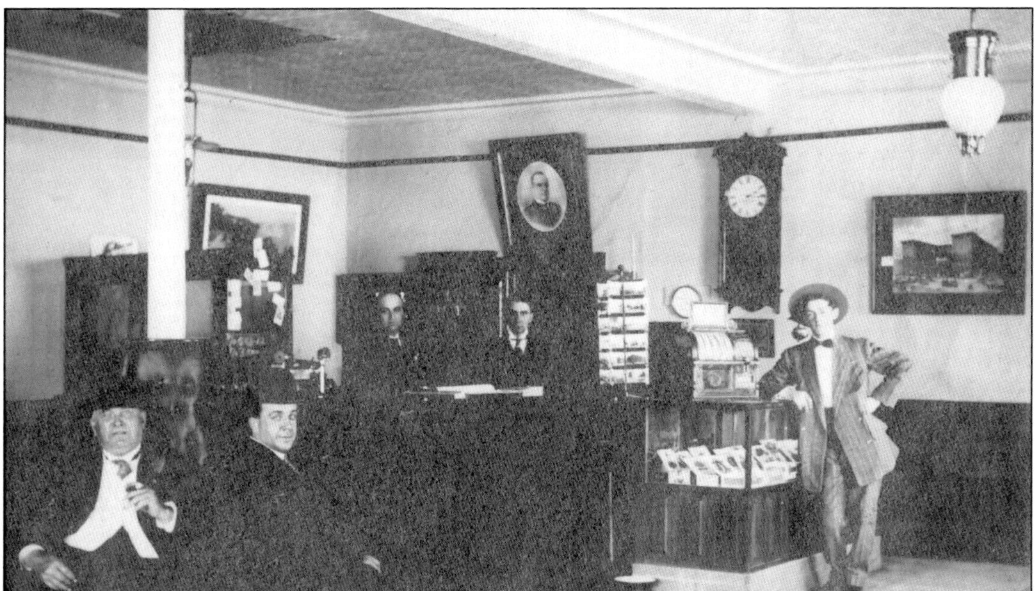

The lobby of the Hotel Pulsher included a cigar display case as well as a display of postcards on the counter. The hotel also offered accommodations for traveling salesmen, and a blackboard on the wall noted the train schedule. (Photograph courtesy of Dave Robertson.)

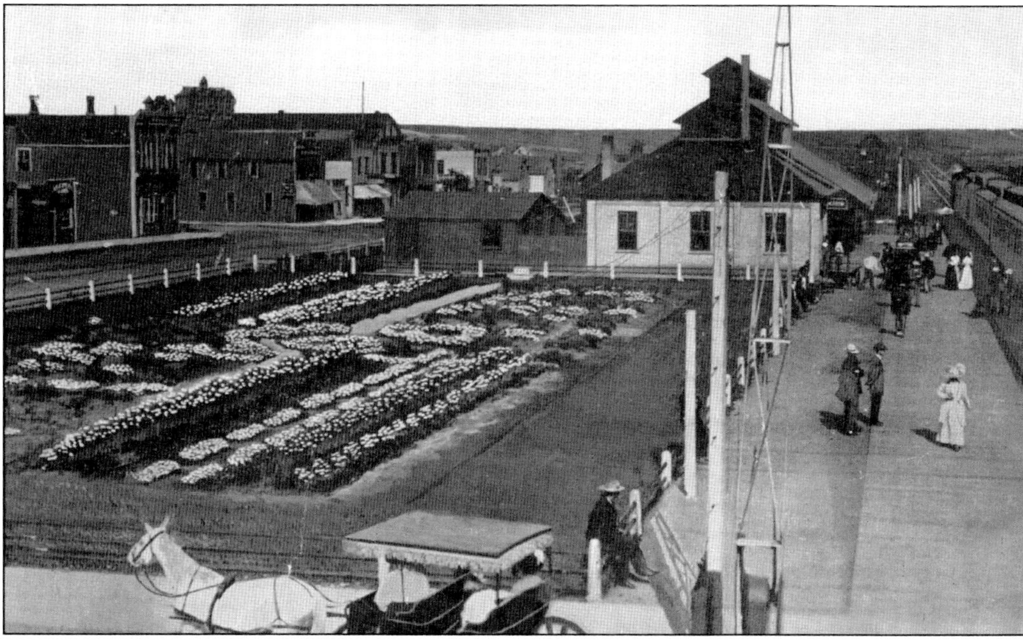

Jamestown's early public school garden was located in the city's original park along the mainline railroad tracks. Students often planted flowers, as seen in this photograph. The school's public garden won several awards before being turned into a parking lot in the 1940s. (Photograph courtesy of Dave Robertson.)

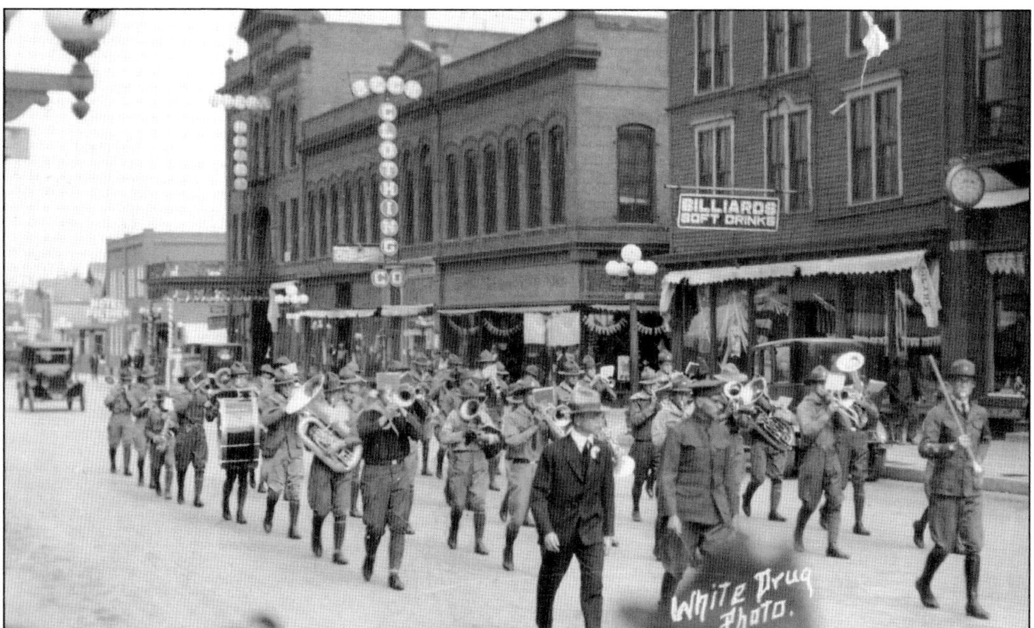

Jamestown residents have never had trouble turning out for a parade. Based on the uniforms and vehicles, this one seems to be from the World War I era. (Photograph courtesy of the Stutsman County Memorial Museum.)

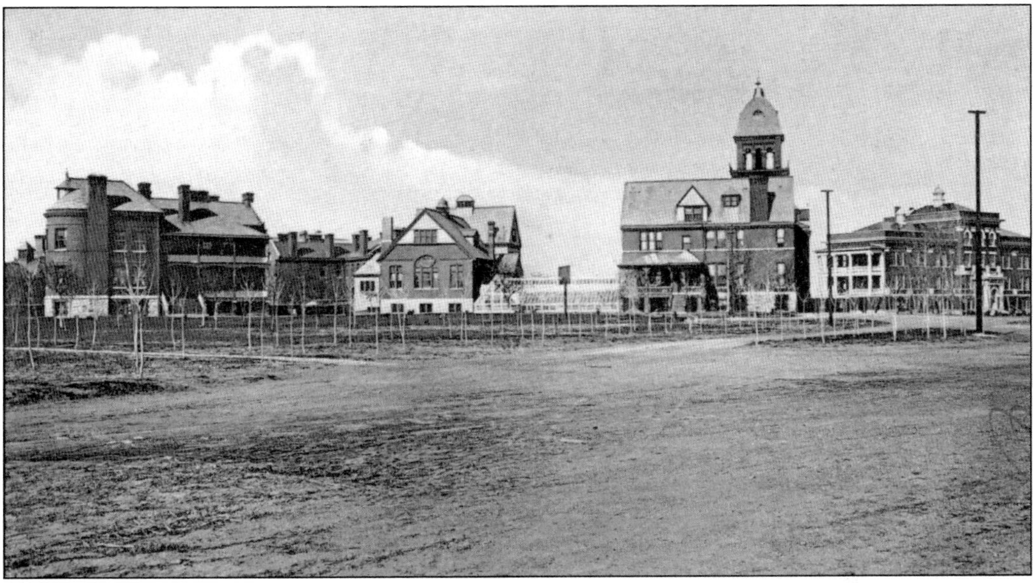
This 1908 postcard of the North Dakota State Hospital shows some of the facility's early buildings. It also shows many of the trees growing on the grounds as saplings at that time. (Photograph courtesy of Dave Robertson.)

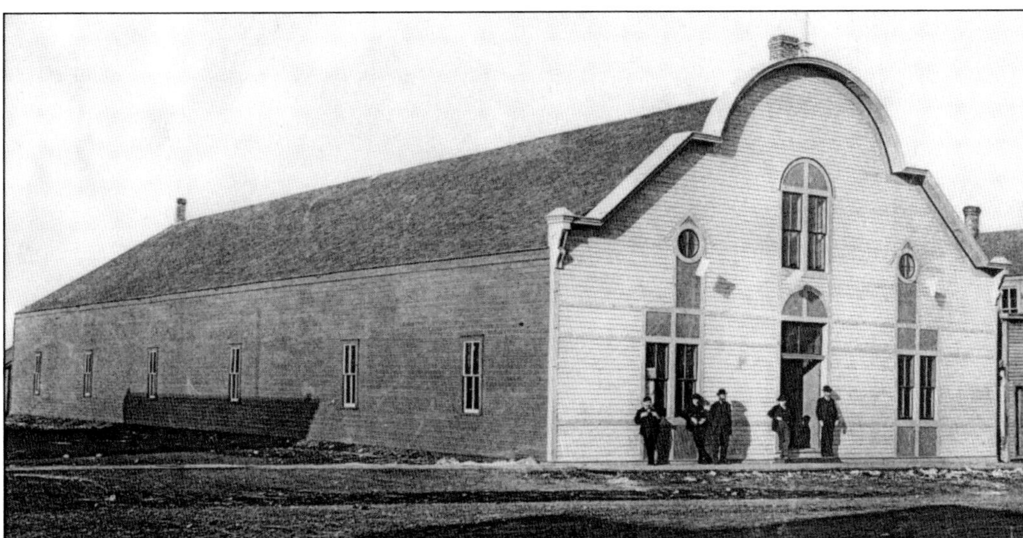
This photograph shows the Rink, a popular roller-skating site built by Anton Klaus in the late 1880s. The building, which also once housed the Elks Club of Jamestown, burned down in the early 1900s. The Elks then built their own lodge on the same tract of land, which they occupied until recently. (Photograph courtesy of the Stutsman County Memorial Museum.)

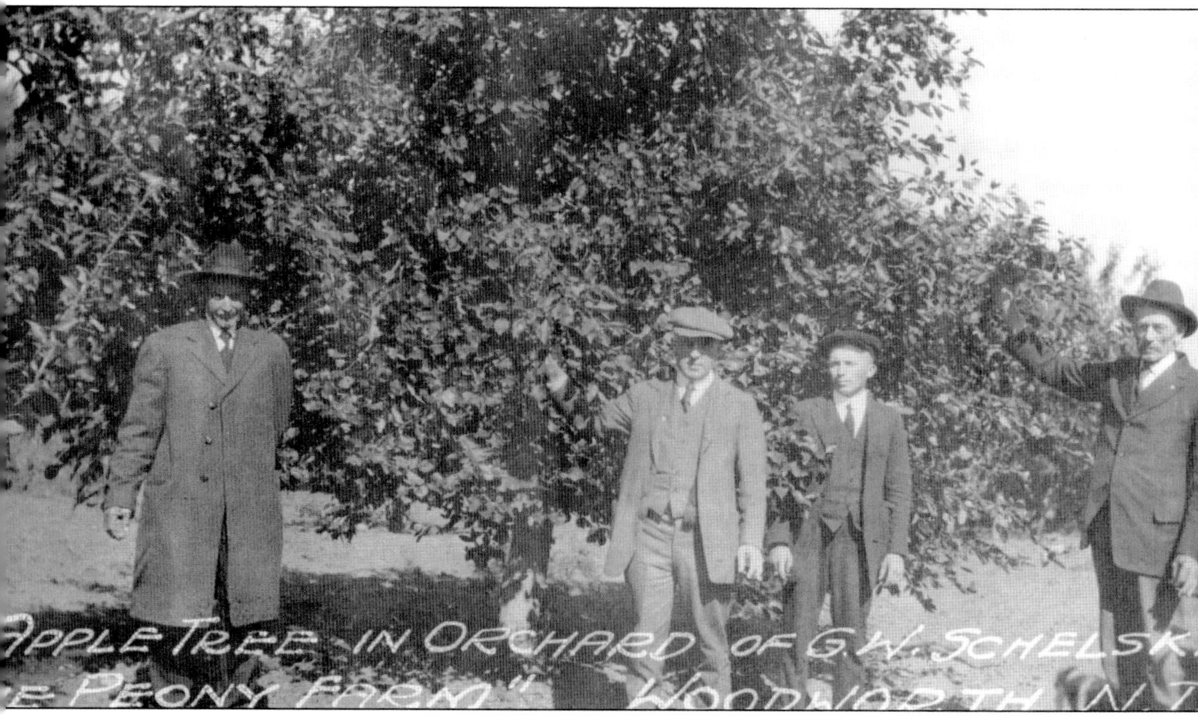

This image shows an apple orchard on G.W. Schelske's peony farm near Woodworth, North Dakota. According to notes on the back of the photograph, Schelske's orchard, which he developed in the 1890s, also produced plums, compass cherries, raspberries, and strawberries. (Photograph courtesy of the Stutsman County Memorial Museum.)

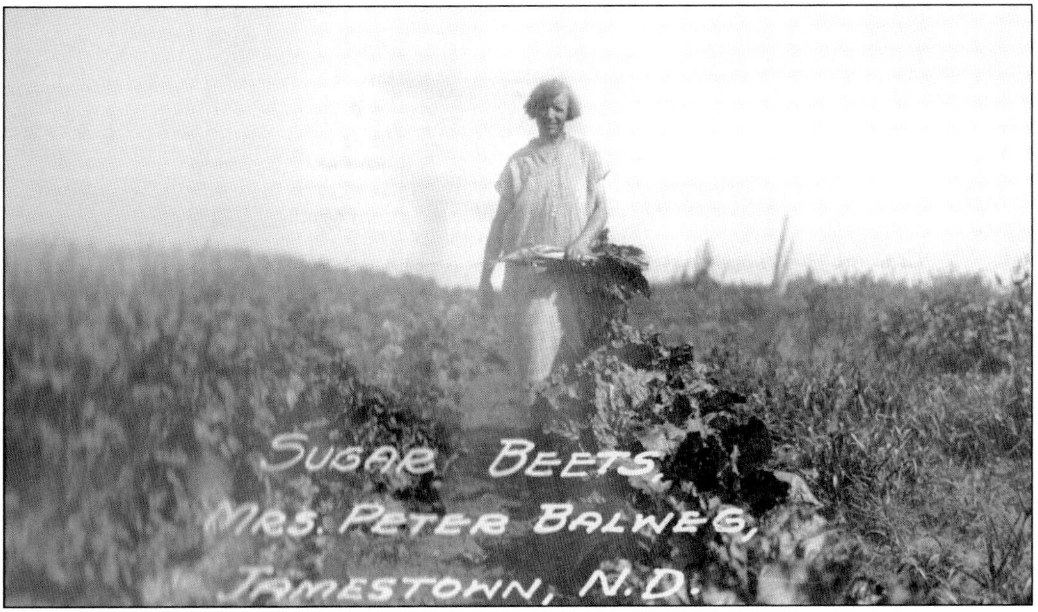

Mrs. Peter Balweg is pictured in her field of sugar beets outside Jamestown. Sugar beets never caught on as a crop in Stutsman County, which was primarily known for wheat and barley until the recent addition of corn and soybeans as cash crops. (Photograph courtesy of the Stutsman County Memorial Museum.)

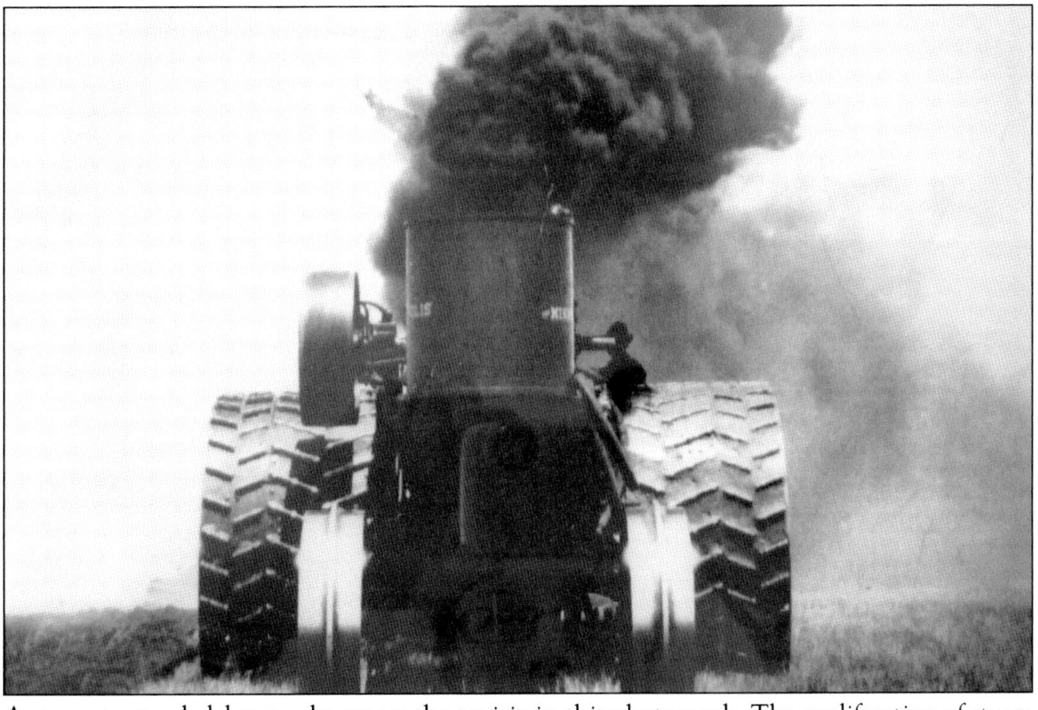

A steam tractor belches smoke across the prairie in this photograph. The proliferation of steam power and advances in the manufacture of plows with hardened steel led to the busting of millions of acres of virgin sod during the first decades of the 20th century. (Photograph courtesy of the Stutsman County Memorial Museum.)

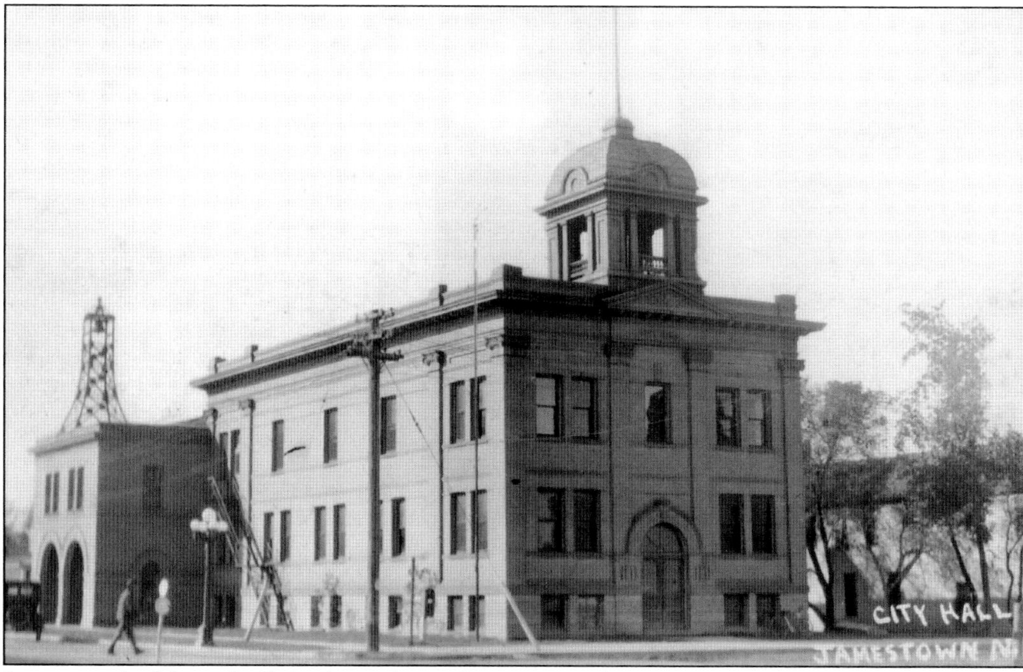

Jamestown's old city hall, built in the early 1900s, is shown here around 1920. It housed the Jamestown Police Department and the fire hall. During World War II, the cupola was utilized as an observation tower. After a fire destroyed a south-side school, the upper level also served as a library and classroom. The building has since been razed, but the cupola was preserved and now sits downtown on the south side of the railroad mainline in a small park near the city's viaduct. (Photograph courtesy of the Stutsman County Memorial Museum.)

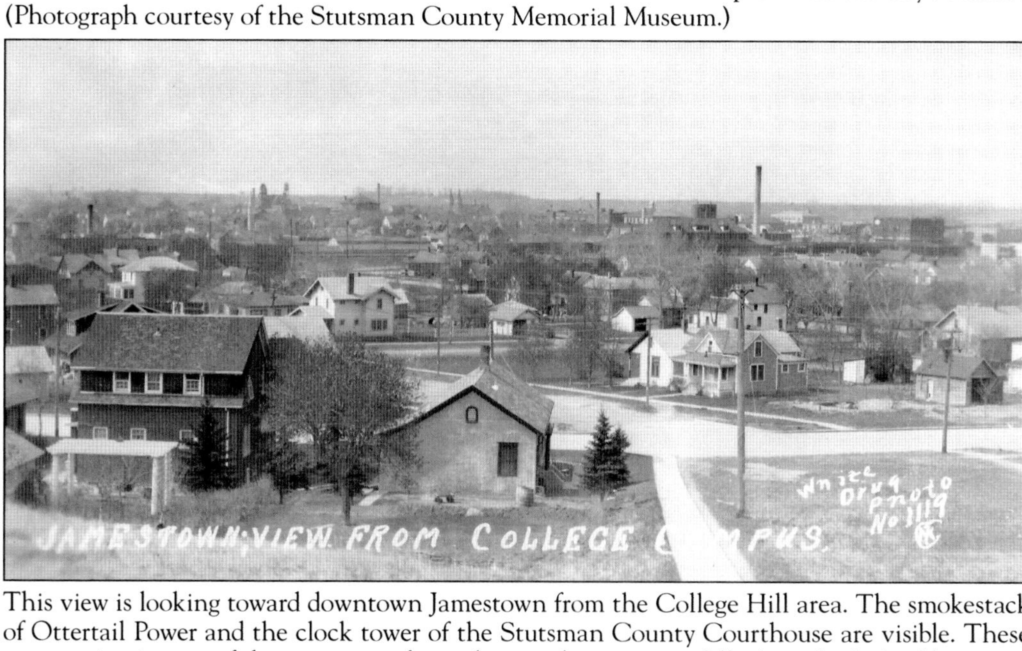

This view is looking toward downtown Jamestown from the College Hill area. The smokestack of Ottertail Power and the clock tower of the Stutsman County Courthouse are visible. These panoramic pictures of the city were often taken in the spring or fall when the lack of leaves on the trees provided better views of the buildings. (Photograph courtesy of the Jamestown Parks & Recreation Department.)

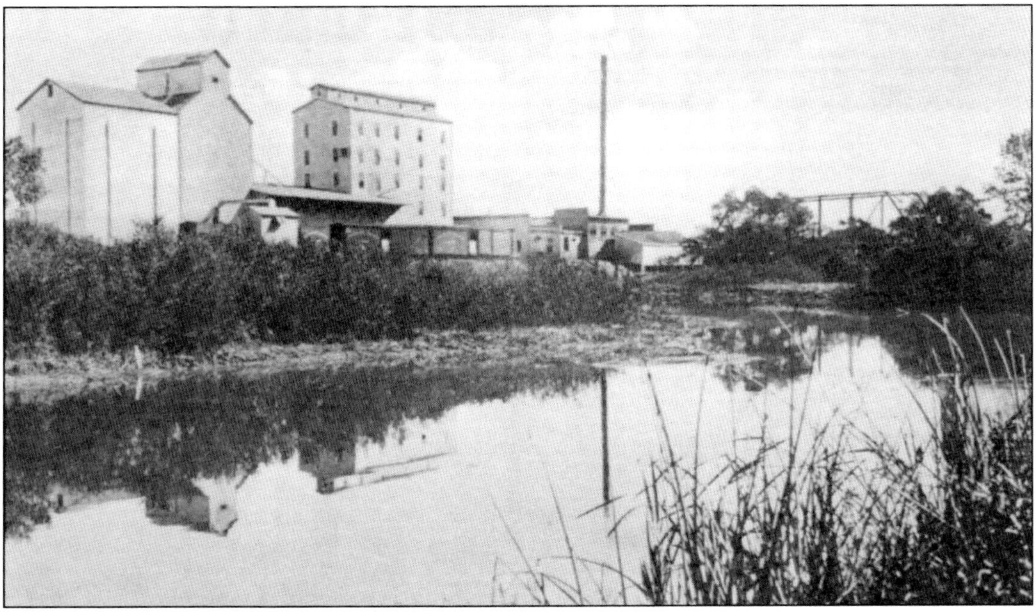

Russell-Miller Milling Company, located next to the James River and close to Klaus Park, is shown in this photograph. These are the backs of the buildings used to store grain and mill it into flour. (Picture postcard courtesy of the Stutsman County Memorial Museum.)

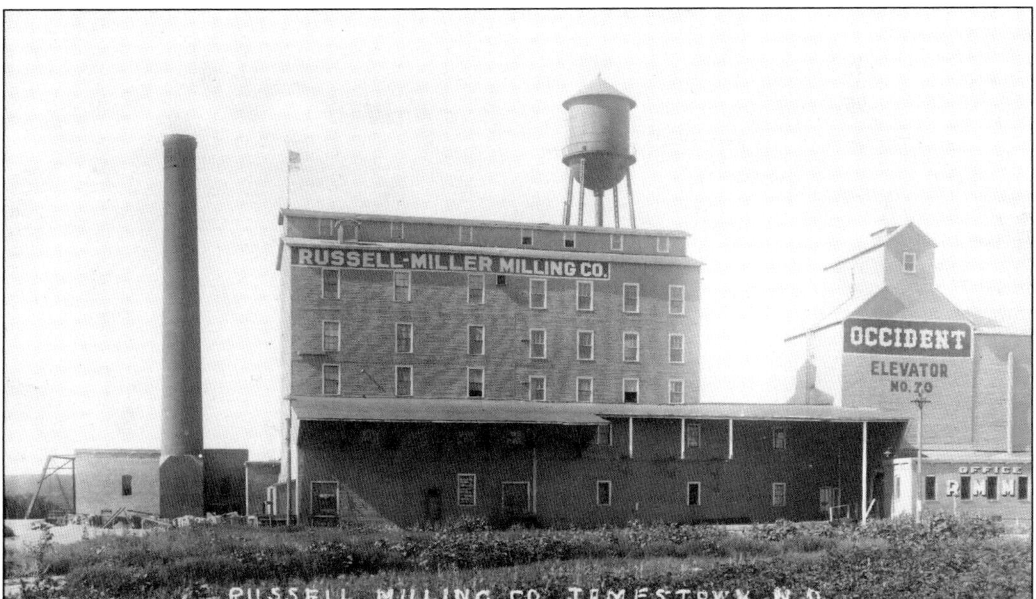

The Russell-Miller Milling Company produced Dakota Maid flour, noted for its quality, at the base of Mill Hill. This picture dates to about 1920. The mills are now gone, but the adjacent hill is still known as Mill Hill. (Photograph courtesy of Dave Robertson.)

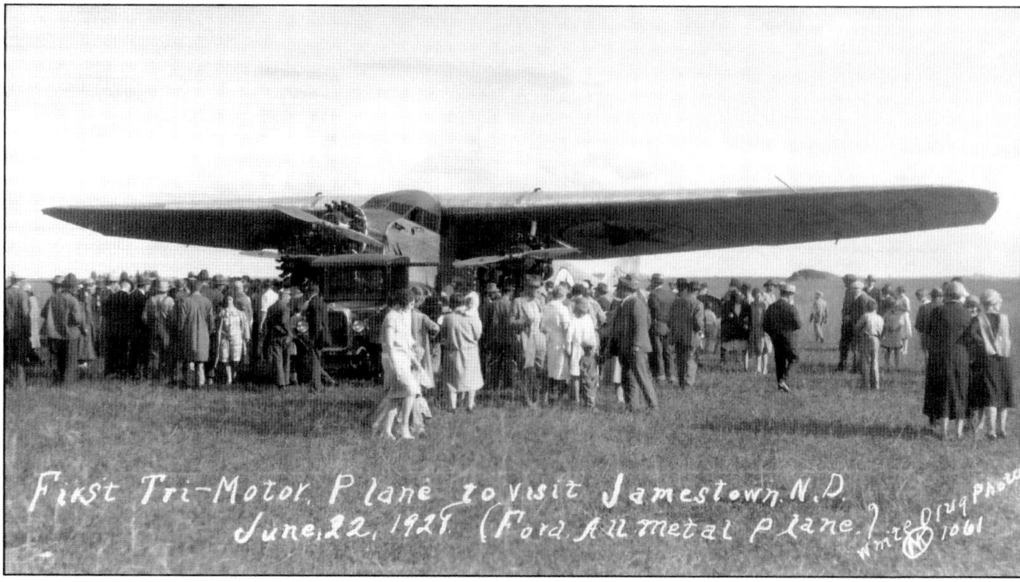

The Texas Oil Company, later known as Texaco, brought a Ford Trimotor plane to visit Jamestown in 1927. The aircraft landed on the grounds of the North Dakota State Hospital and drew visitors from the community. (Photograph courtesy of the Jamestown Parks & Recreation Department.)

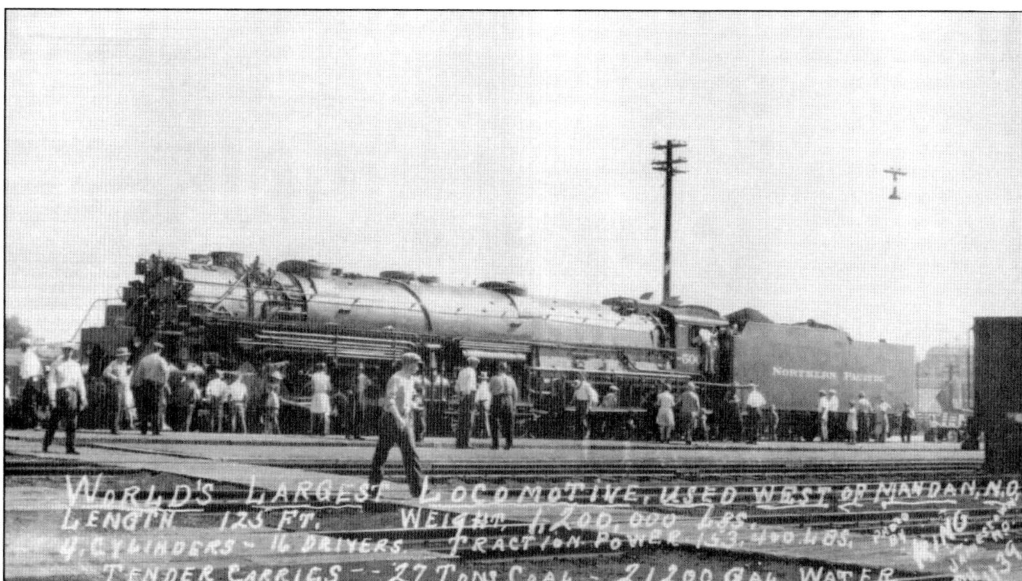

The notation on this photograph labeled it the "world's largest locomotive used west of Mandan, ND." At 125 feet long, this engine was a beast. While the engine and tender commonly made runs west of Jamestown, this photograph shows the engine in Jamestown on what was probably a promotional stop. (Photograph courtesy of Dave Robertson.)

Two

A City Matures

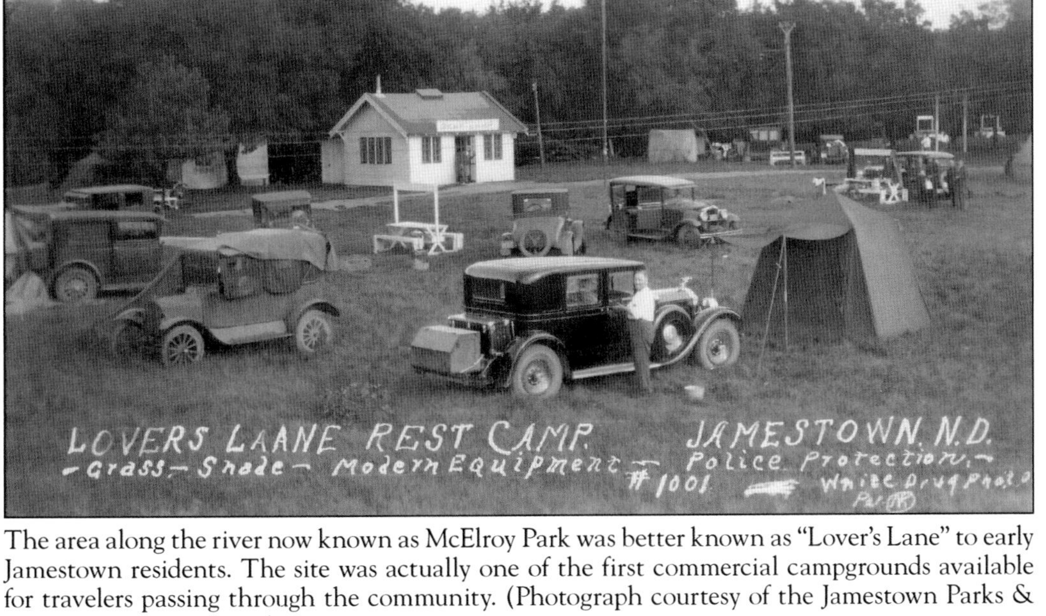

The area along the river now known as McElroy Park was better known as "Lover's Lane" to early Jamestown residents. The site was actually one of the first commercial campgrounds available for travelers passing through the community. (Photograph courtesy of the Jamestown Parks & Recreation Department.)

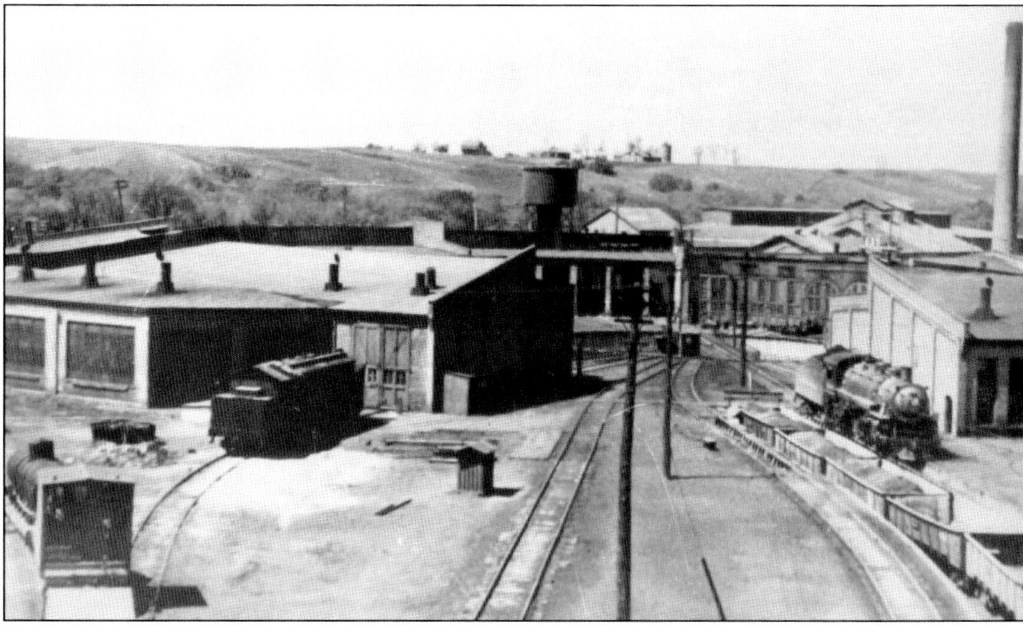

This photograph offers a view into the Northern Pacific Railroad yard. The turntable and roundhouse are visible in the center, with a farm on the horizon. (Photograph courtesy of the Stutsman County Memorial Museum.)

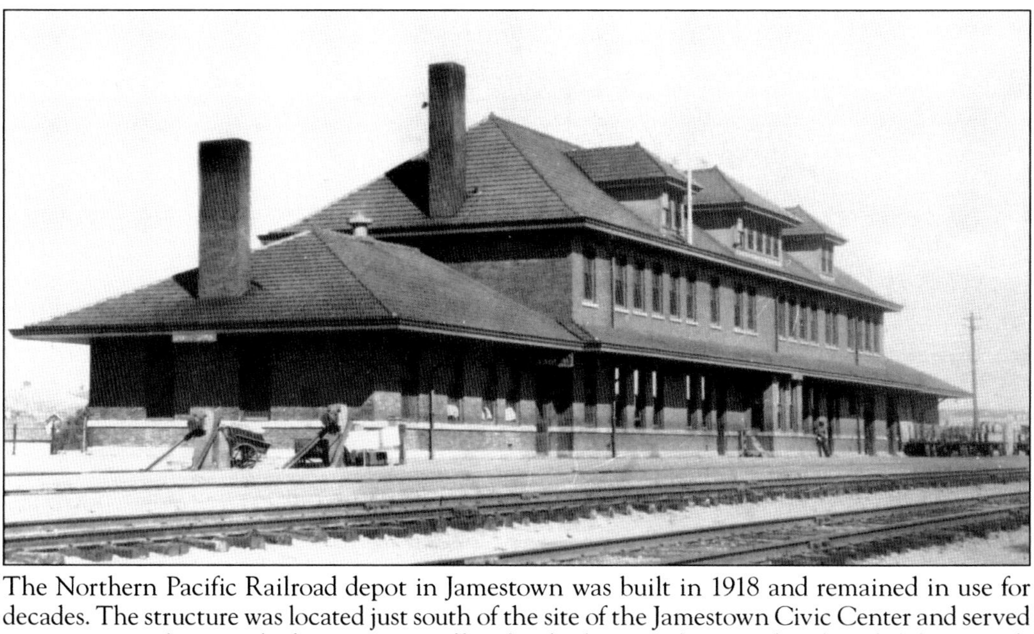

The Northern Pacific Railroad depot in Jamestown was built in 1918 and remained in use for decades. The structure was located just south of the site of the Jamestown Civic Center and served as a passenger depot and administrative office for the line until it was abandoned. (Photograph courtesy of the Stutsman County Memorial Museum.)

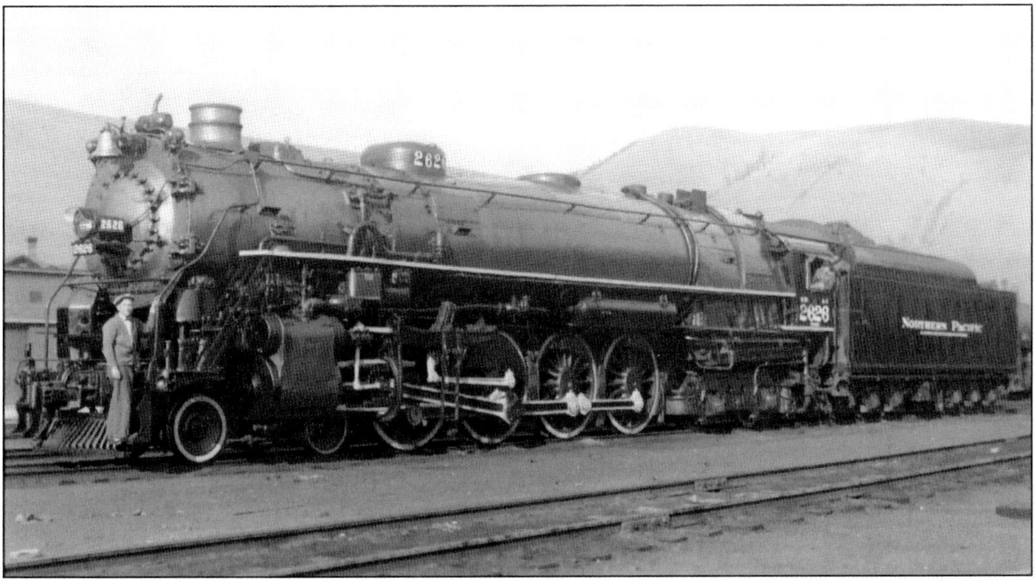

This is a photograph of one of the Northern Pacific's heavy steam engines. Note the coal car coupled to the engine. According to Northern Pacific records, this engine reached a top speed of 88 miles per hour during a 1931 run in Montana. (Photograph courtesy of the Stutsman County Memorial Museum.)

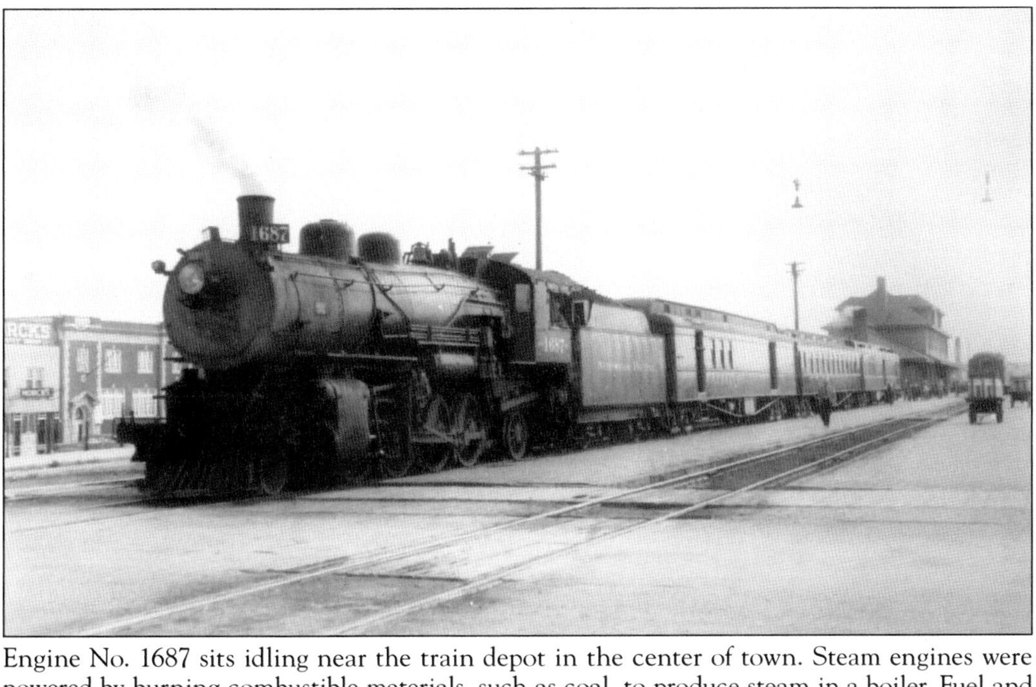

Engine No. 1687 sits idling near the train depot in the center of town. Steam engines were powered by burning combustible materials, such as coal, to produce steam in a boiler. Fuel and water were carried on the locomotive or in cars pulled behind it. (Photograph courtesy of the Stutsman County Memorial Museum.)

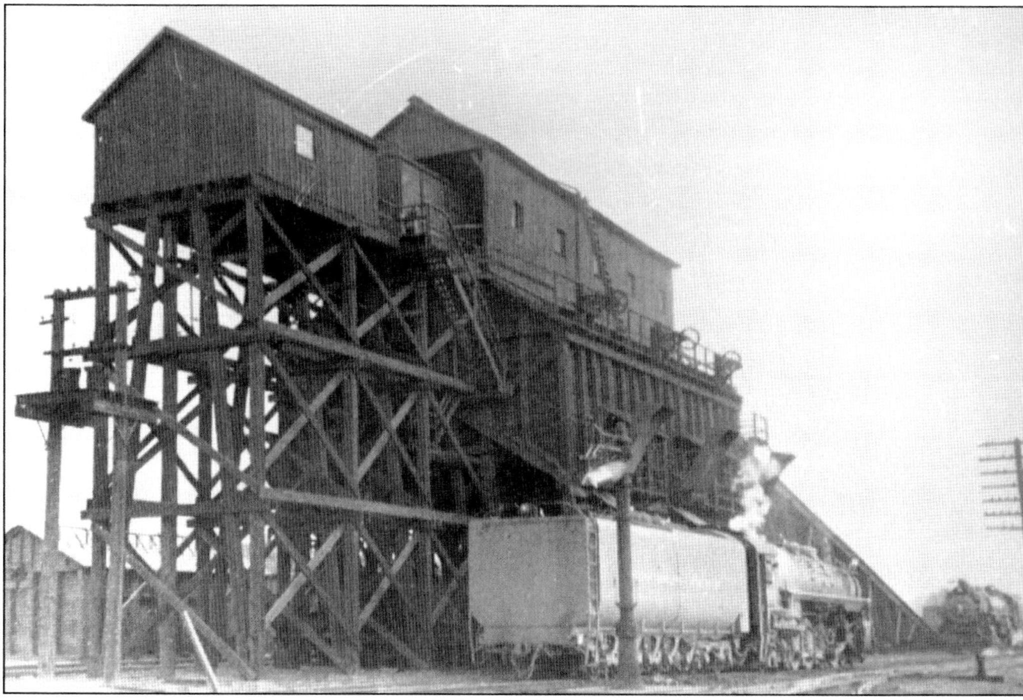

The elevated coal bunkers in Jamestown provided fuel for the engines in the age of steam locomotives. Coal cars were winched up the ramp before dumping into the bins below, and coal tenders were then filled from the bins. (Photograph courtesy of the Stutsman County Memorial Museum.)

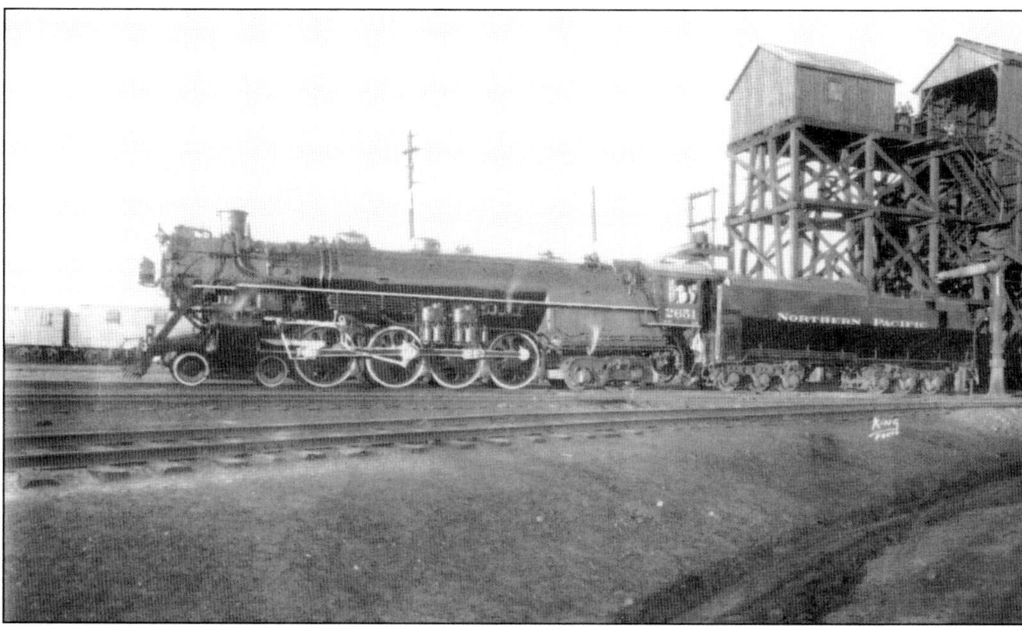

This photograph, probably from the 1940s, shows a steam-powered engine and train at the coal-loading facility near the Jamestown roundhouse. Use of the facility ceased when diesel engines were adopted in the early to mid-1950s. (Photograph courtesy of the Stutsman County Memorial Museum.)

A thick, wintry plume of smoke billows from this steamer as it heads down the track near Jamestown. The plume coming from the engine was a mixture of water steam and coal exhaust and was more notable in cold weather. (Photograph courtesy of the Stutsman County Memorial Museum.)

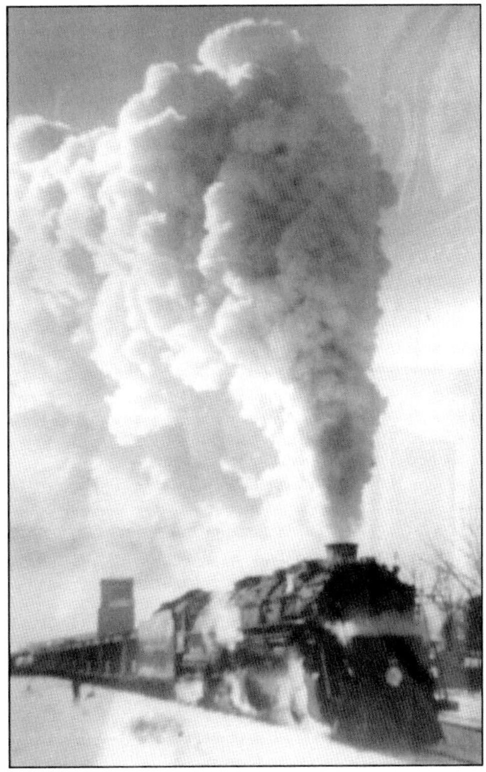

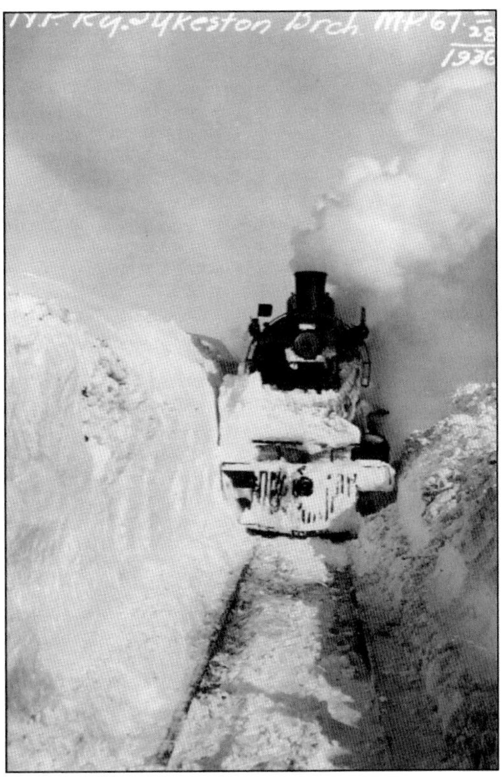

Winters in North Dakota can be harsh, with bone-chilling cold and deep snow. This steam engine is making a cut through a deep bank of snow on the prairie outside Jamestown. Early snow-removal efforts often included hiring local workers to shovel the snow from the tracks. (Photograph courtesy of the Stutsman County Memorial Museum.)

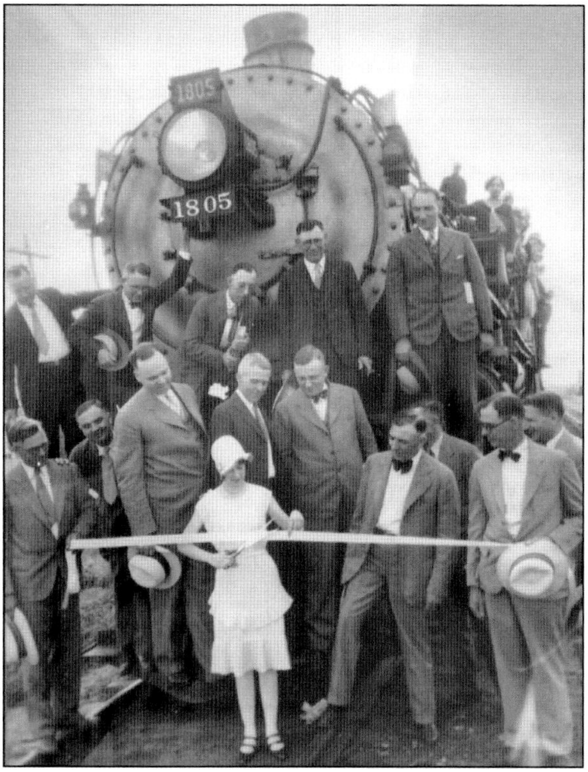

This photograph depicts a ribbon cutting held by the Midland Continental Railroad. Though only remnants of the railroad still exist, one interesting site is the Midland Continental Railroad Depot Transportation Museum in Wimbledon, North Dakota, not far from Jamestown. It is the only remaining Midland Continental depot left and once was the home of singer Peggy Lee and her father. Lee was born in Jamestown in 1920. (Photograph courtesy of the Stutsman County Memorial Museum.)

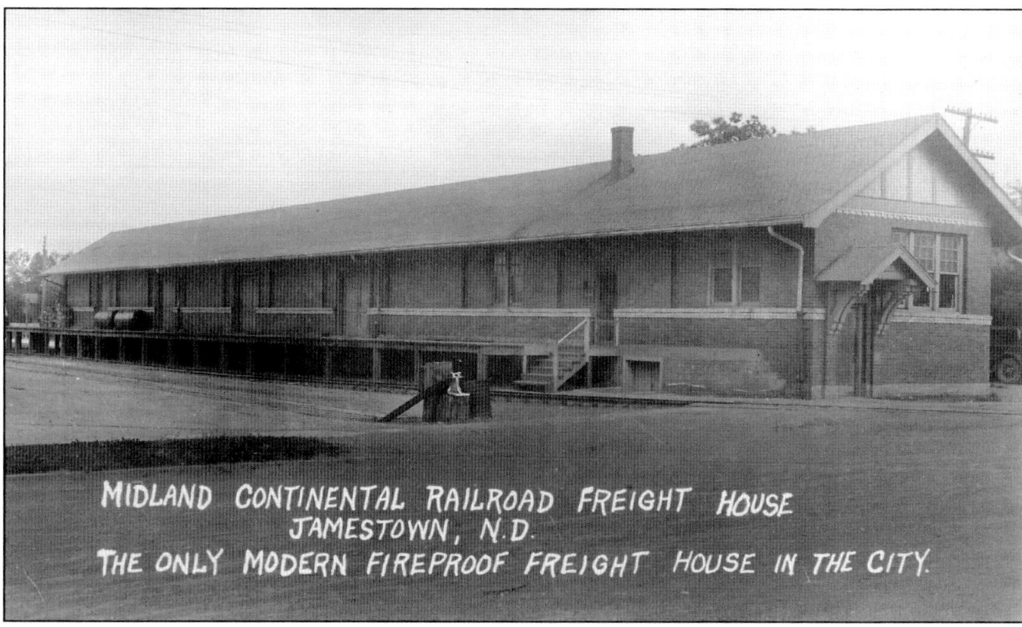

This photograph shows one of the Midland Continental Railroad's buildings, a freight house, in Jamestown. The Midland Continental had intended to connect Winnipeg, Manitoba, to Galveston, Texas, but only about 50 miles of track, all in North Dakota, were laid. The railroad was headquartered in Jamestown until operations ceased in the 1970s. (Photograph courtesy of Dave Robertson.)

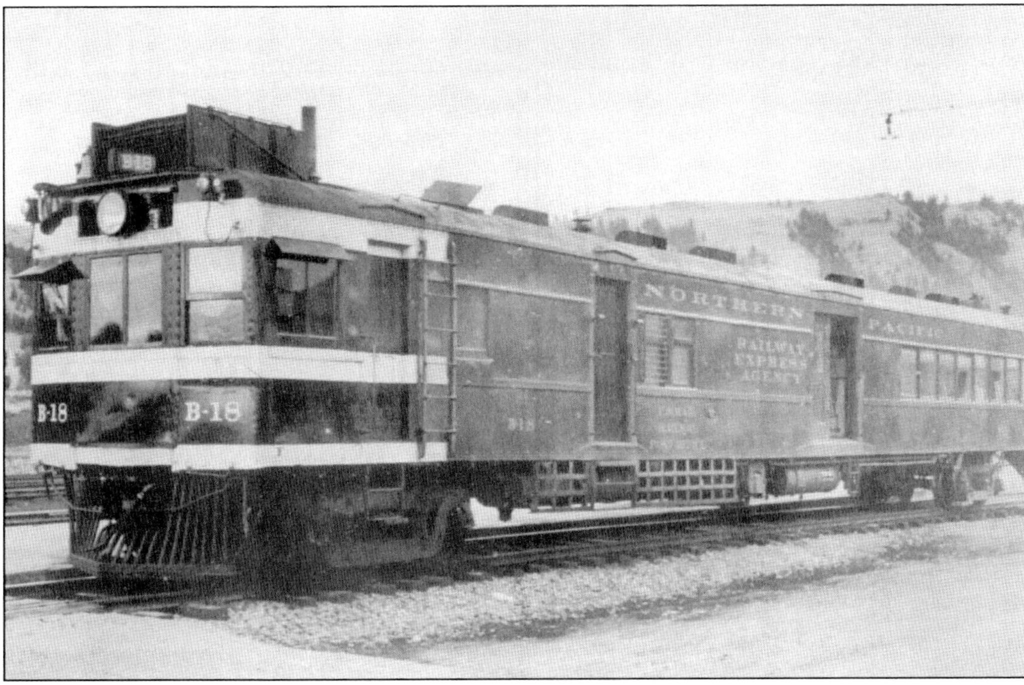

In later years, demand for rail freight diminished. In order to handle mail and cream contracts, the Northern Pacific utilized the "Galloping Goose," a type of combination car and engine that was operated by an engineer and conductor. (Photograph courtesy of Dave Robertson.)

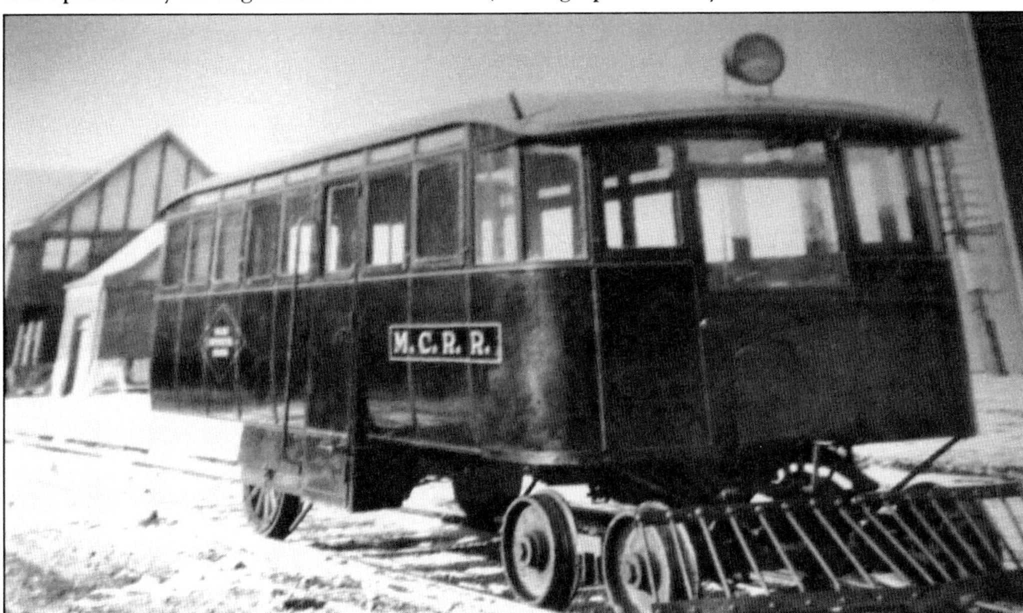

The Midland Continental Railroad operated a dinkey as its vehicle for daily trips across its tracks. The dinkey not only accommodated mail and cream, but passengers as well. It, along with the Galloping Goose, allowed the rail lines to maintain daily service to small communities without the expense of operating full trains. (Photograph courtesy of the Stutsman County Memorial Museum.)

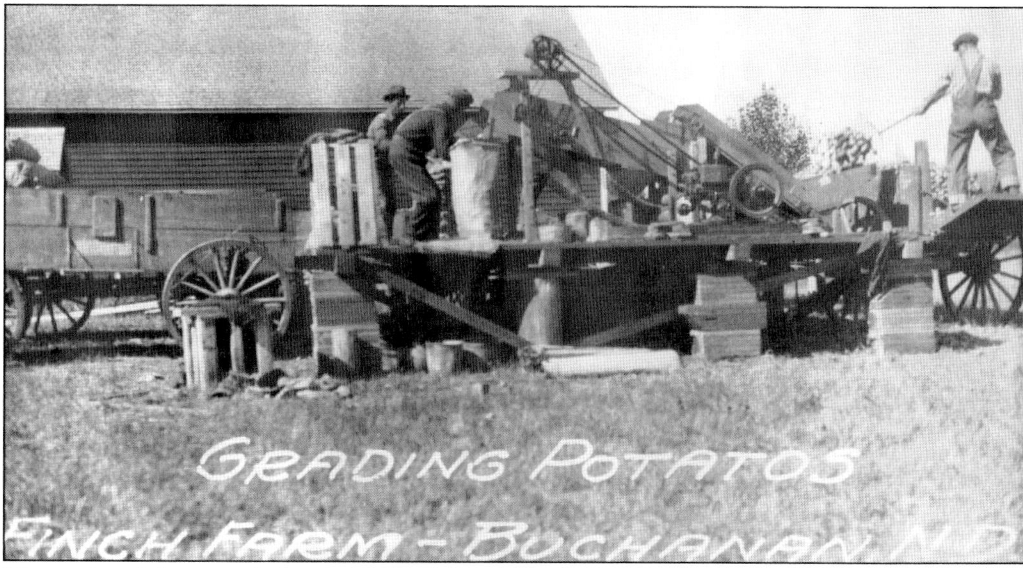

This undated photograph shows the Finch family grading potatoes on a Buchanan, North Dakota, farm. According to notations on the back of the picture, the Finches also grew alfalfa, sweet clover, corn, and wheat in addition to raising cattle and hogs. In the past, farm families' operations were far more diversified than they typically are today, with a greater variety of crops and a wider range of animals. (Photograph courtesy of the Stutsman County Memorial Museum.)

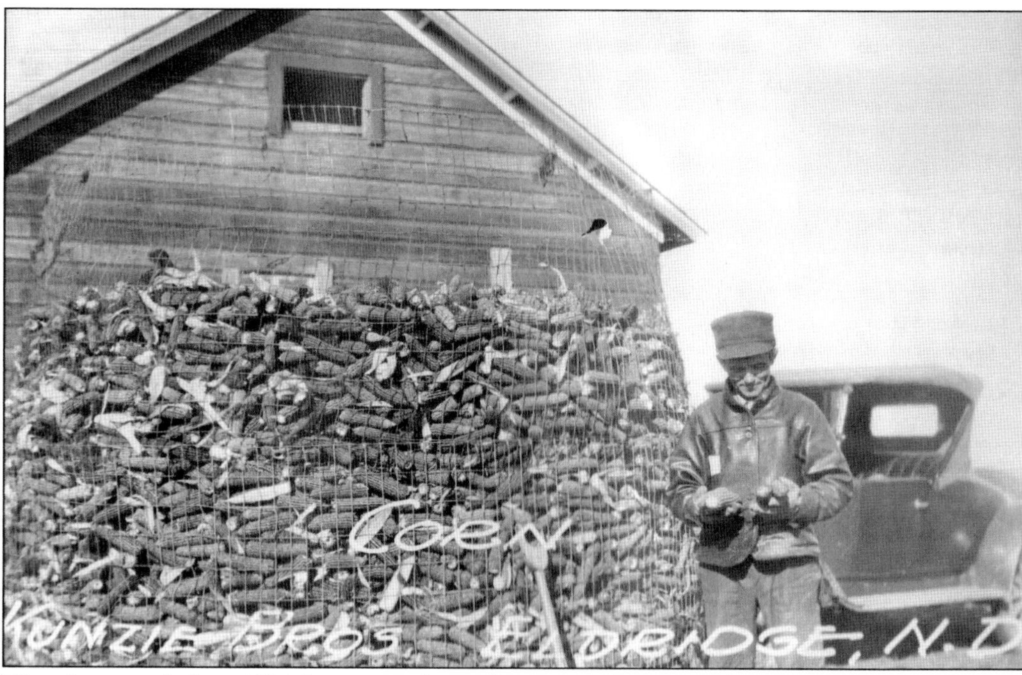

This photograph from 1924 shows a seed-corn harvest at the Kunzie brothers' farm near Eldridge, North Dakota. According to the back of the photograph, the Kunzies harvested 1,420 bushels of corn valued at $3.75 a bushel. After filling their 100-ton silo, the brothers still had 1,189 bushels available for feed. (Photograph courtesy of the Stutsman County Memorial Museum.)

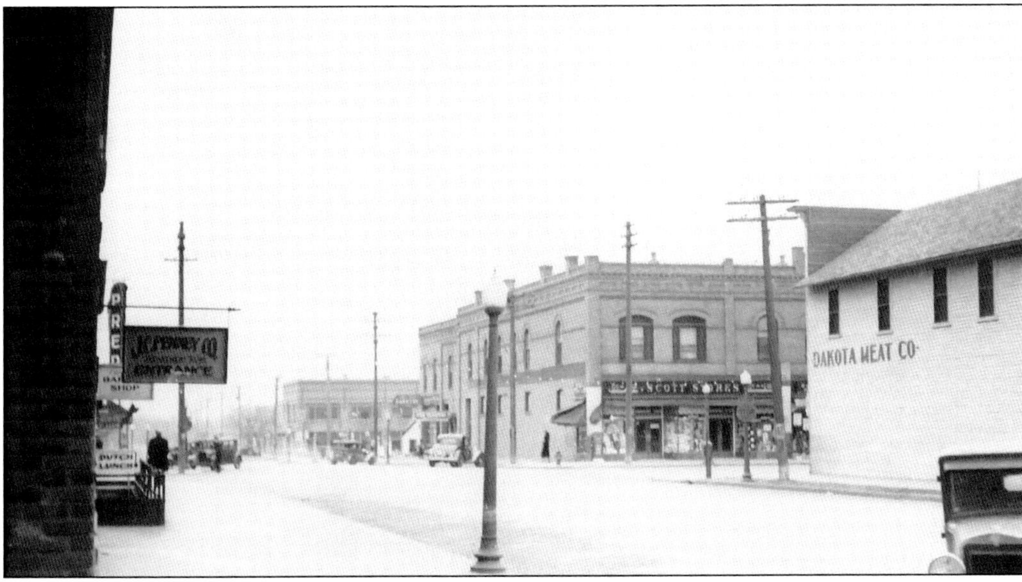

The Dakota Meat Company was a going concern in Jamestown for many years. The company's First Avenue outlet store thrived downtown during the 1930s and 1940s. (Photograph courtesy of Dave Robertson.)

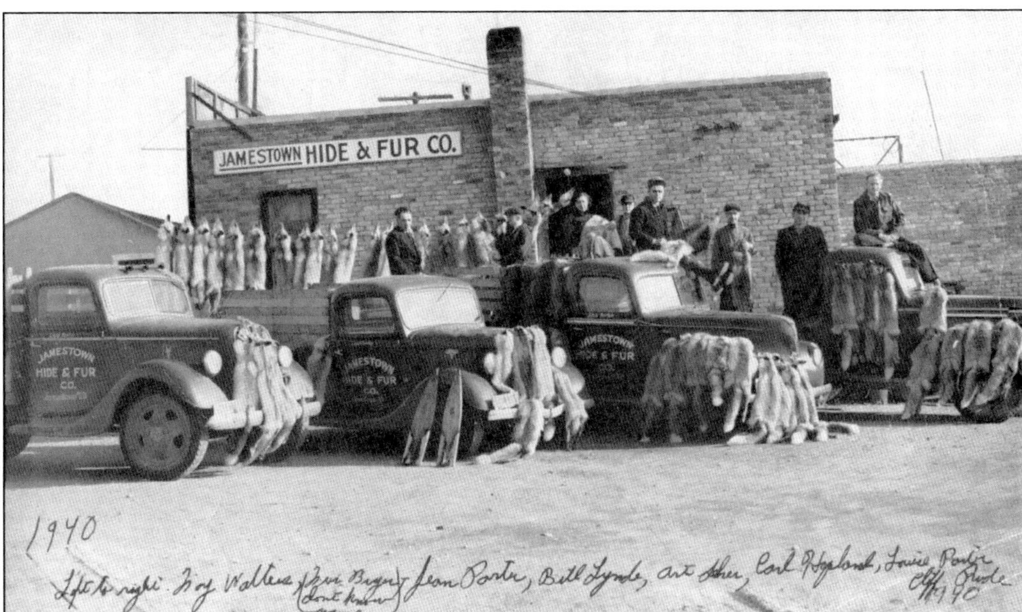

This 1940 photograph demonstrates how important fur trapping was for many people in the region at the time. Dozens of coyote pelts hang from the fenders and windows of pickups. While trapping is not what it used to be, some trappers still bring their furs to sell to Porter Brothers Company, which is located on the west side of Jamestown. (Photograph courtesy of Leonard Rude collection.)

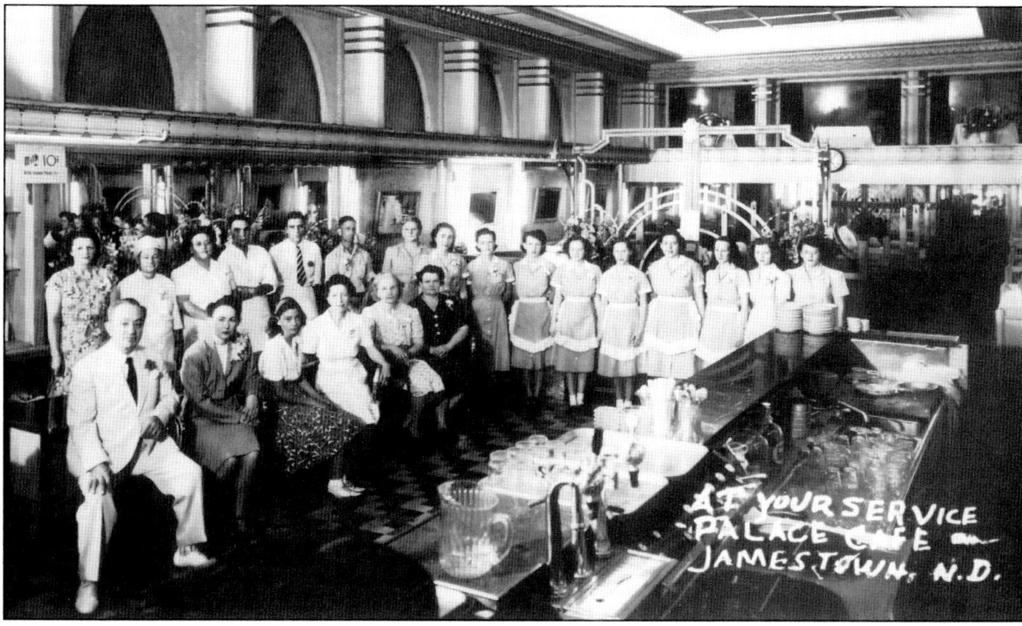

The Palace Café, located at the present site of the Buffalo City Rotisserie Grill, was noted as one of the premier eateries in Jamestown. This photograph from the late 1940s shows the management and staff. (Photograph courtesy of Dave Robertson.)

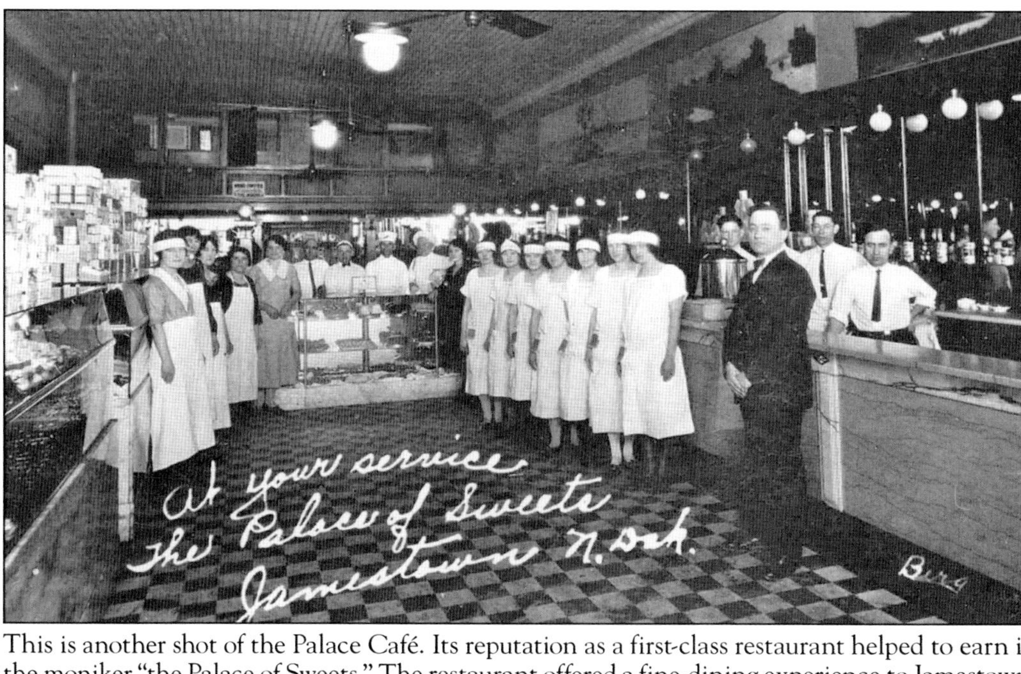

This is another shot of the Palace Café. Its reputation as a first-class restaurant helped to earn it the moniker "the Palace of Sweets." The restaurant offered a fine-dining experience to Jamestown residents. (Picture postcard courtesy of the Stutsman County Memorial Museum.)

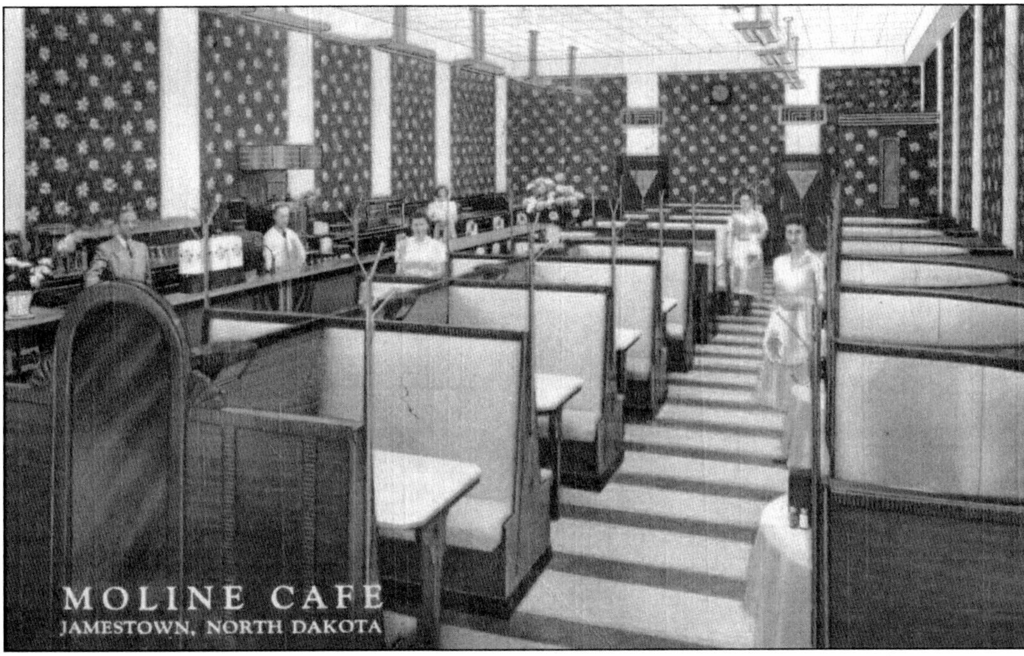

The Moline Café, another favorite downtown eatery, is shown in this postcard. This restaurant featured booths and tables and offered a more casual dining experience. (Picture postcard courtesy of the Stutsman County Memorial Museum.)

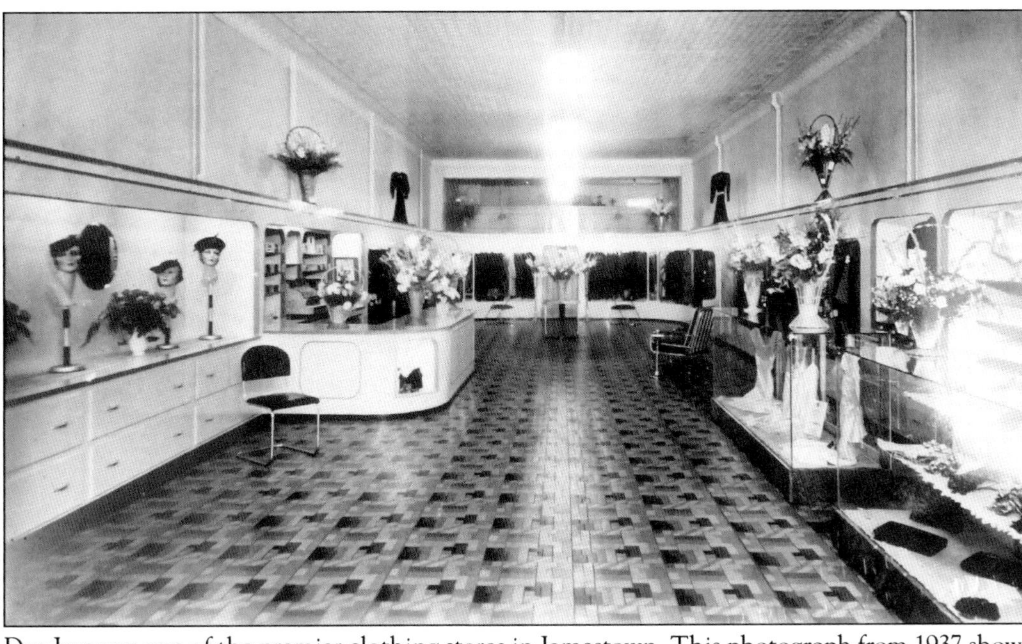

Dee Jays was one of the premier clothing stores in Jamestown. This photograph from 1937 shows some of its decor and inventory. The space has since been incorporated into the site currently utilized by the Buffalo City Rotisserie Grill. (Photograph courtesy of Dave Robertson.)

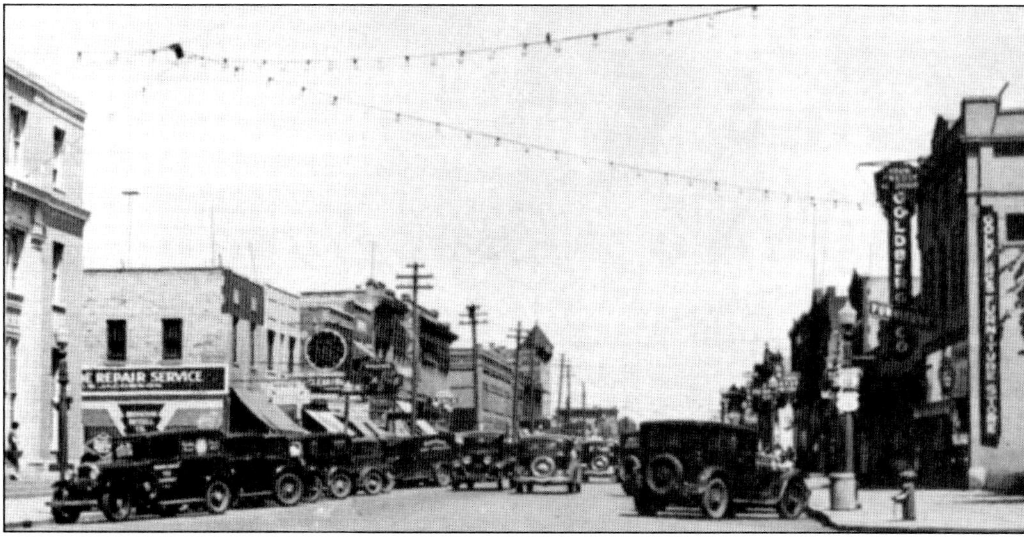

This c. 1930 photograph shows a bustling city main street with lots of traffic and lots of business activity. The diagonal parking of that era was later replaced with parallel parking when the street was modified to accommodate four lanes of traffic. (Photograph courtesy of the Stutsman County Memorial Museum.)

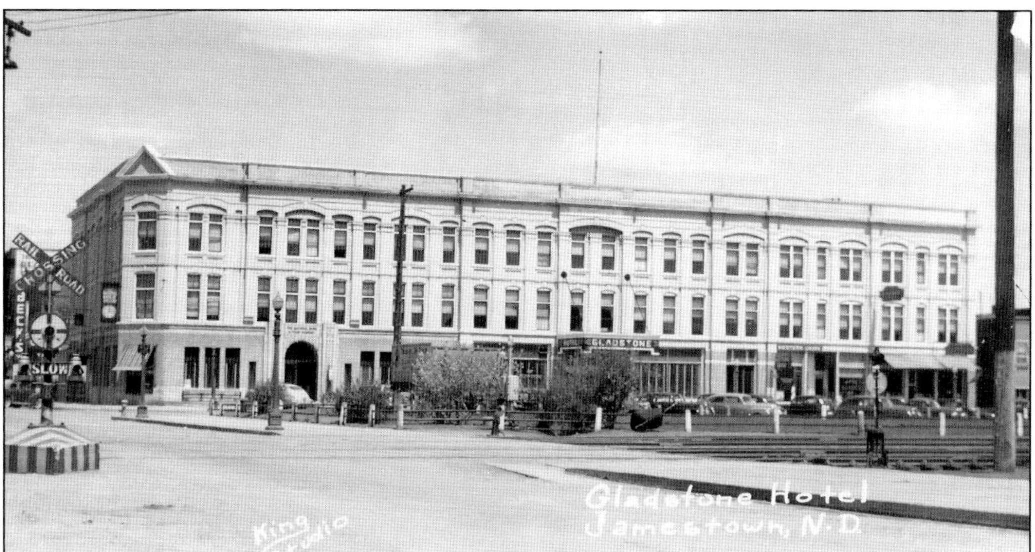

This photograph shows the Gladstone Hotel in the 1920s. The hotel was one of the largest between Minneapolis and the west coast and was well known by travelers on the Northern Pacific mainline as it was located on the north side of the track just a couple blocks from the train depot. (Photograph courtesy of the Stutsman County Memorial Museum.)

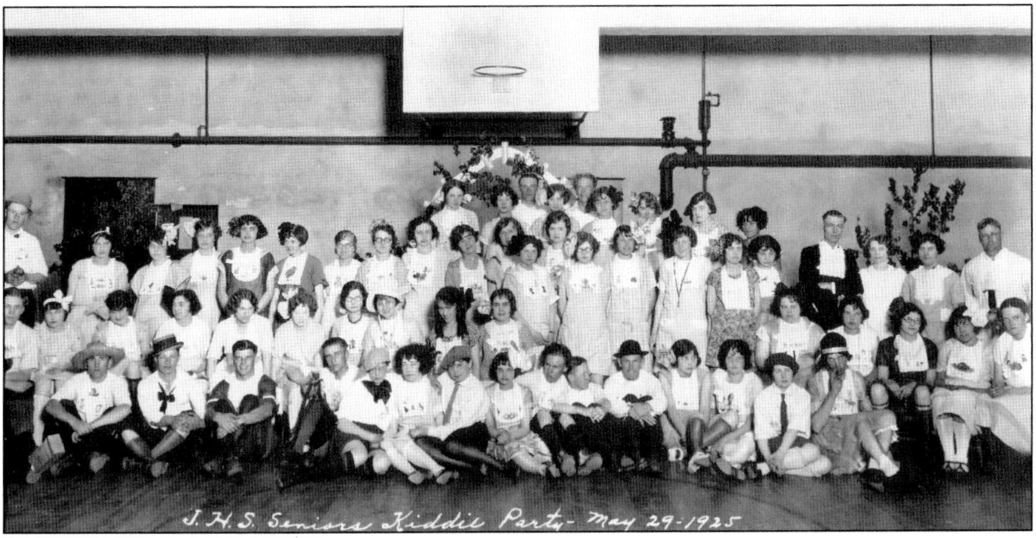

Late in the 1925 school year, the seniors at Jamestown High School gathered for an event called a "kiddie party." The students, who were approaching graduation, dressed as children for the day. (Photograph by Oscar Berg, courtesy of Bruce Berg.)

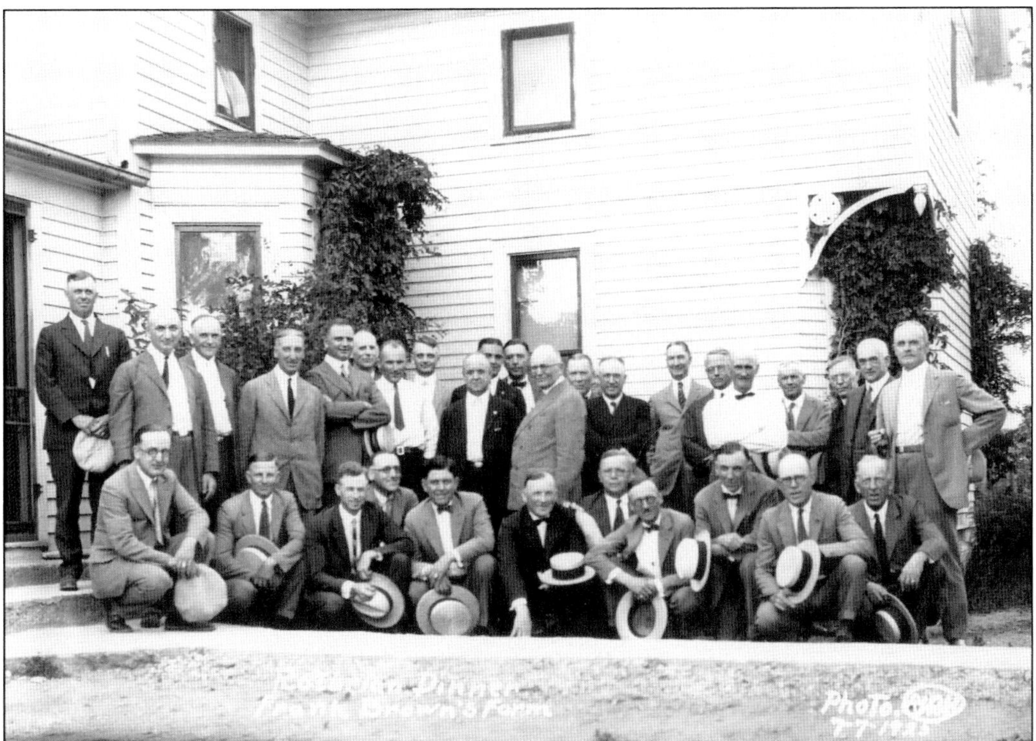

The 1925 Jamestown Rotary Club posed for this picture in front of the home of Frank Brown. The group, which was one of the more active organizations in the community, continues to exist today. (Photograph courtesy of Kent Horton.)

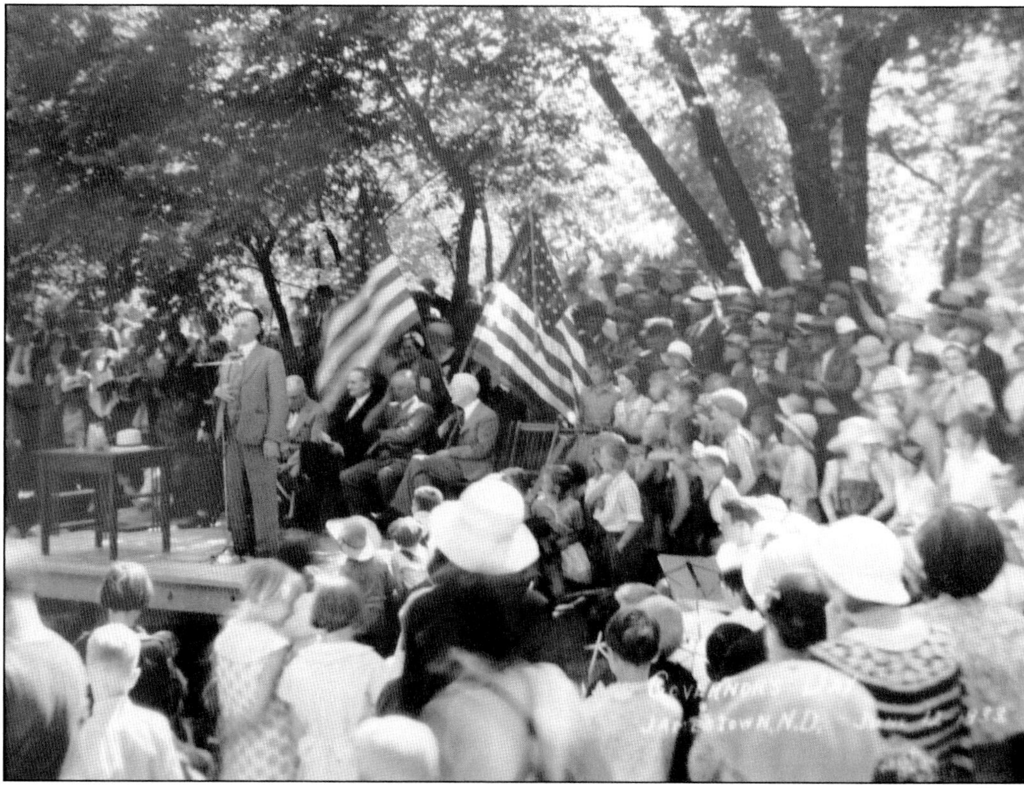

Citizens and political heavyweights gather in a city park on June 12, 1933, to listen to speeches during a Governor's Day celebration. Patriotic events have always been popular in Jamestown. (Photograph courtesy of the Stutsman County Memorial Museum.)

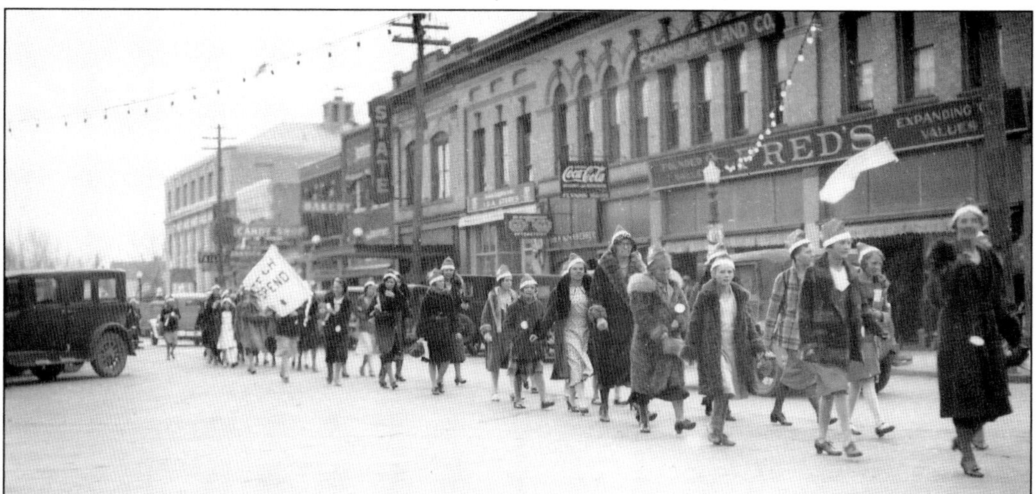

The 4-H clubs of Stutsman County held a parade as part of their conference in November 1932. Each club wore a distinctive club hat as they marched through downtown Jamestown. (Photograph courtesy of the Jamestown Parks & Recreation Department.)

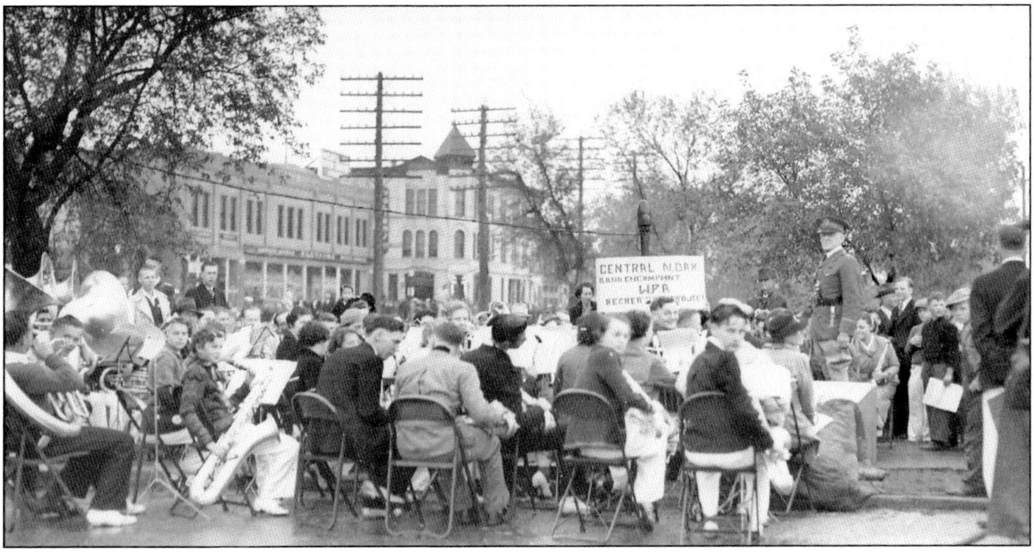

The Jamestown College band, along with others, performed in the city's parks. In the background, the James River National Bank is visible. The sign advertising the Central North Dakota Band Encampment, which was a Works Progress Administration project, helps date this photograph to the 1930s. (Photograph courtesy of the Jamestown Parks & Recreation Department.)

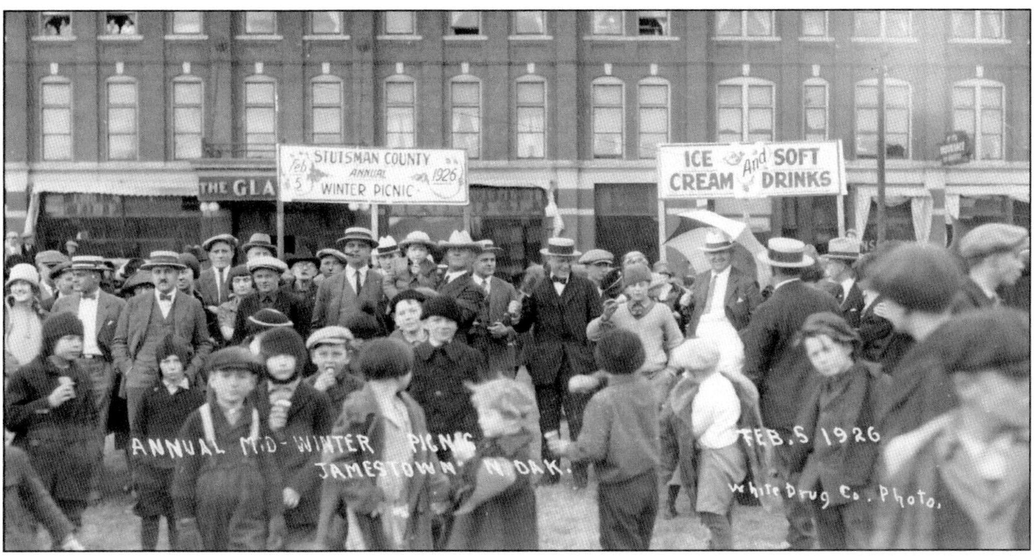

The 1926 winter picnic was held on the streets in front of the Gladstone Hotel. The event brought together the community during months when weather kept most people homebound. (Photograph courtesy of the Jamestown Parks & Recreation Department.)

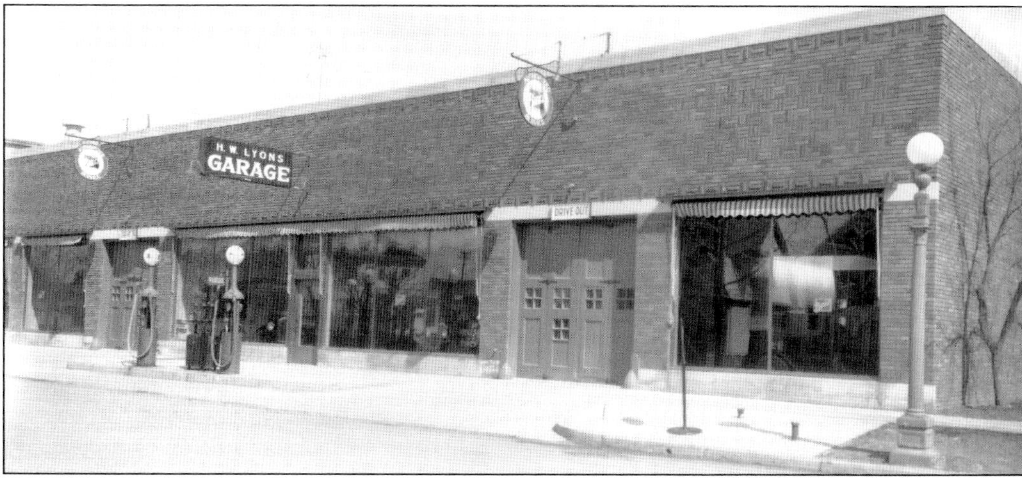

The Lyons Garage, connected to an early Buick dealership, is shown here. The building still stands on Main Street and is now used as a shopping mall. (Photograph courtesy of Bruce Berg.)

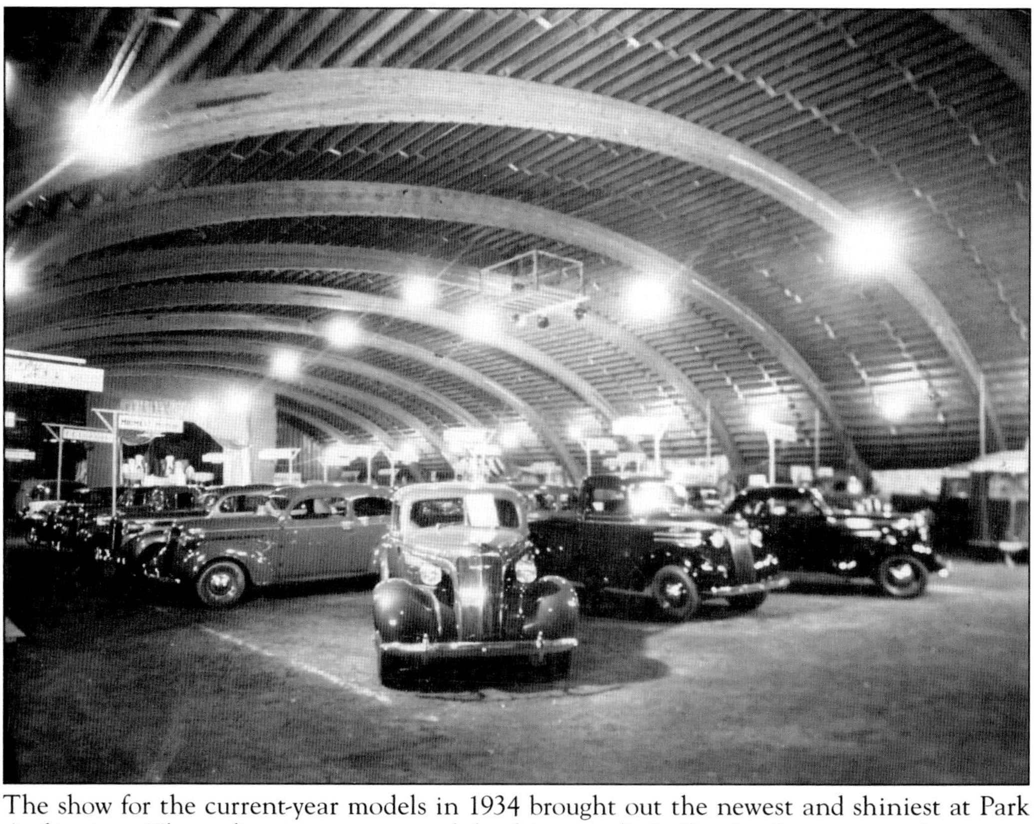

The show for the current-year models in 1934 brought out the newest and shiniest at Park Auditorium. The auditorium was part of the fairground's facility in the area now known as McElroy Park. This building, which was associated with the county fairgrounds at that time, was demolished in the 1950s. (Photograph courtesy of Kent Horton.)

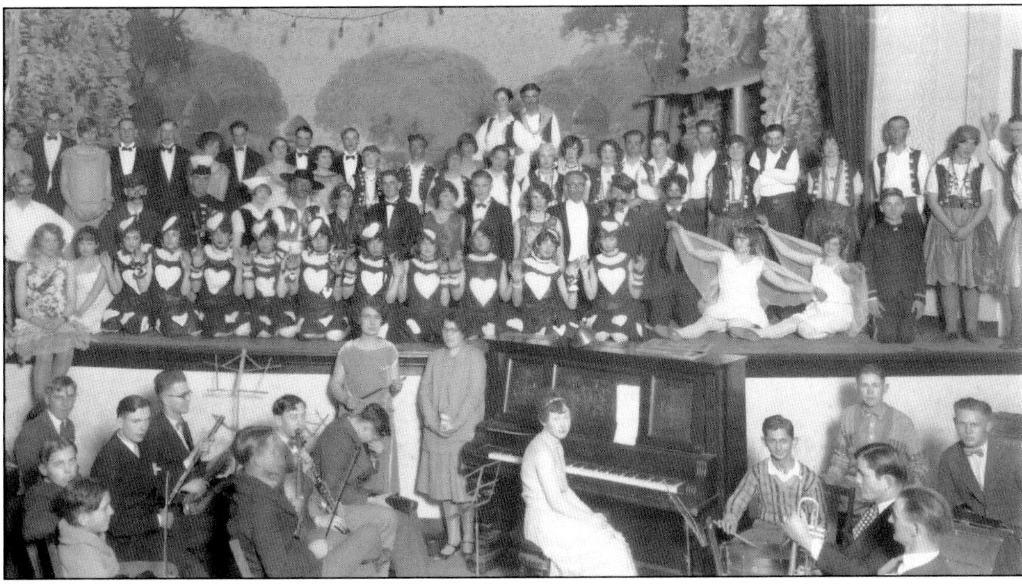

Given the number of hearts on the costumes in this late 1920s photograph, this must have been a Valentine's Day celebration with a Jamestown High School orchestra performance. Local musical and theater performances served as entertainment in the days before television or radio. (Photograph by Oscar Berg, courtesy of Bruce Berg.)

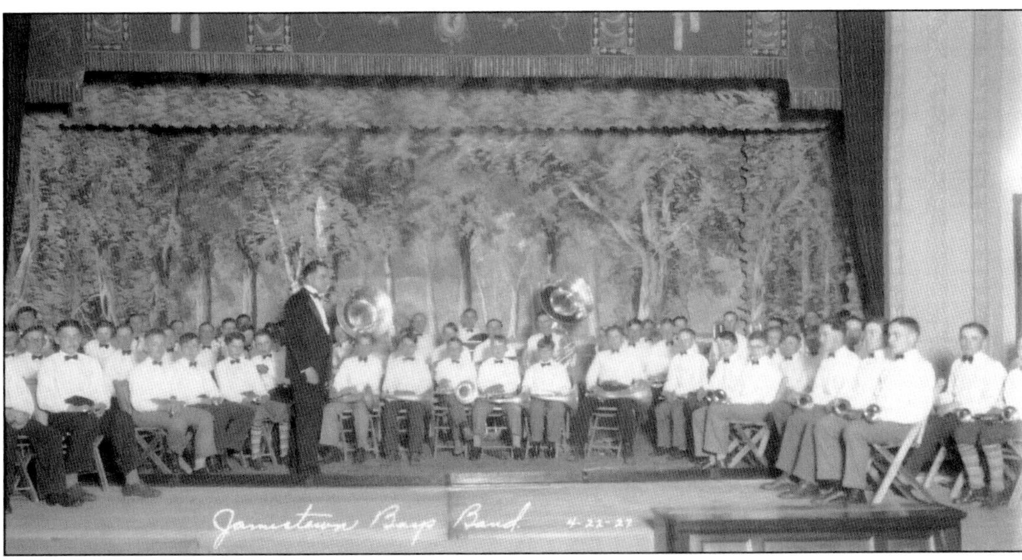

This photograph from April 1927 depicts the public school's boys' band at Thompson Auditorium. The school not only provided education, it also entertained the community through its bands, sports teams, and drama productions. (Photograph by Oscar Berg, courtesy of Bruce Berg.)

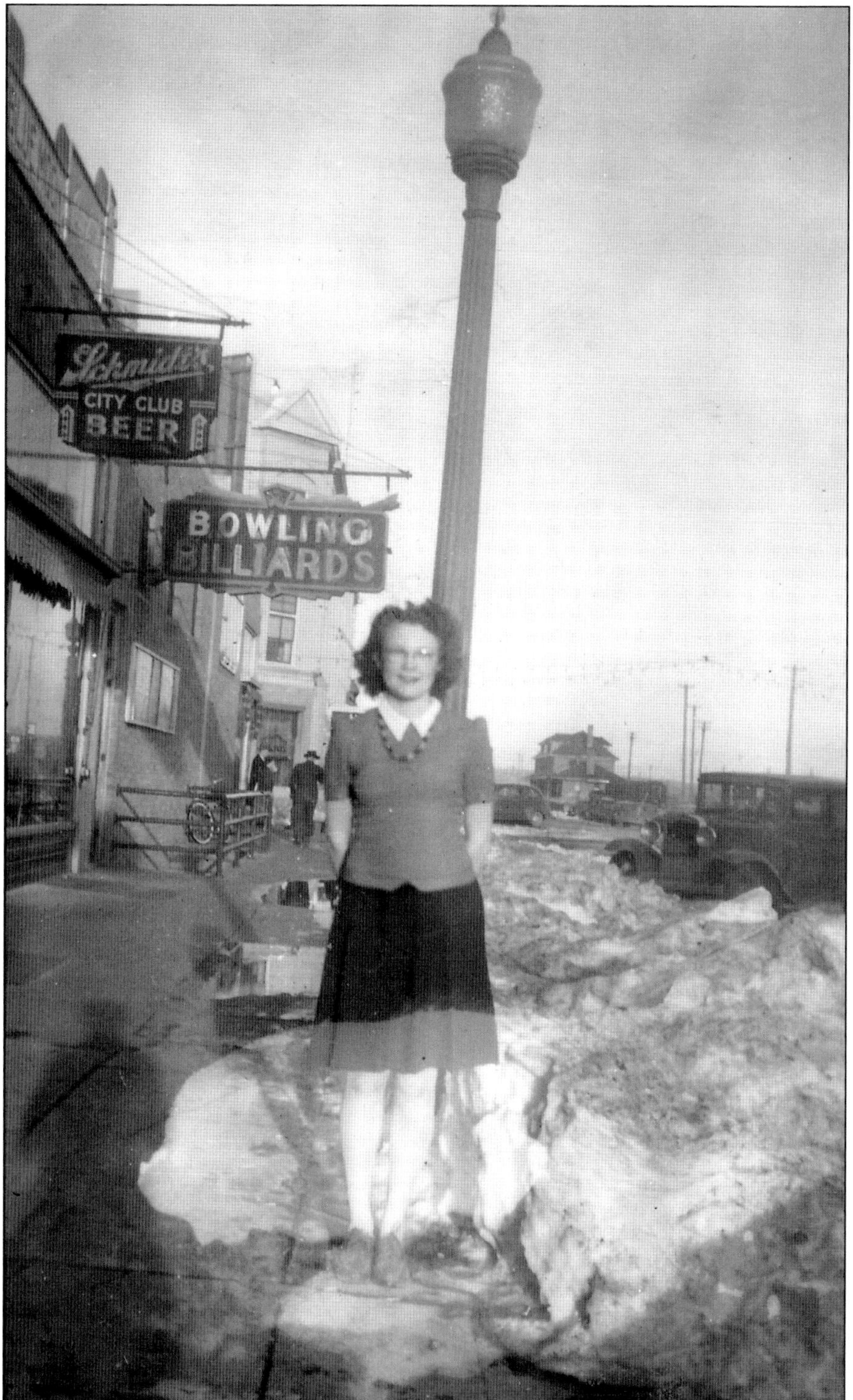

Francis Rude stands in front of the Jamestown Café and a bowling-and-billiards hall. In the background is the Northern Pacific Railroad's depot. (Photograph courtesy of the Leonard Rude collection.)

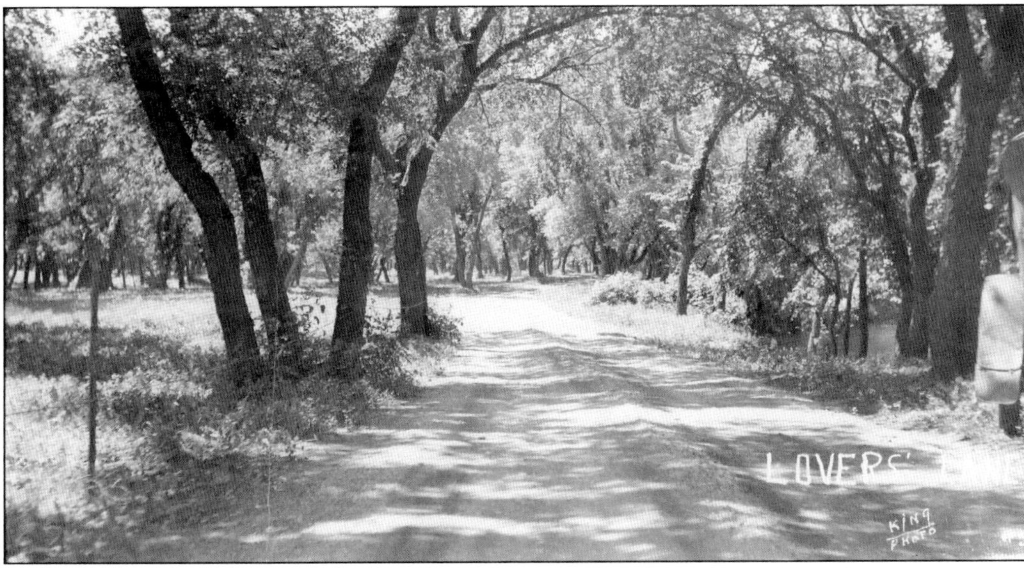

Sometimes, it seems that every community in the country has a "lovers' lane." Jamestown's was located in Klaus Park, and driving the road through the park today will likely take one over at least a portion of it. (Photograph courtesy of Dave Robertson.)

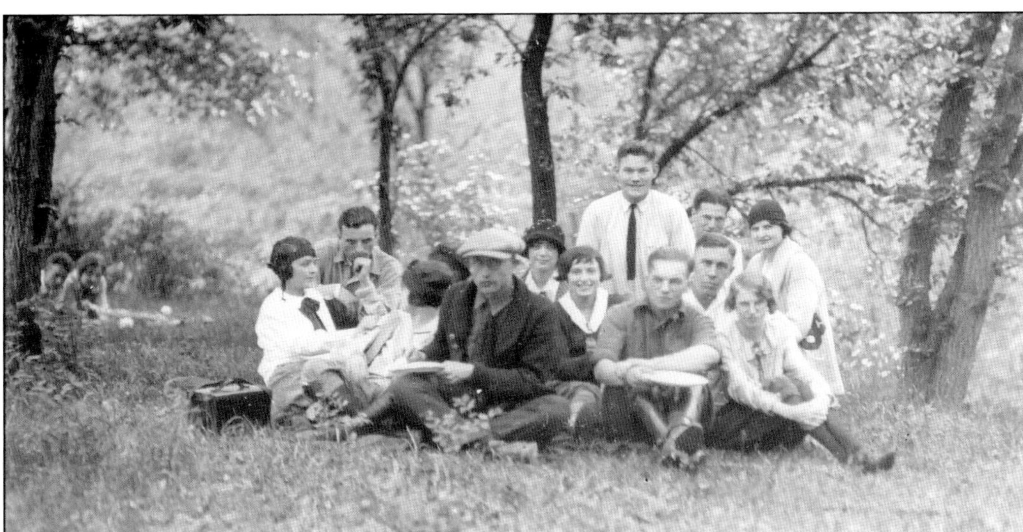

College students pose in Klaus Park, which served as a camping location for those ready and willing to pitch a tent. (Photograph courtesy of Dave Robertson.)

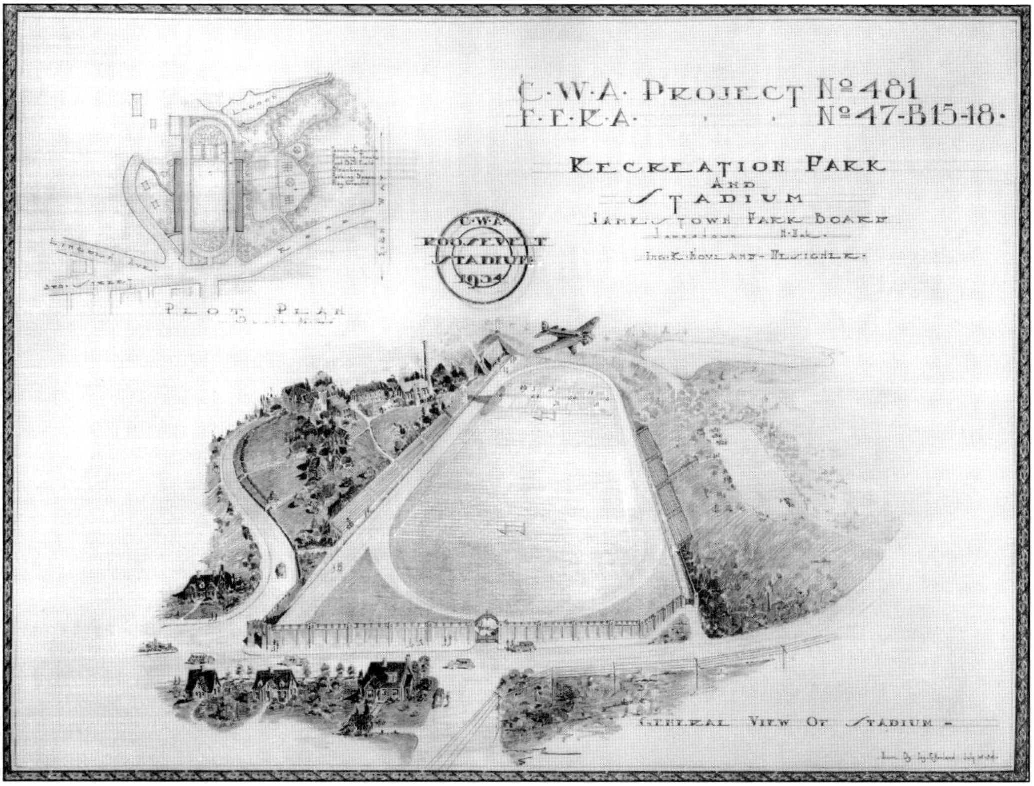

This image shows an architect's rendering of a project that would become the Jamestown College football stadium, constructed by the WPA during the 1930s under the name of Roosevelt Stadium. The structure has seen revisions through the years but is still in use. (Photograph courtesy of the Jamestown Parks & Recreation Department.)

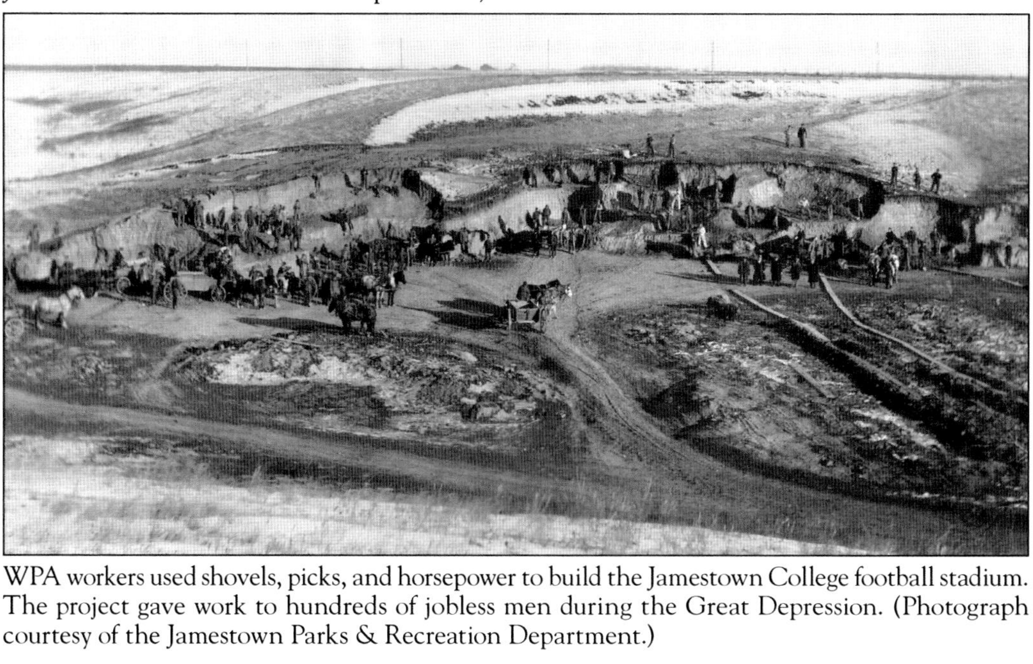

WPA workers used shovels, picks, and horsepower to build the Jamestown College football stadium. The project gave work to hundreds of jobless men during the Great Depression. (Photograph courtesy of the Jamestown Parks & Recreation Department.)

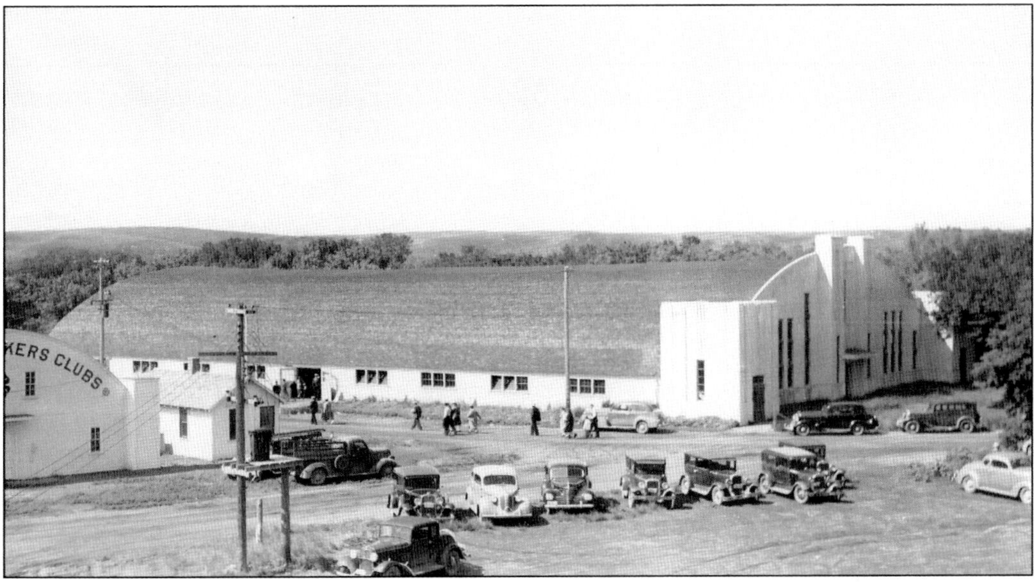

The Jamestown Park Auditorium was the scene of many events. This c. 1930 photograph shows some of the 4-H buildings associated with the fairground to the left. The 4-H buildings remain, but are now used for storage. (Photograph courtesy of the Jamestown Parks & Recreation Department.)

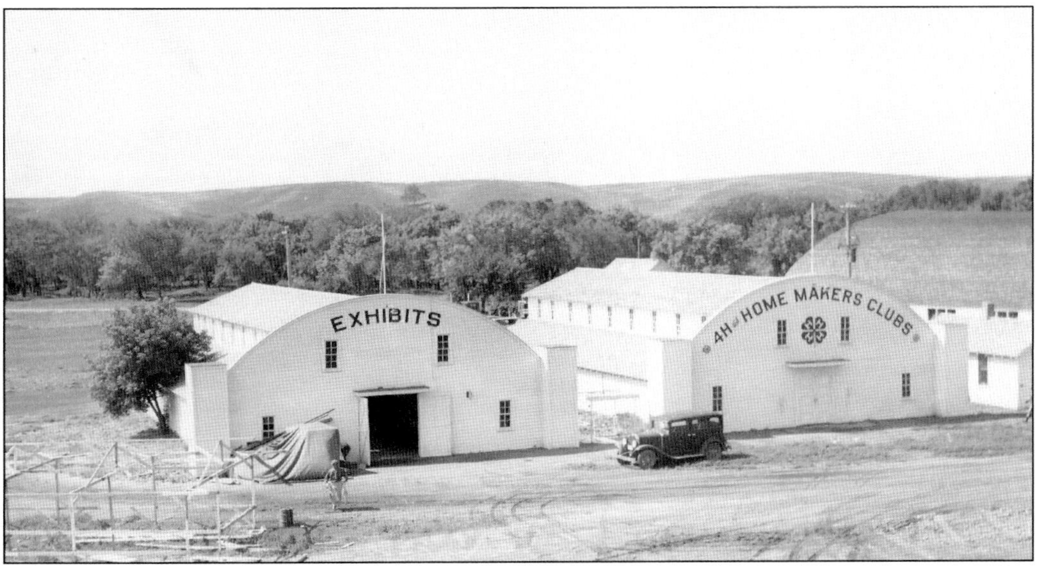

The exhibit buildings of the original Stutsman County Fair still stand in McElroy Park. To the right in this photograph is the Park Auditorium. The fairgrounds are now located on the north side of Jamestown, just west of Jamestown Dam. (Photograph courtesy of the Jamestown Parks & Recreation Department.)

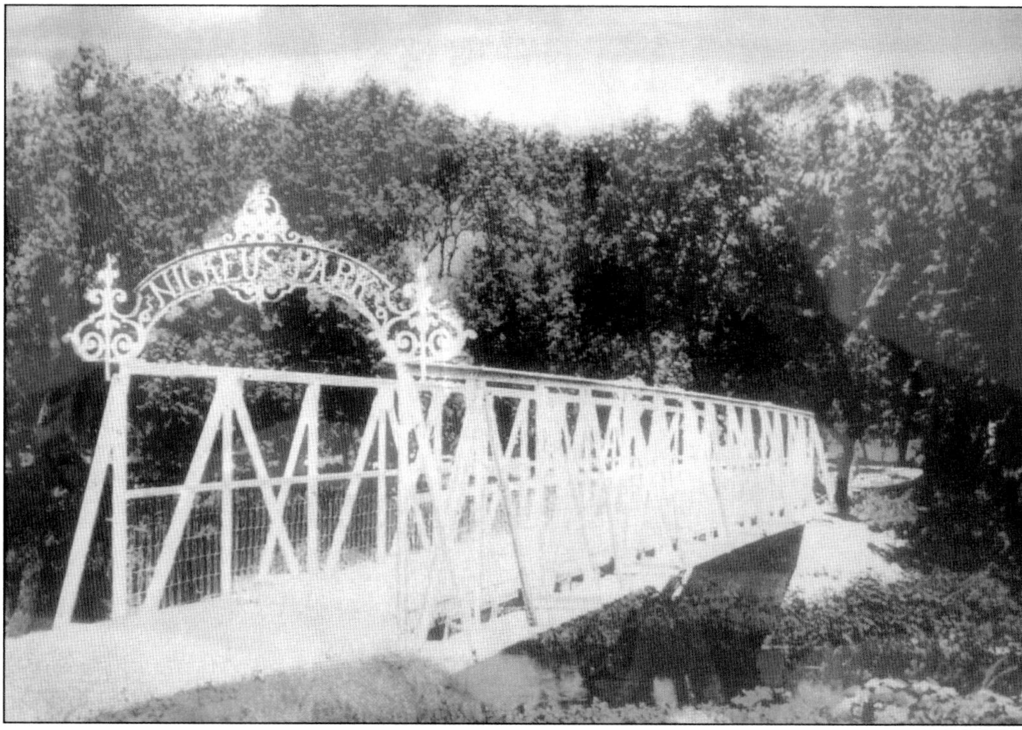

The Nickeous Park footbridge still straddles the James River between First Avenue North and the park, though the ornate cast-iron sign above the bridge is now gone. (Photograph courtesy of the Stutsman County Memorial Museum.)

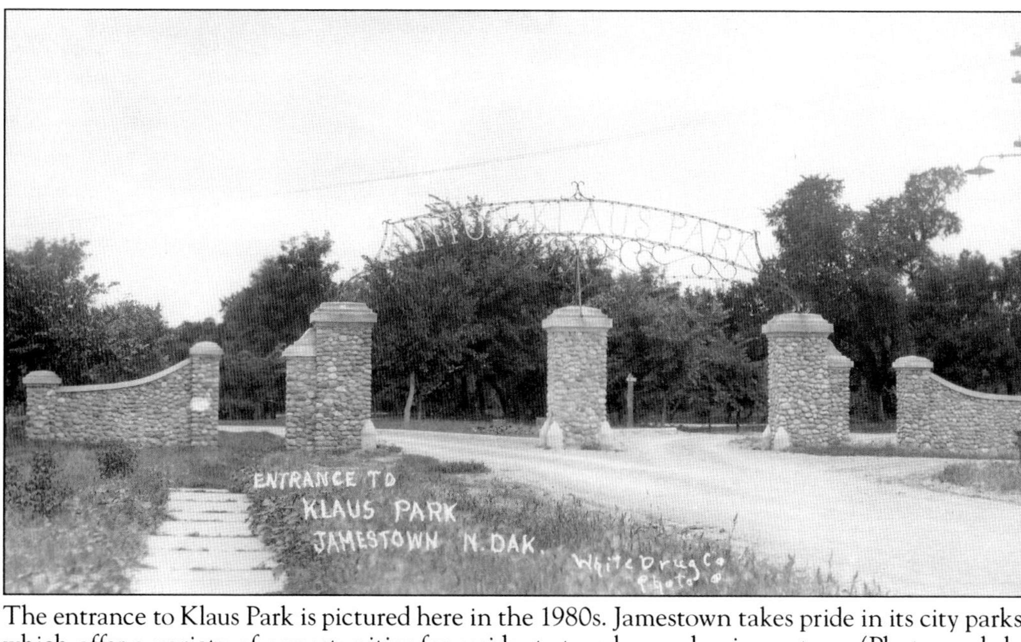

The entrance to Klaus Park is pictured here in the 1980s. Jamestown takes pride in its city parks, which offer a variety of opportunities for residents to relax and enjoy nature. (Photograph by Tom Domek.)

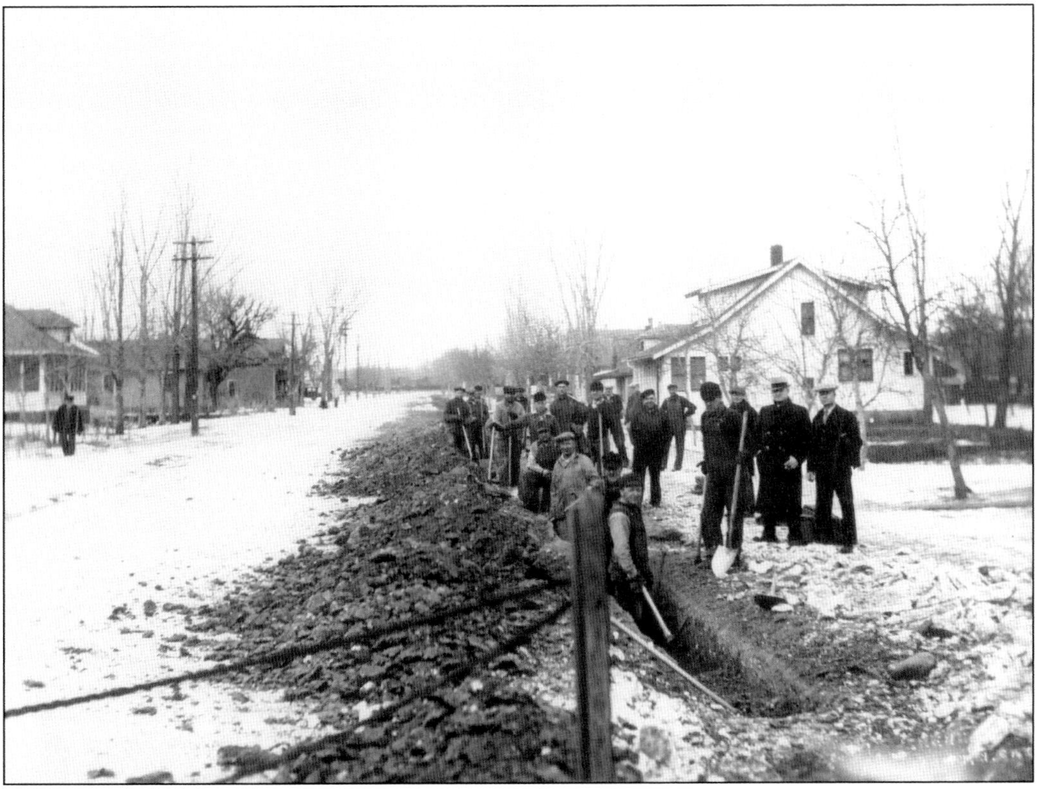

During the drought years of the 1930s, water levels were improved with the addition of a water line from a downtown well to the stretch of river used as a swimming hole. This photograph shows a WPA crew digging the trench in February 1934. (Photograph courtesy of the Jamestown Parks & Recreation Department.)

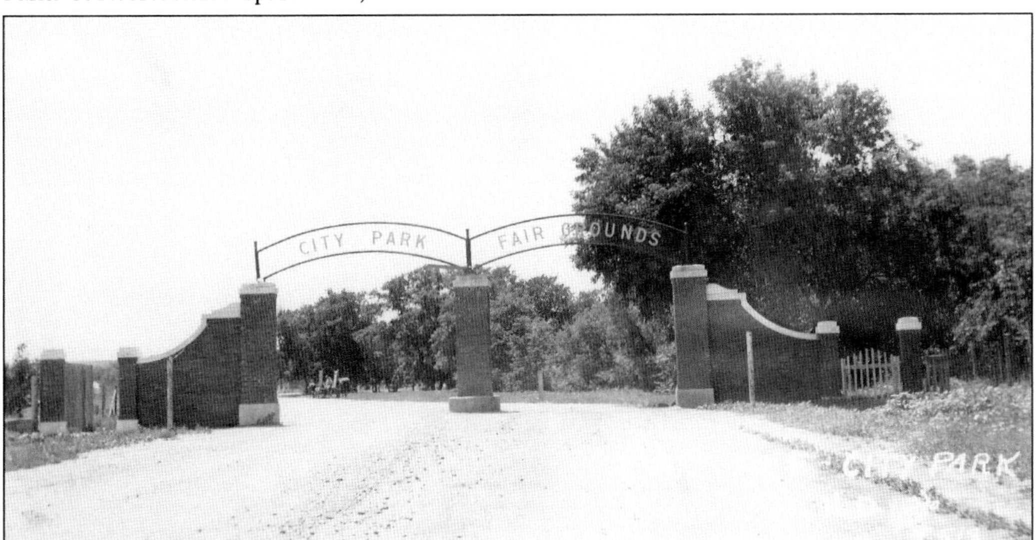

This entrance gate welcomed visitors to the City Park and Fair Grounds. The fairgrounds were moved from the park in the 1960s and the park is now known as McElroy Park. (Photograph courtesy of the Jamestown Parks & Recreation Department.)

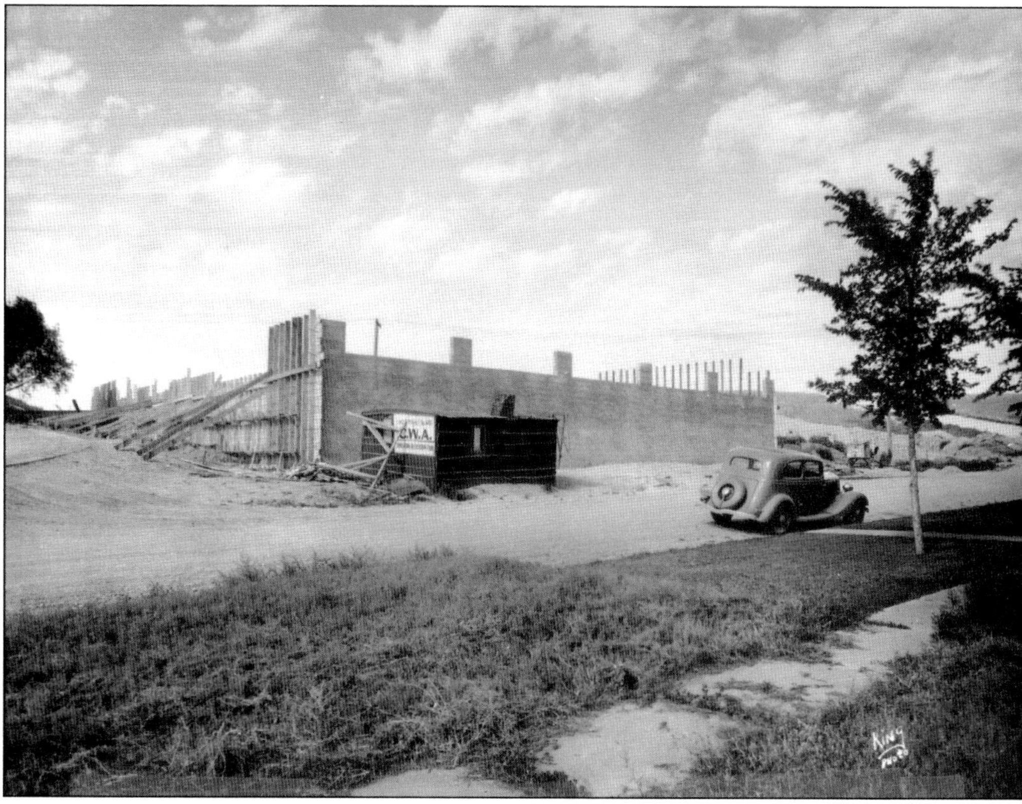

The retaining walls around the Jamestown College football field, then called Roosevelt Stadium, are under construction in this Great Depression–era photograph. (Photograph courtesy of the Jamestown Parks & Recreation Department.)

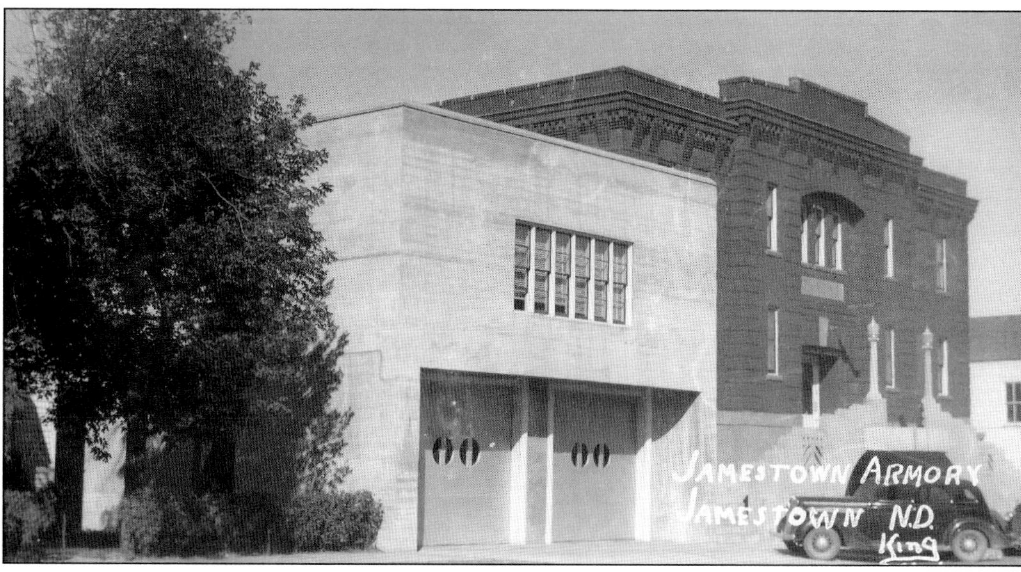

Jamestown Armory, which served the community until being demolished in the 1990s, is pictured here around 1940. It functioned as a training center for the National Guard as well as a community and teen center. (Photograph courtesy of the Jamestown Parks & Recreation Department.)

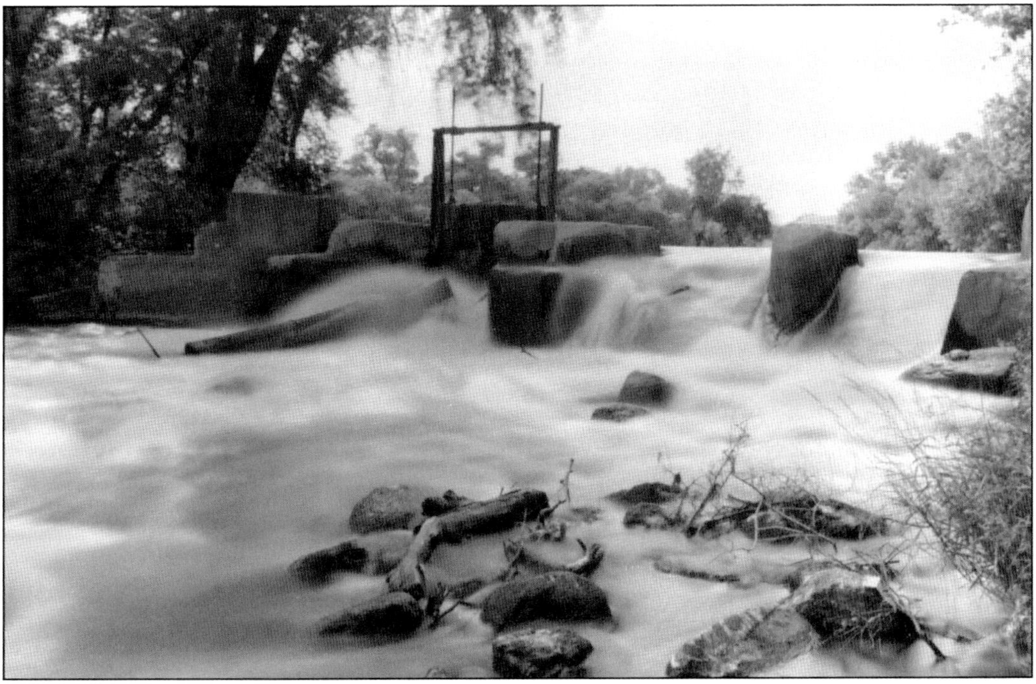

The Ice House Dam is shown in this photograph from the early 1980s. In the early years, ice was cut from behind the dam in winter to be used to cool food and other perishable products during the summer. Deliverymen distributed the ice throughout the community. (Photograph by Tom Domek.)

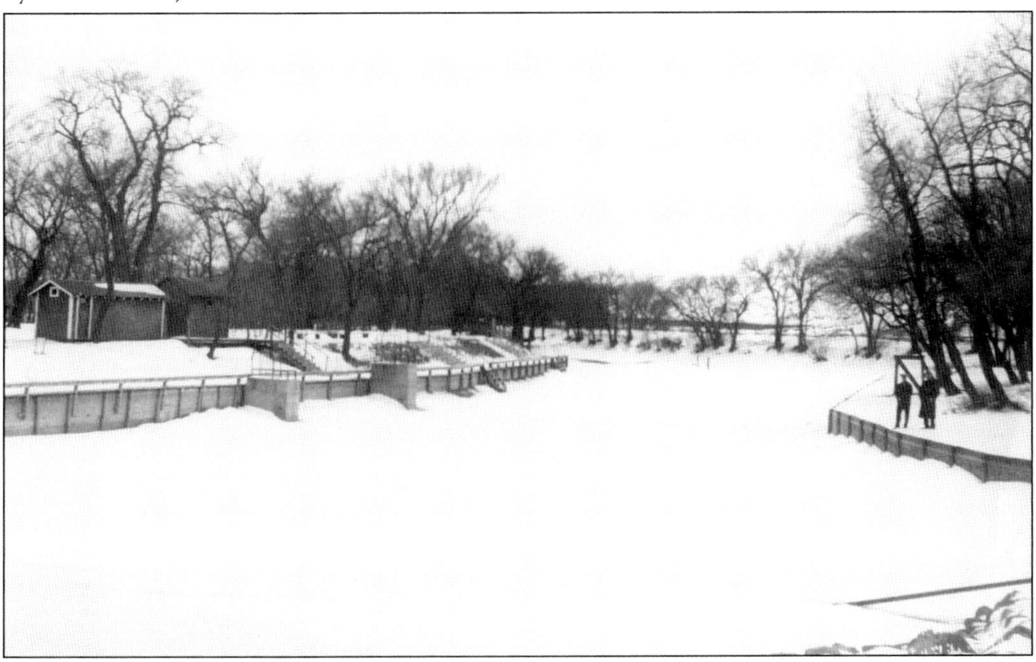

Jamestown used a stretch of the James River as a swimming hole through the 1950s. This photograph shows some of the work done on the swimming hole by the WPA during the 1930s. (Photograph courtesy of the Jamestown Parks & Recreation Department.)

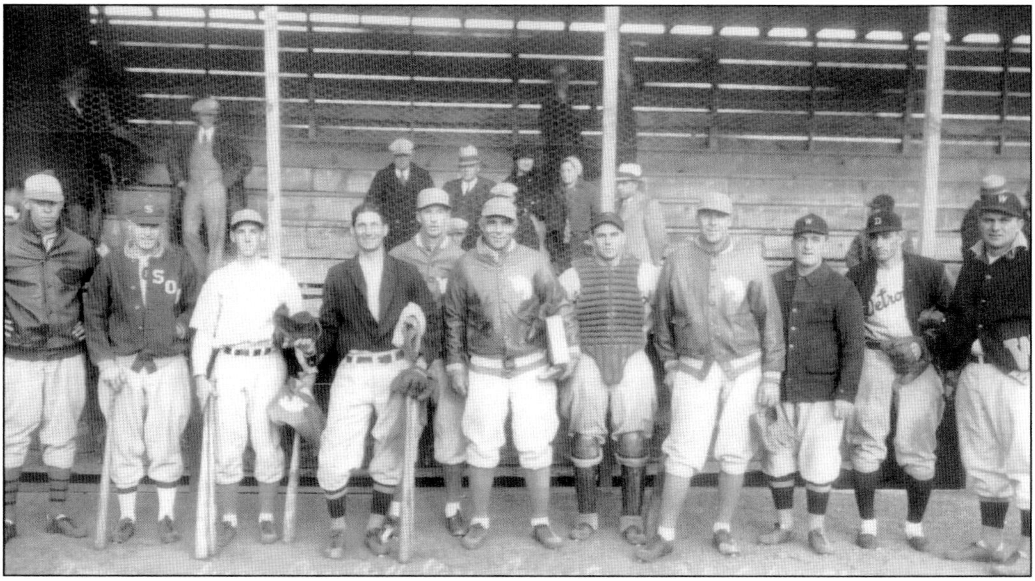

The all-stars of Major League Baseball paid a visit to Jamestown in 1932 to play the local squad. The local team, including several Negro League veterans and other professional athletes, defeated the big leaguers. (Photograph by Oscar Berg, courtesy of Bruce Berg.)

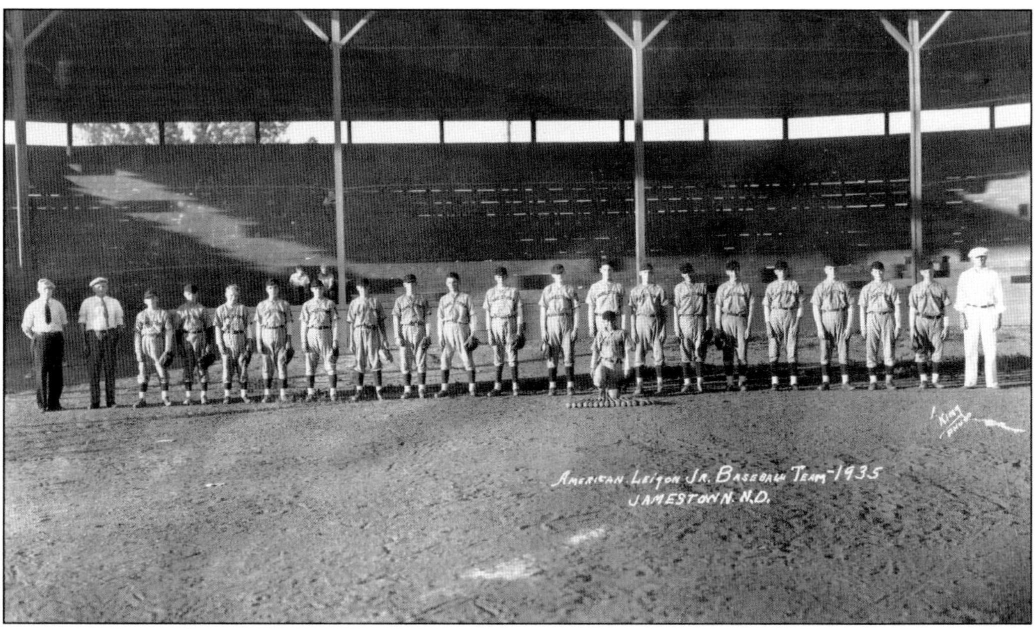

Baseball has long been a favorite pastime for generations of Jamestown residents. This photograph shows the city's 1935 Junior American Legion team. (Photograph courtesy of the Stutsman County Memorial Museum.)

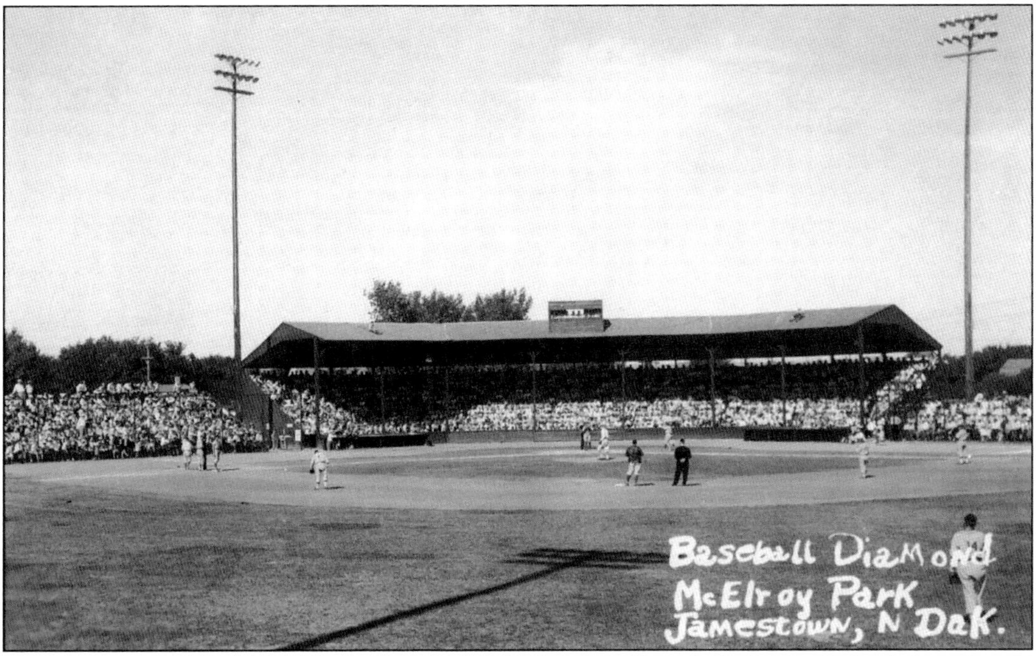

Spectators fill the bleachers at the baseball field near McElroy Park. Built in the 1930s, the old stadium was later named for Jack Brown, a well-respected local sports booster. This stadium burned in the 1980s but was rebuilt at the same location with a similar design. (Photograph courtesy of the Stutsman County Memorial Museum.)

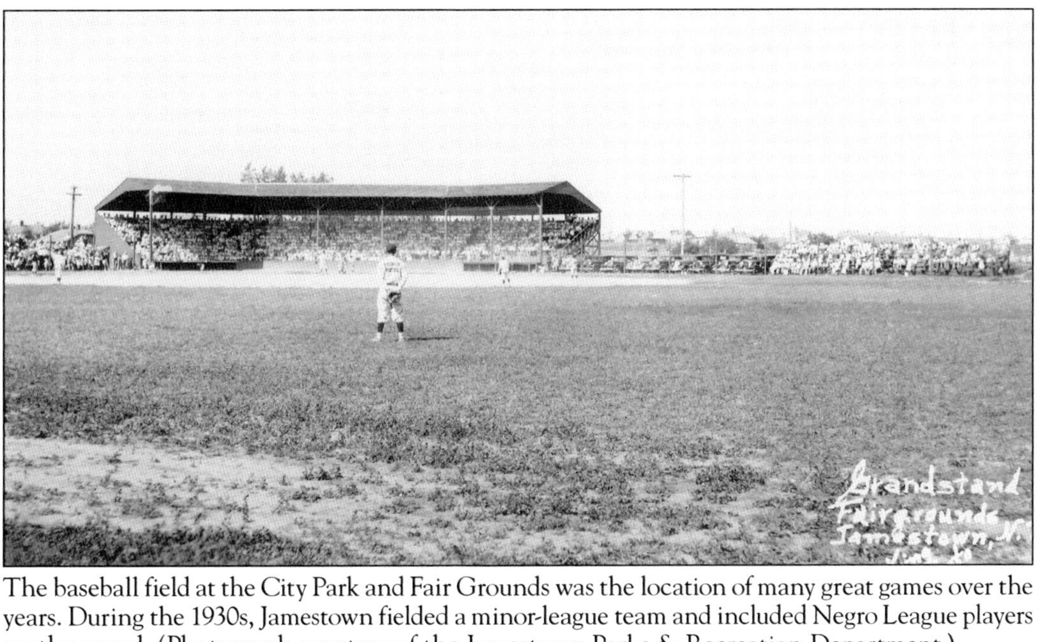

The baseball field at the City Park and Fair Grounds was the location of many great games over the years. During the 1930s, Jamestown fielded a minor-league team and included Negro League players on the squad. (Photograph courtesy of the Jamestown Parks & Recreation Department.)

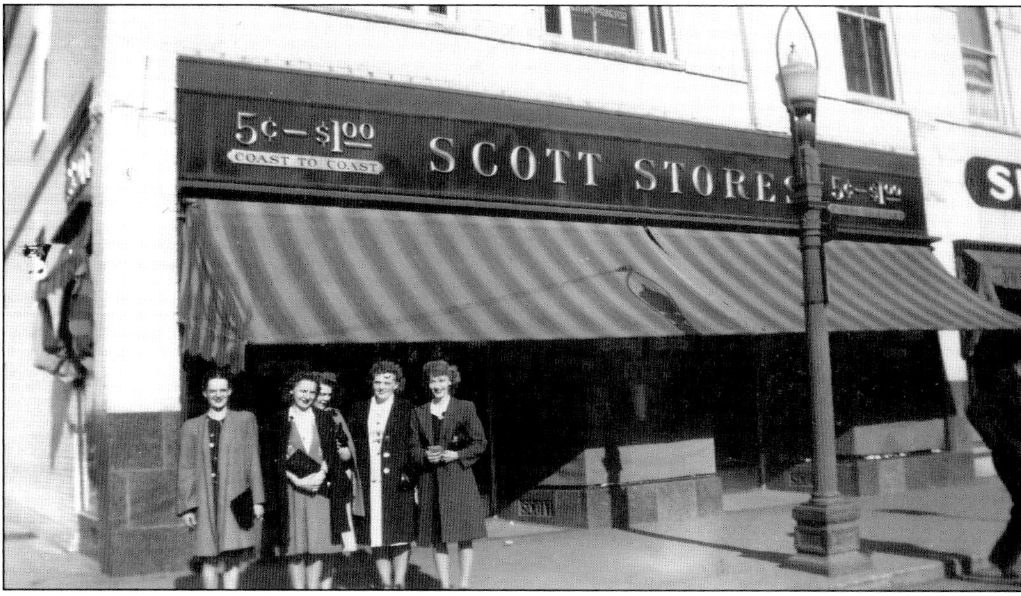

The Scott Store, a local five-and-dime, is shown here around 1947. (Photograph courtesy of Leonard Rude collection.)

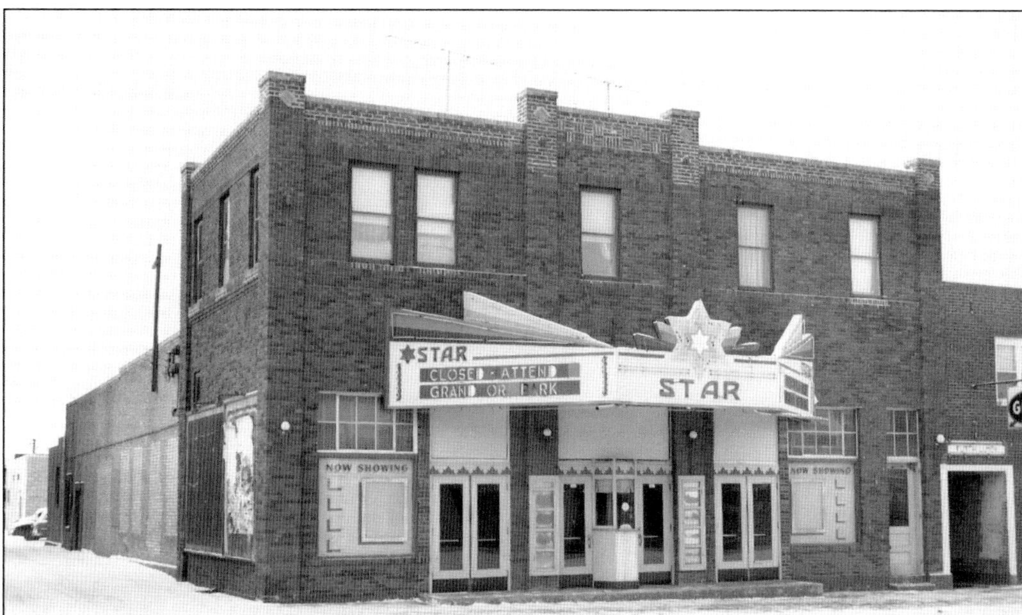

The Star Theater in downtown Jamestown served as competition for the majestic Grand Theater and provided an additional movie screen for those interested in attending the newest Hollywood blockbuster. (Photograph courtesy of Dave Robertson.)

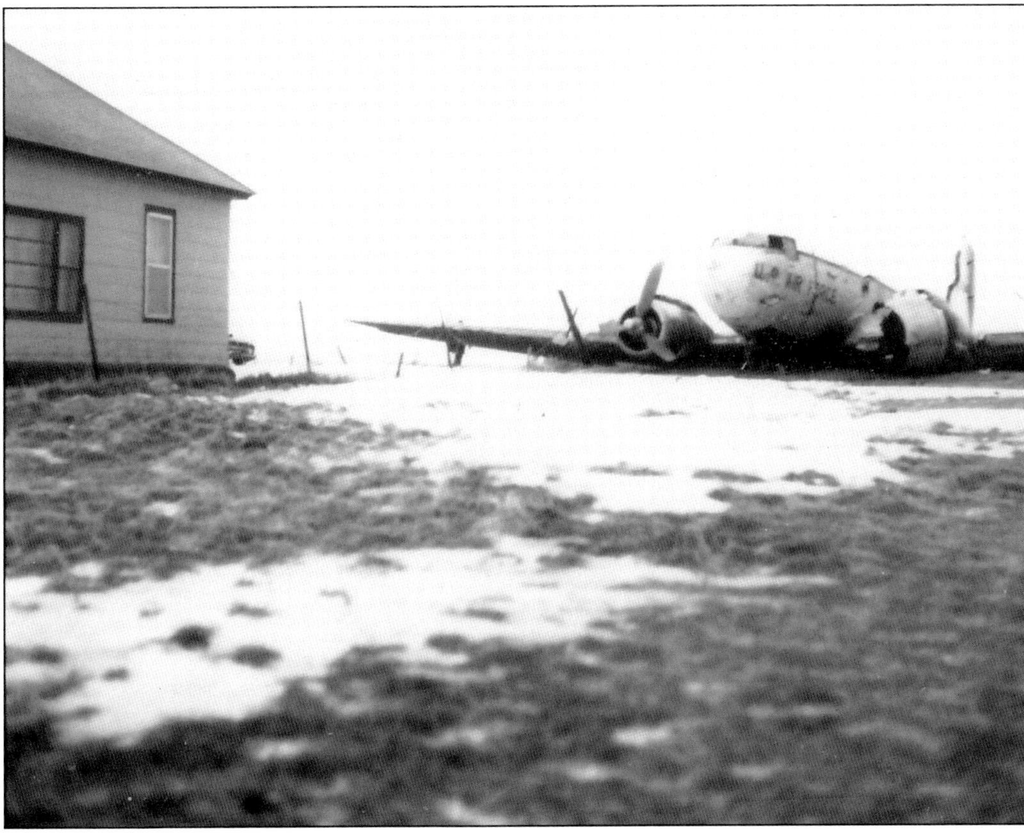

Bad weather and poor judgment led to the crash of this C-47 Air Force transport plane on the outskirts of Jamestown on January 4, 1962. Only slight injuries were reported in the incident, though the wreckage came within 40 feet of this occupied home. (Photograph courtesy Kent Horton.)

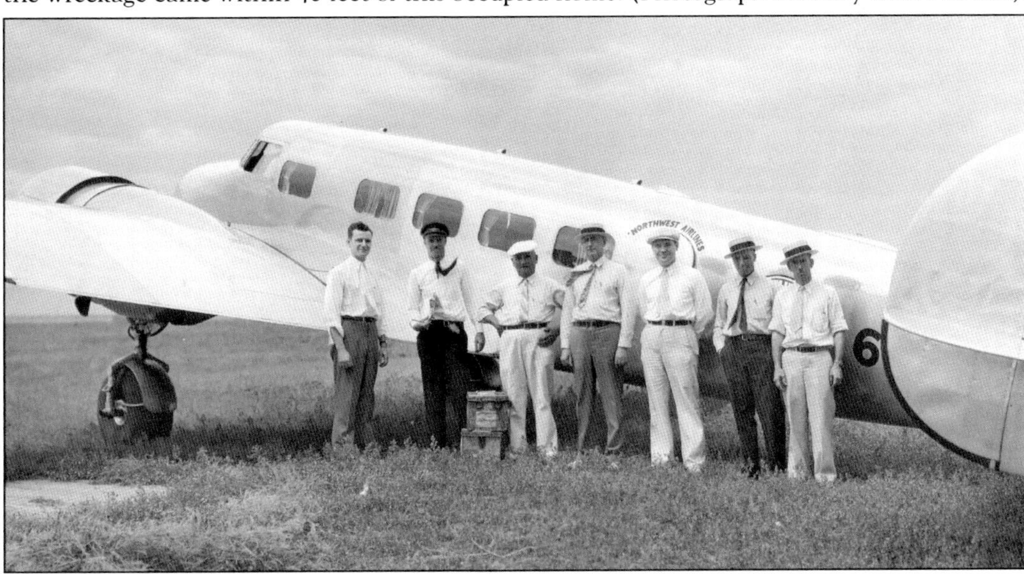

This photograph shows one of the original planes of Northwest Airways servicing Jamestown in 1932. (Photograph courtesy of the Stutsman County Memorial Museum.)

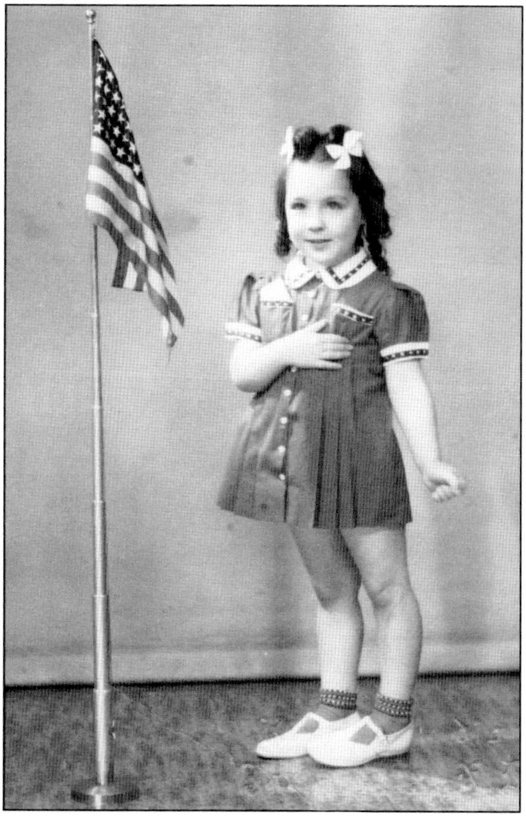

Little cutie Barbara Jean Arneson pledges her allegiance as a young patriot in the 1940s. (Photograph courtesy of Fay Domek.)

St. John's Catholic Academy today looks much like it did in the 1940s, when this photograph was taken. A convent was also located on the campus, and the nuns who lived there also taught the students in the school building. (Photograph courtesy of Fay Domek.)

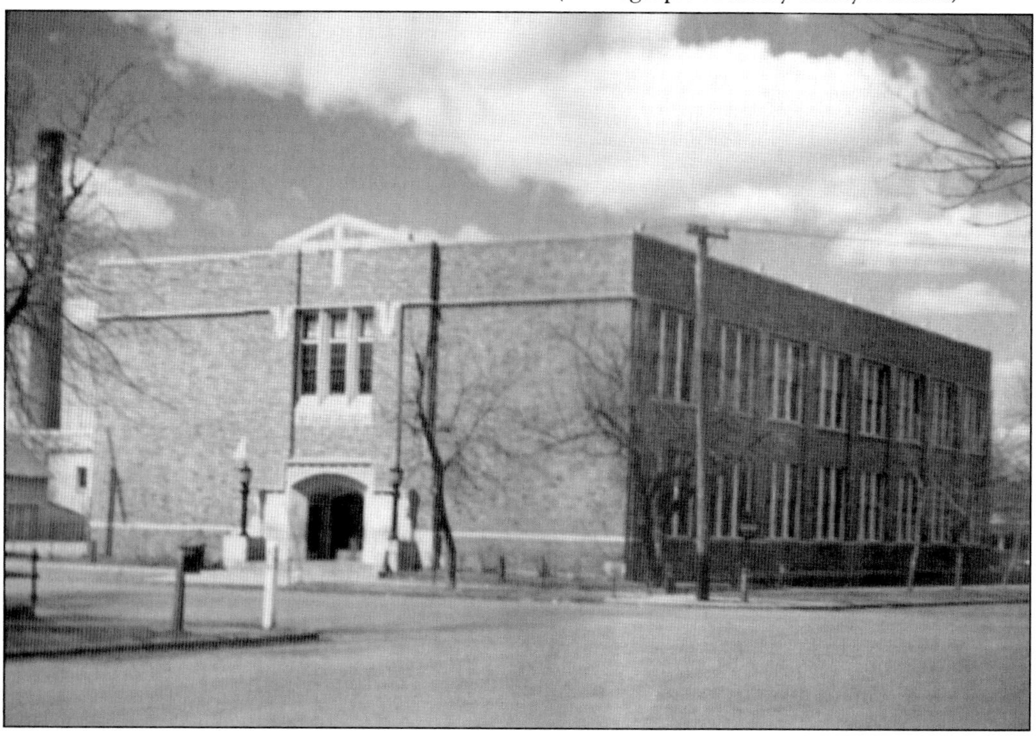

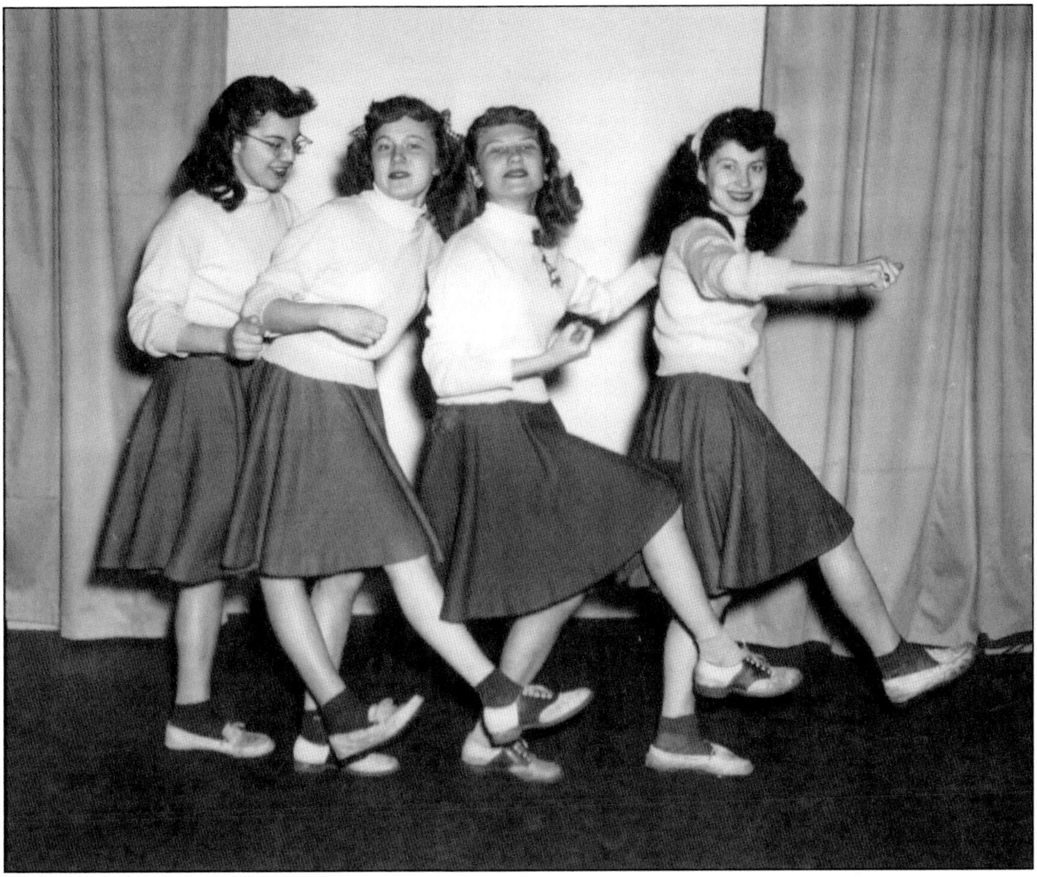

A quartet of St. John's Academy cheerleaders perform for the camera in the early 1940s. (Photograph courtesy of Fay Domek.)

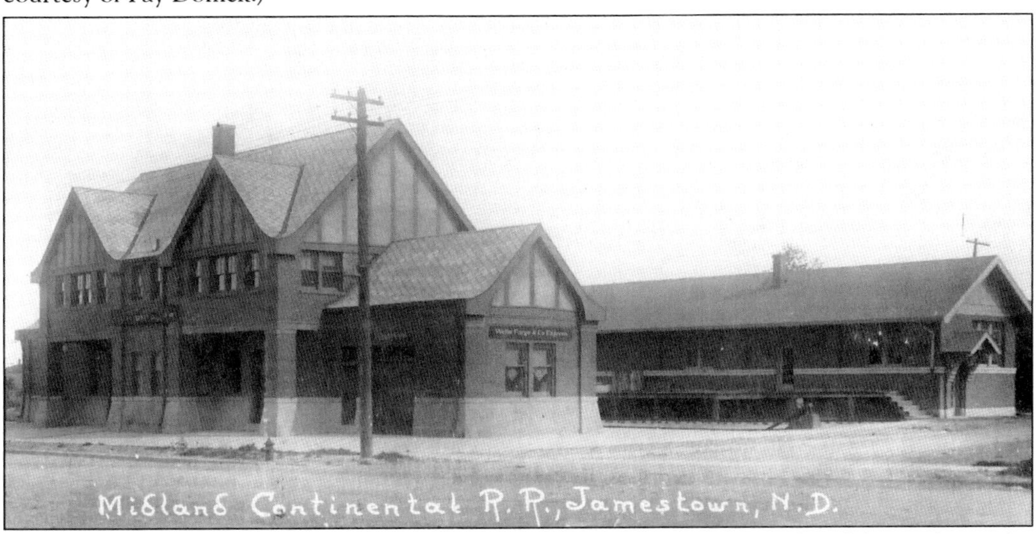

This photograph shows the headquarters for the Midland Continental Railroad, located near the Ottertail Power Company. The line operated from the World War I era to the 1970s. (Photograph courtesy of Kent Horton.)

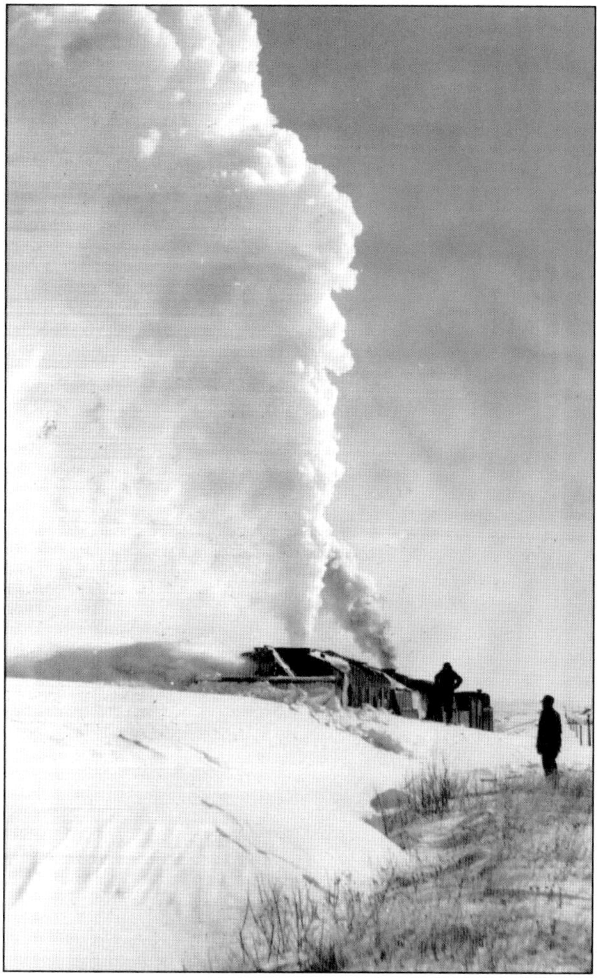

A snowplow clears a railroad line outside of Sykeston, North Dakota, in this photograph from 1943. Rotary plows such as this were large snow blowers with few safety features, and they occasionally caused damage to items that blew with the snow onto the tracks. (Photograph courtesy of the Stutsman County Memorial Museum.)

This photograph was also taken along the branch line to Sykeston in 1943. The rotary plows posed a risk to structures, livestock, or people who stood too close to the track being cleared. (Photograph courtesy of the Stutsman County Memorial Museum.)

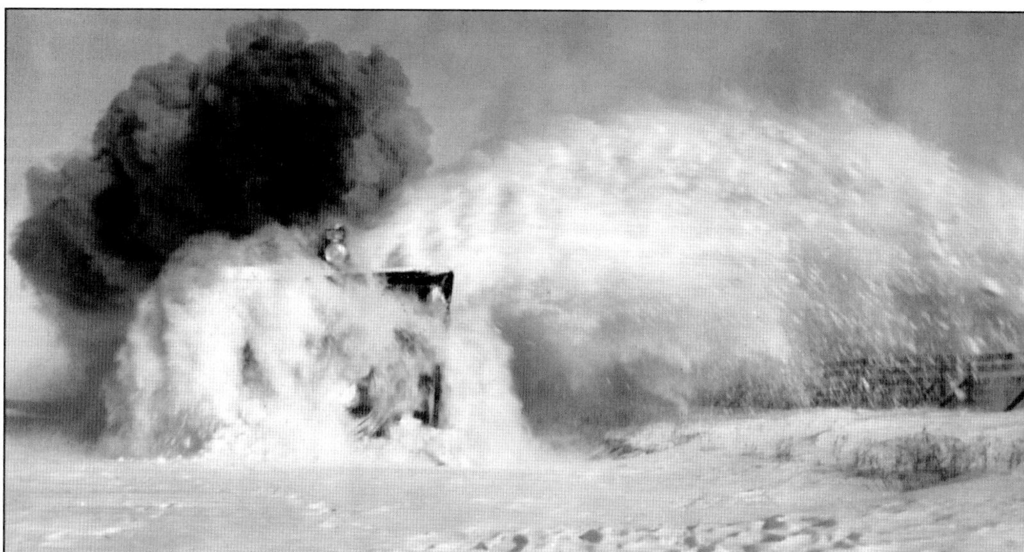

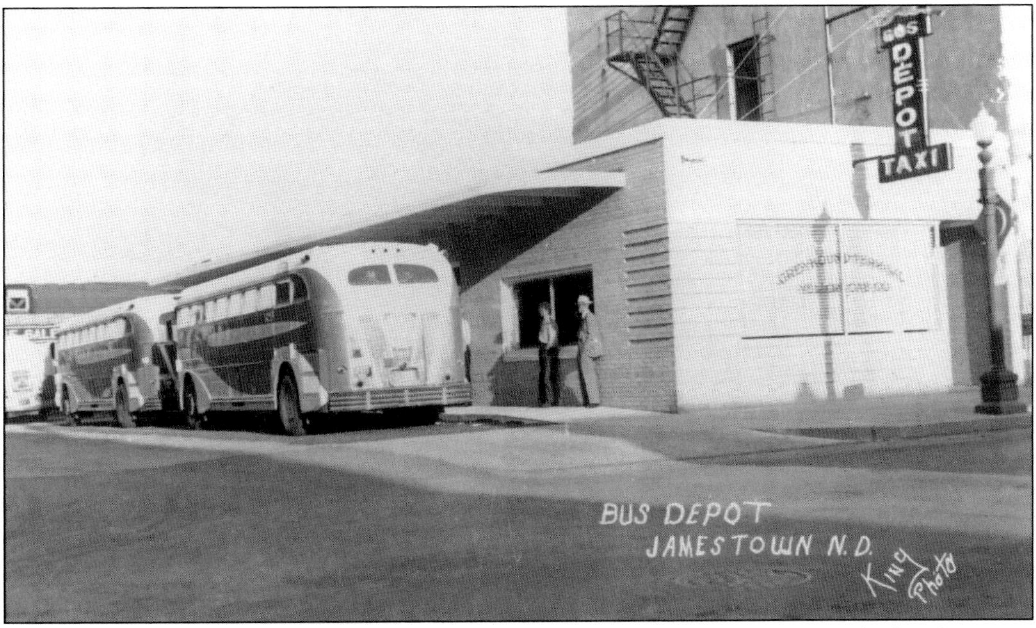

Located near the Gladstone Hotel, the Jamestown bus depot also served as the headquarters of the taxi service. Eugene (left) and E.B. Allen are pictured in this 1948 image. (Photograph courtesy of Dave Robertson.)

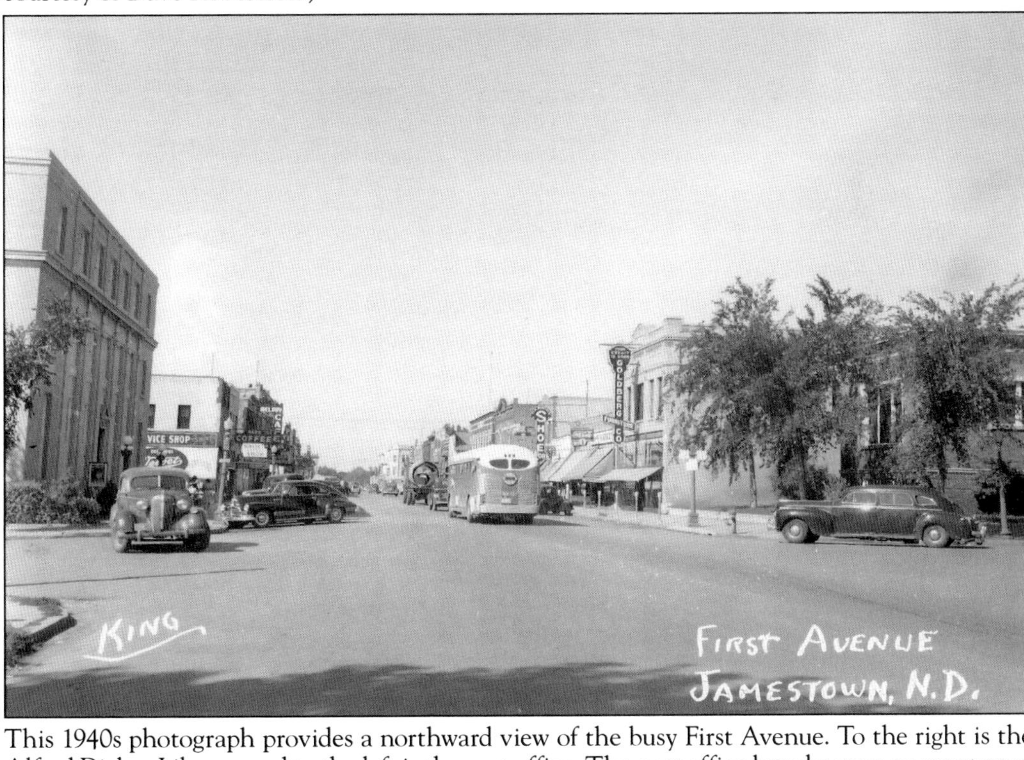

This 1940s photograph provides a northward view of the busy First Avenue. To the right is the Alfred Dickey Library, and to the left is the post office. The post office later became an apartment complex and is now called the Post House. (Photograph courtesy of the Jamestown Parks & Recreation Department.)

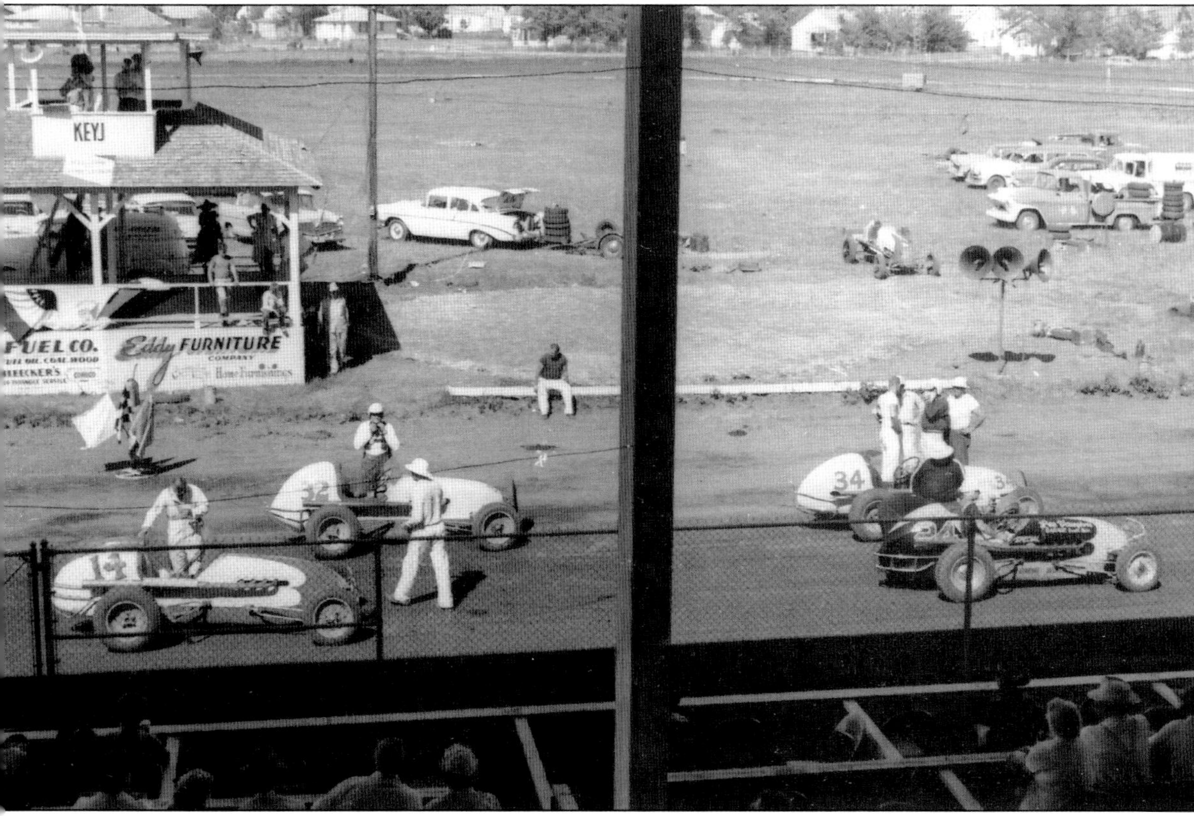

Racing has always been a part of the sporting scene in Jamestown. This shot from the 1950s shows sprint cars at the track that was part of the fairgrounds at the current McElroy Park. (Photograph courtesy Kent Horton.)

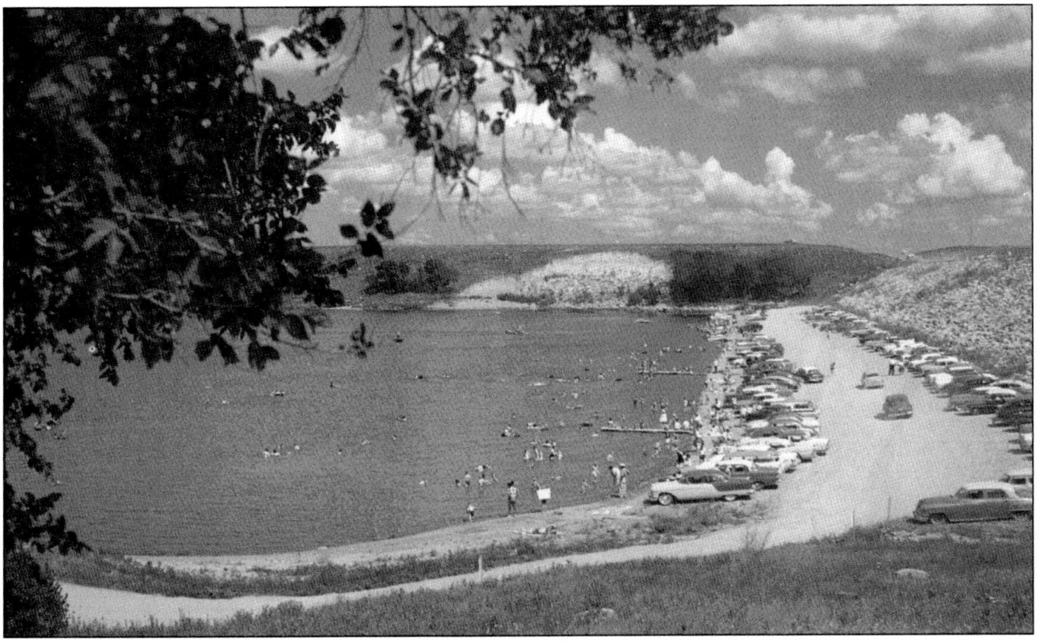

This photograph from the 1950s shows a partially filled Jamestown Reservoir with cars parked on the slope of the dam. The water level of the fully filled dam is about 20 feet higher than is pictured here. A swimming beach was later developed a few miles to the north, near a marina on the east side of the dam. (Photograph courtesy of Dave Robertson.)

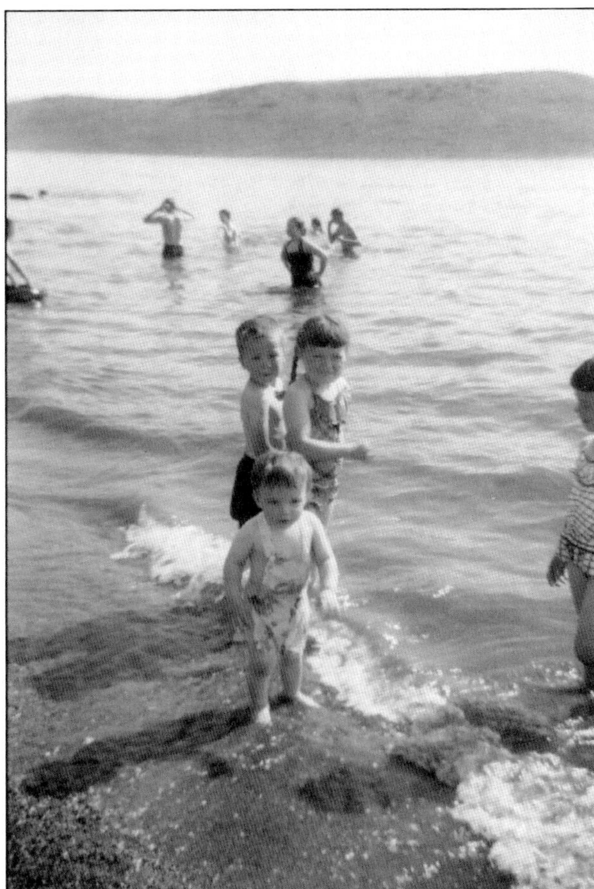

These children, pictured in 1958, play in the sand at the beach on Jamestown Reservoir, north of town. They are, from left to right, Mark Wagner, Lance Domek, Barbara Domek, and Marianne Wagner. (Photograph courtesy of Fay Domek.)

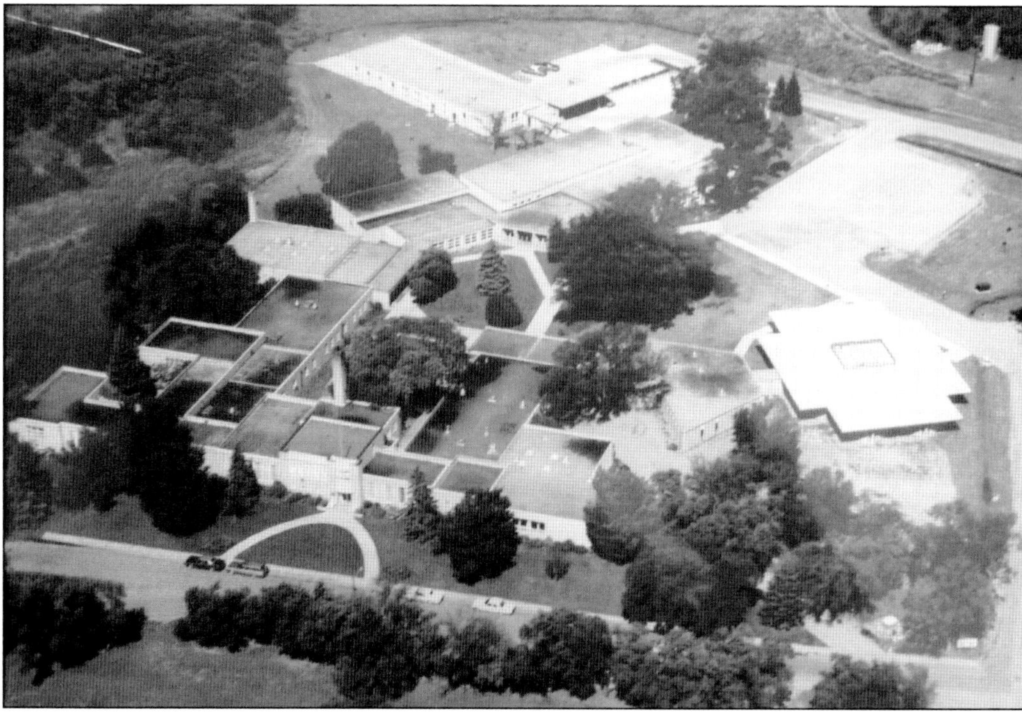

The first buildings of the present-day Anne Carlsen Center were built between 1940 and 1941. At that time, the campus was known as the "Crippled Children's School." In 1948, Dr. Anne Carlsen was named principal of the school and soon became its superintendent. Over the years, many buildings and programs were added on the six-acre campus. This aerial view dates to around the 1960s. (Photograph courtesy of the Stutsman County Memorial Museum.)

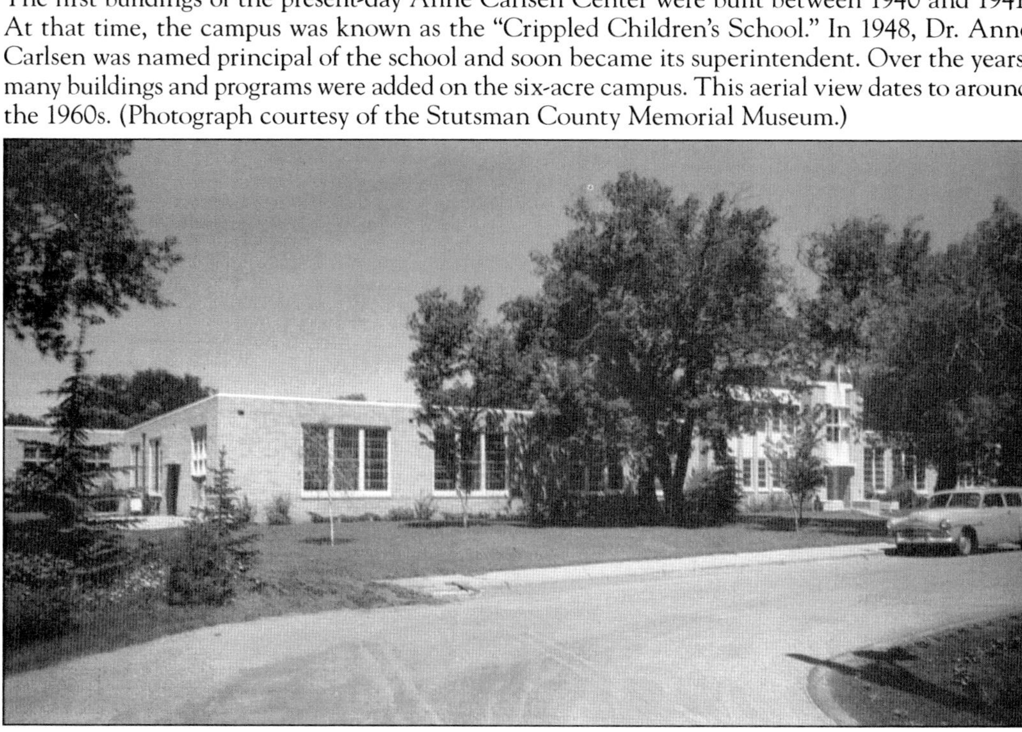

The Anne Carlsen Center, which continues to operate in the northwest corner of Jamestown, has been providing quality education to children with physical disabilities since the 1940s. (Photograph courtesy of Dave Robertson.)

Byron "Scoop" Hansen stands next to a printing press at the *Jamestown Sun* newspaper around 1958. Hansen was editor of the newspaper from 1925 until 1973. Over the years, the *Sun* was known by various names, including the *Jamestown Alert*, the *Jamestown Weekly Alert*, the *Jamestown Morning Alert*, the *Jamestown Sun & Daily Alert*, and finally, the *Jamestown Sun*. (Photograph courtesy of the Stutsman County Memorial Museum.)

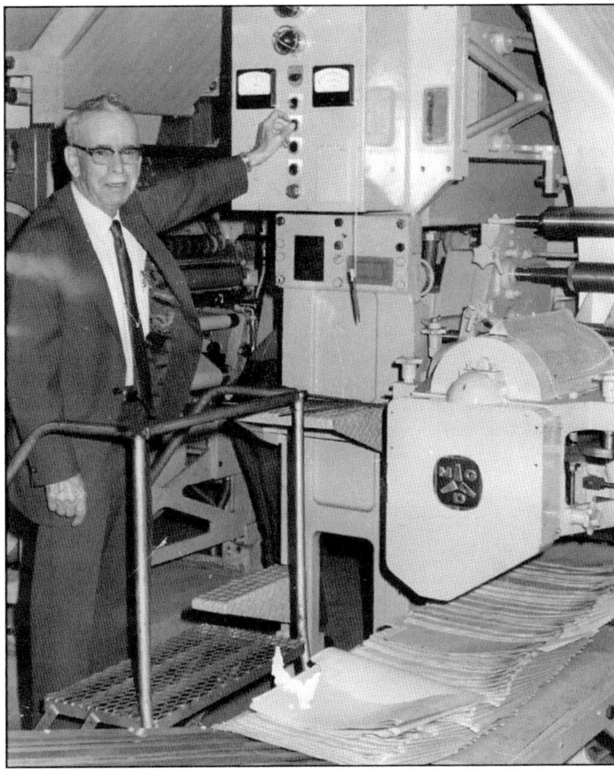

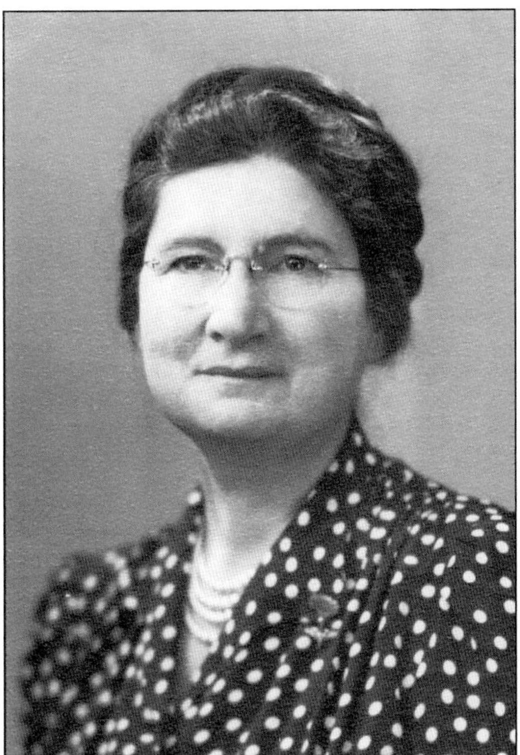

One of Jamestown's best-read reporters was Eva Plunkett (1888–1976), a pioneer newswoman who wrote for the *Jamestown Sun*. She worked for the newspaper for 30 years, reporting on a continuous stream of news about the city. (Photograph courtesy of the Stutsman County Memorial Museum.)

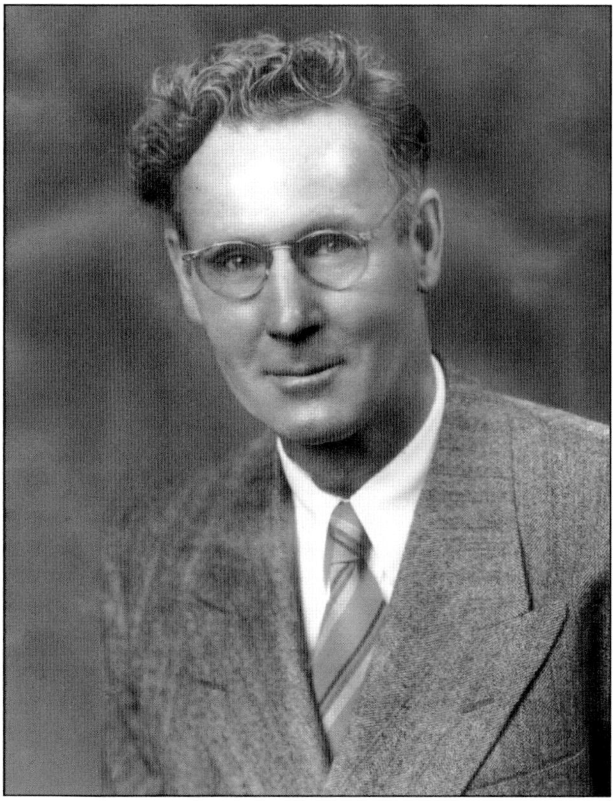

James A. Kirkpatrick was born in Detroit Lakes, Minnesota, in 1898, but was raised near Beach, North Dakota, in the North Dakota badlands. He served in World War I before moving to Jamestown, where he opened a sign business. While his commercial venture was successful, he began doing oil paintings with Old West themes, perhaps inspired by his boyhood days in Beach. He produced more than 3,000 paintings, nearly all of which were sold or donated to others. His work is on display at the Smithsonian Institution and the US Senate in Washington, DC. (Photograph courtesy of the Stutsman County Memorial Museum.)

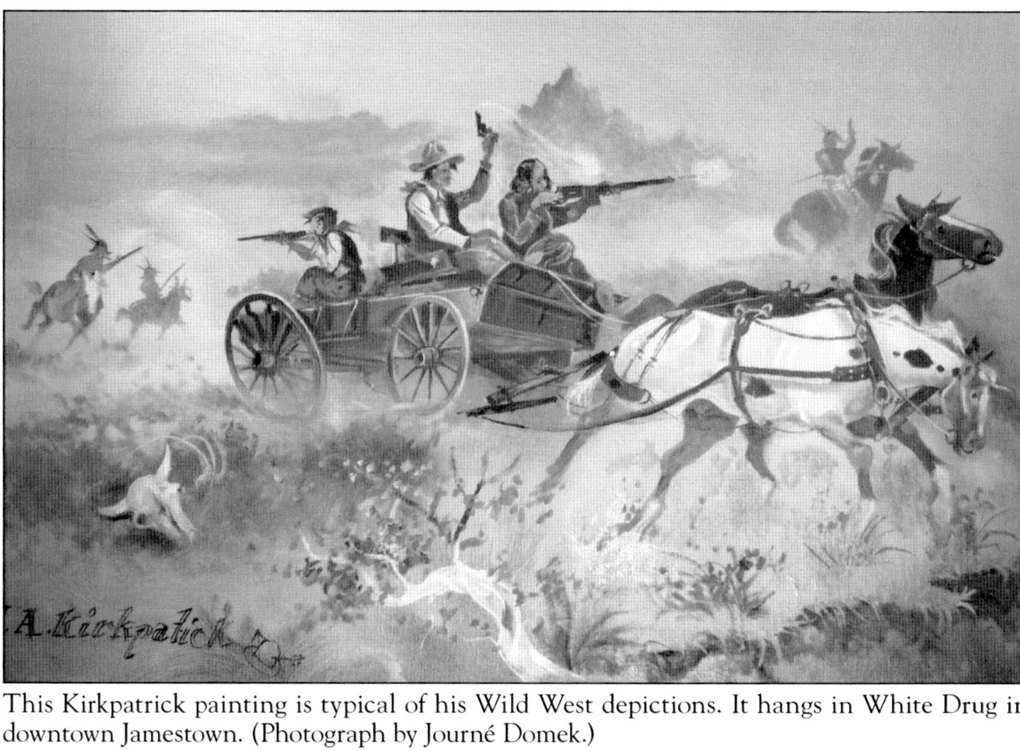

This Kirkpatrick painting is typical of his Wild West depictions. It hangs in White Drug in downtown Jamestown. (Photograph by Journé Domek.)

Jamestown's favorite son, Louis L'Amour, published 117 novels—mostly westerns—45 of which became movies. L'Amour was born in Jamestown in 1908 but left at the age of 15 to travel the world and satisfy his wanderlust. (Picture postcard courtesy of the Stutsman County Memorial Museum.)

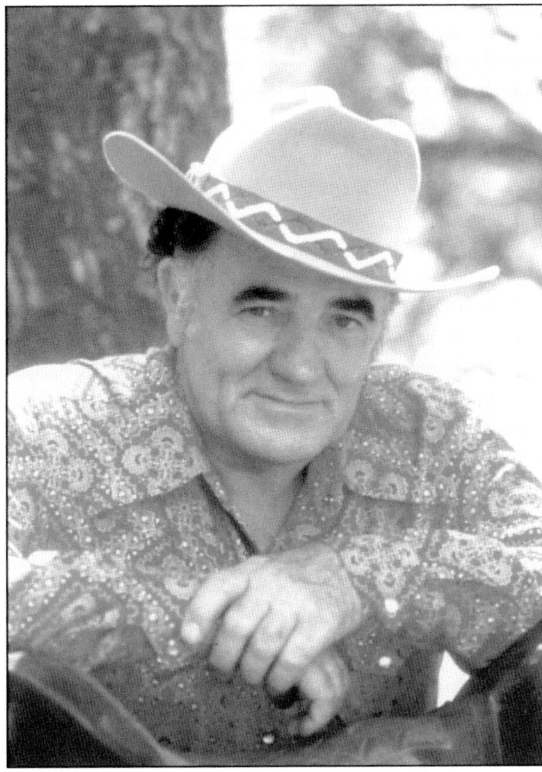

A crowd gathers outside the Louis L'Amour Writer's Shack at Frontier Village. The city takes great pride in its favorite author and in 1989 even named an elementary school after him. (Photograph courtesy of the Frontier Village Visitors Center.)

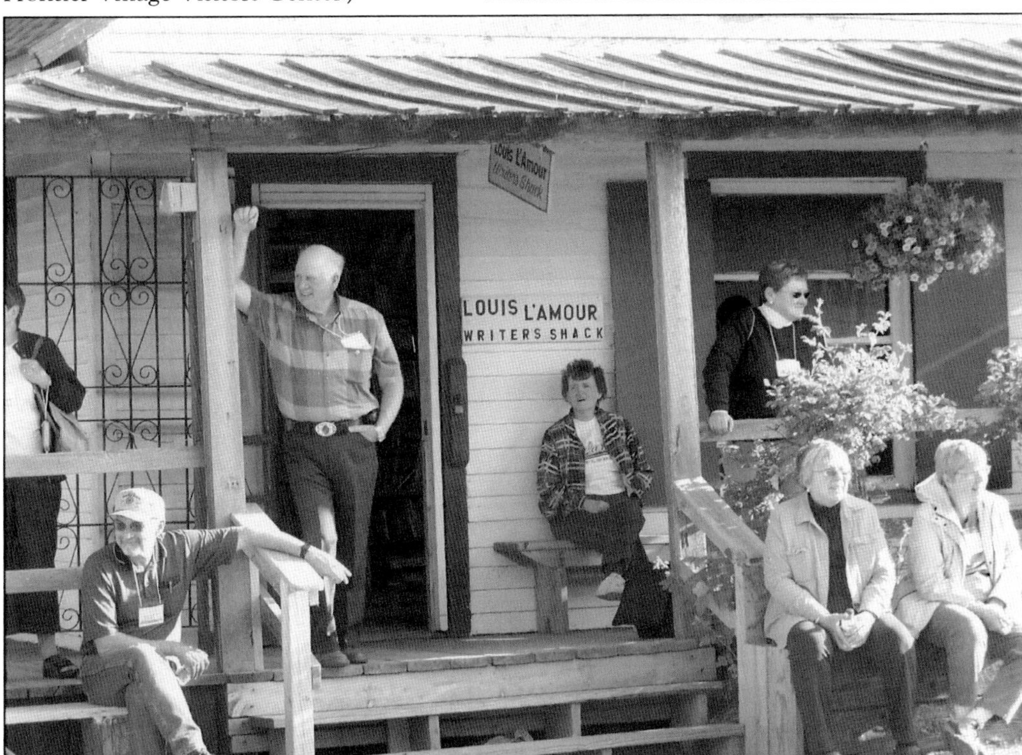

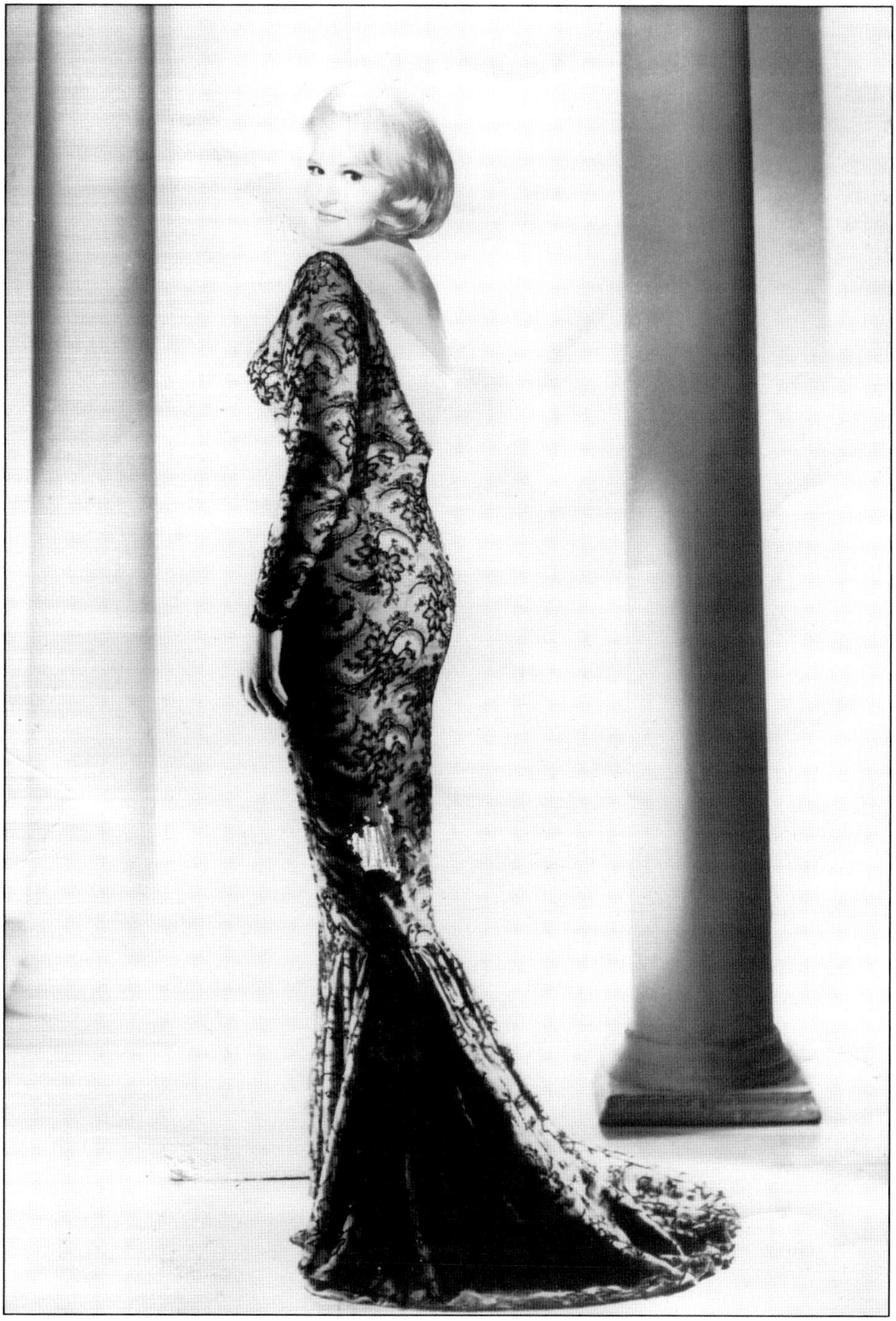

Blues and jazz artist Peggy Lee (whose given name was Norma Delores Egstrom) was born in Jamestown in 1920. She rose to fame singing for the Benny Goodman Band in the early 1940s. Her hits included such classics as "Why Don't You Do Right?" and "Fever." The sultry singer also acted in films and lent her voice to animated hits like Disney's *Lady and the Tramp*. Lee was a three-time Grammy winner and was also the inspiration for Miss Piggy of *The Muppet Show*. The beautiful siren died in 2002. (Photograph courtesy of the Stutsman County Memorial Museum.)

Three

A Way to Look Back

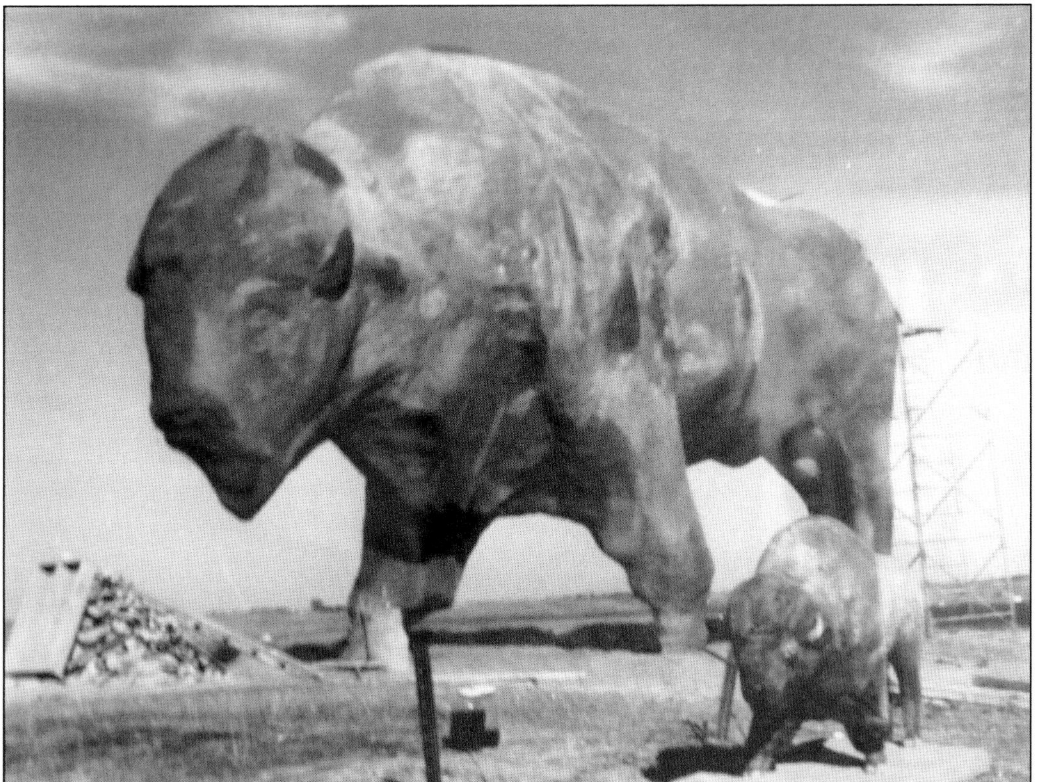

Jamestown is home to the *World's Largest Buffalo*, a massive concrete structure built in 1959. In this early photograph, the sculptor's model sits adjacent to the real McCoy. The sculpture overlooks the south side of the city. (Photograph courtesy of the Frontier Village Visitors Center.)

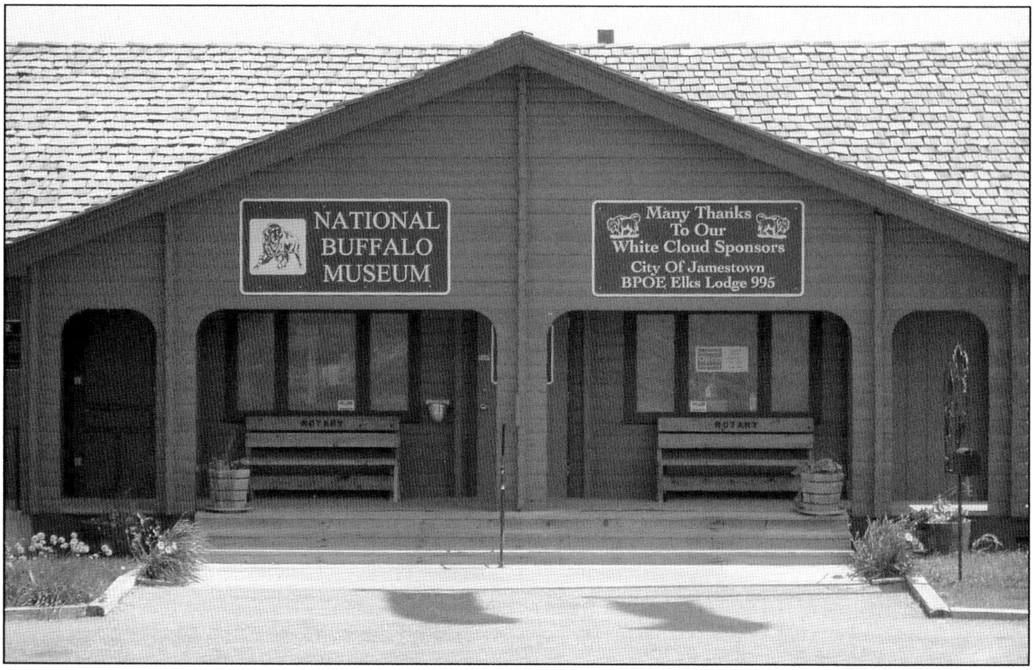

The National Buffalo Museum, located next to Frontier Village, is a first-rate museum with 6,000 square feet devoted to the American bison. Some 250 acres adjacent to the museum showcase a bison herd that includes three albino buffalo. Many Plains tribes revere albino buffalo as sacred. (Photograph by Journé Domek.)

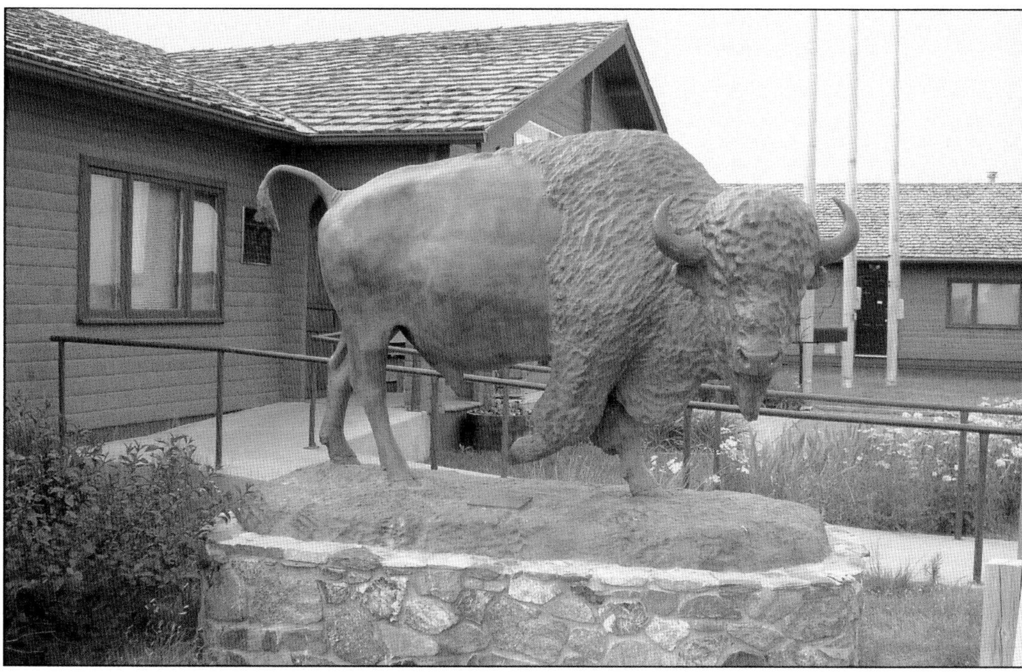

This bronze statute stands guard at Jamestown's National Buffalo Museum, an educational facility that celebrates the animal known as the "Great Monarch of the Plains." (Photograph courtesy of Frontier Village Visitors Center.)

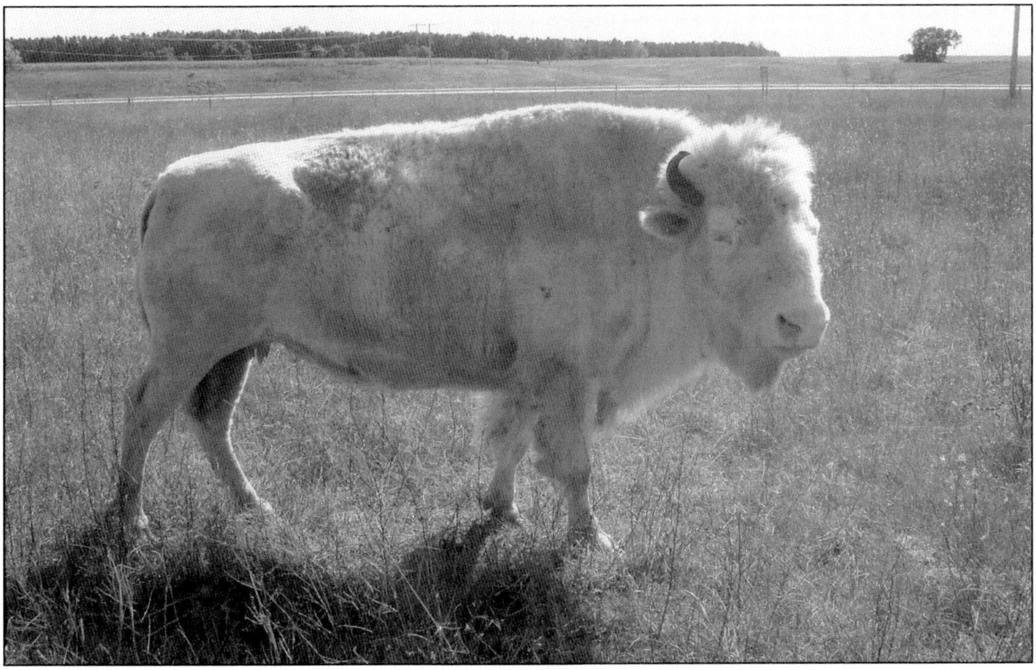

White Cloud, an albino bison, can be found outside of the National Buffalo Museum. The site has been home to three white buffalo (the other two are named Dakota Miracle and Dakota Legend), but White Cloud is probably the most famous. (Photograph courtesy of the National Buffalo Museum.)

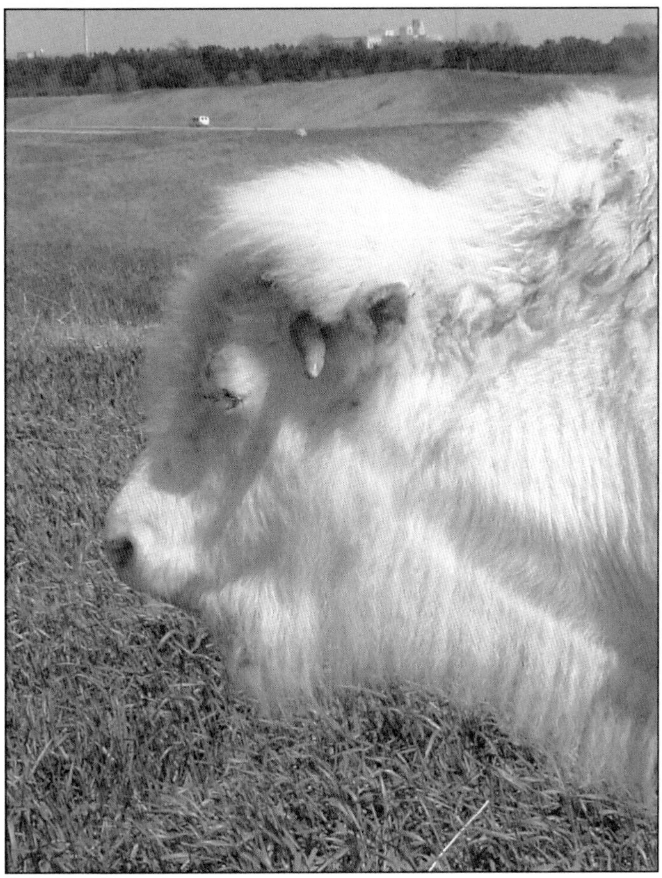

This is a close-up view of White Cloud, who of course has pink eyes. Millions of bison once roamed the prairies of the Great Plains. Today, there are approximately 30 grazing the acreage around the National Buffalo Museum. In this photograph, the North Dakota State Hospital can be seen in the background. (Photograph courtesy of the Frontier Village Visitors Center.)

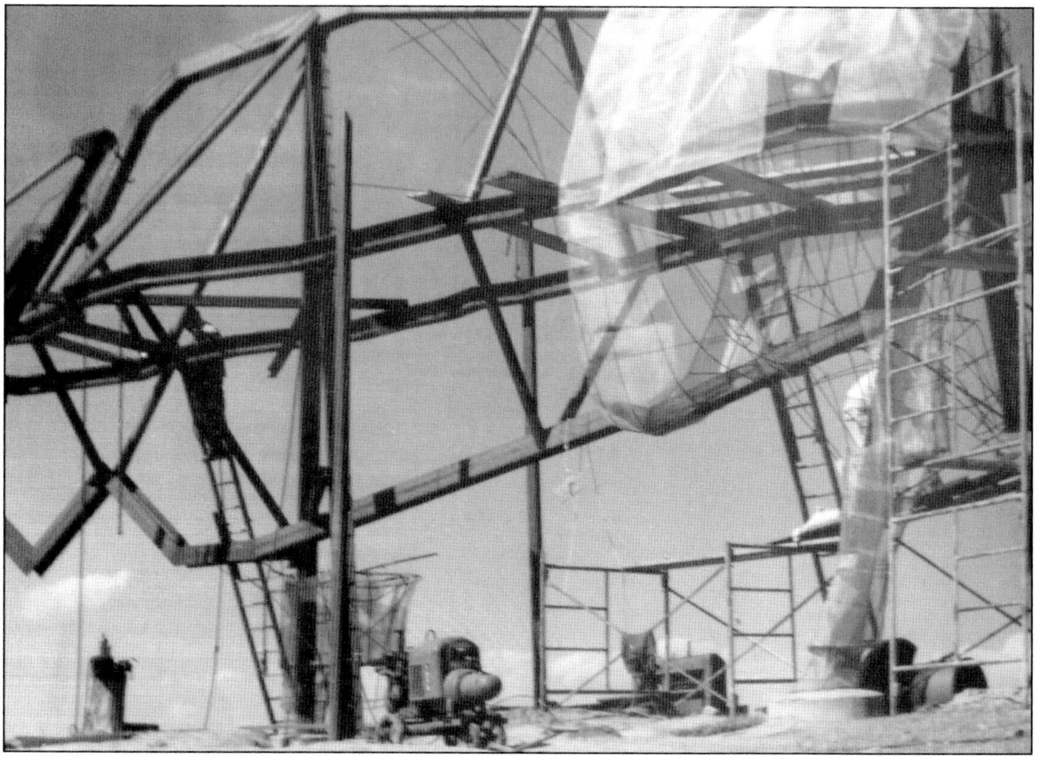

This photograph from 1959 shows the *World's Largest Buffalo* in the initial stages of construction. The concrete structure was commissioned by local businessman Harold Newman in 1959. Art students from Jamestown College provided the labor under supervision of the designer, Elmer Peterson. (Photograph courtesy of the National Buffalo Museum.)

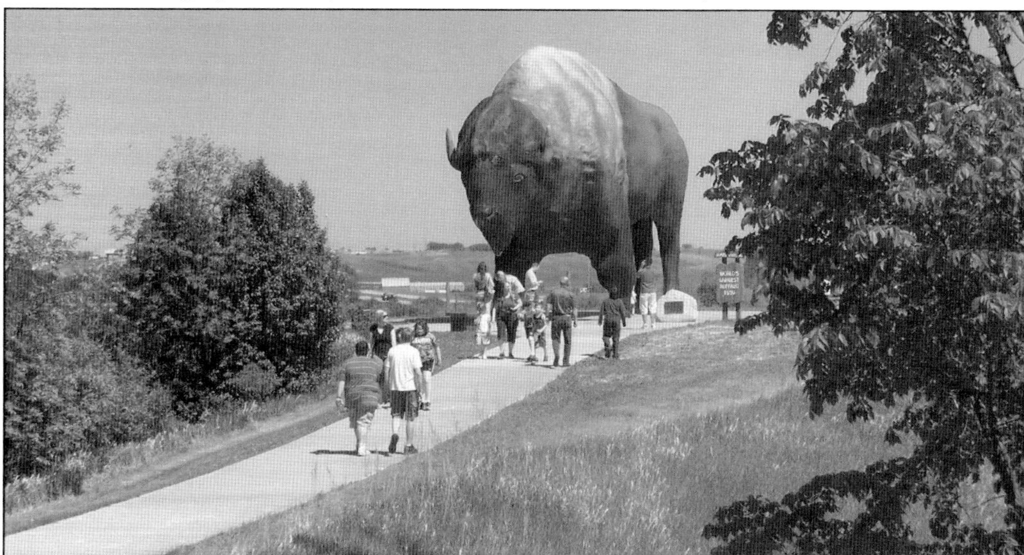

A walkway and interpretive signs lead visitors to the *World's Largest Buffalo*. The statue, which is 26 feet high and 46 feet long, weighs around 60 tons. It can be seen from Interstate 94, which is less than a mile from the site. (Photograph courtesy of the Frontier Village Visitors Center.)

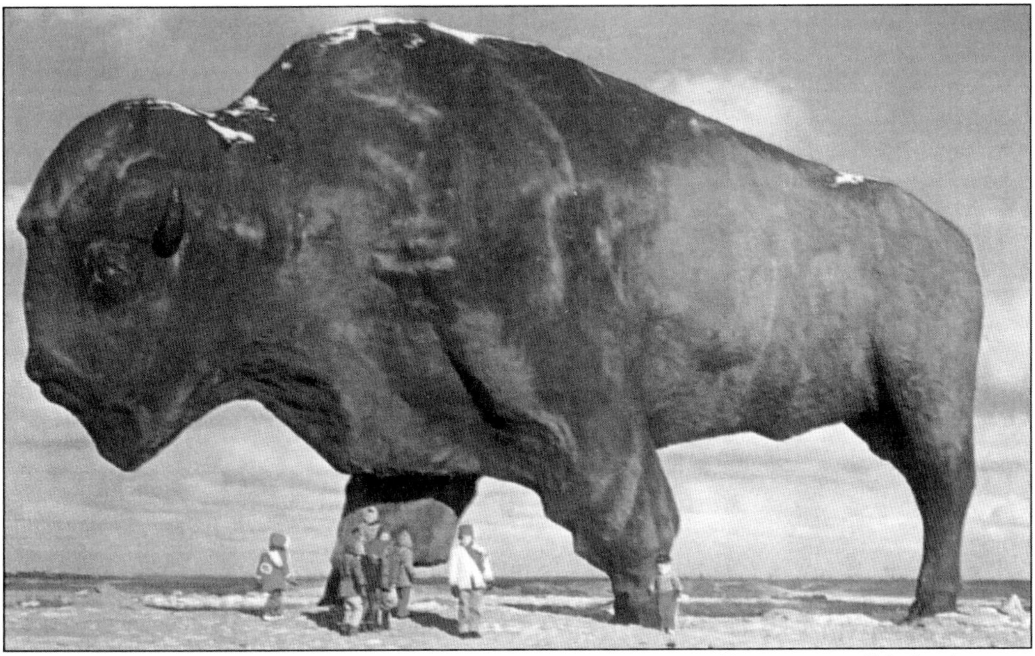

The sight of children posing beneath Jamestown's behemoth, the *World's Largest Buffalo*, has become quite common over the years. Here, the statue still bears its original paint, dating this photograph to around the early 1960s. (Photograph courtesy of the Frontier Village Visitors Center.)

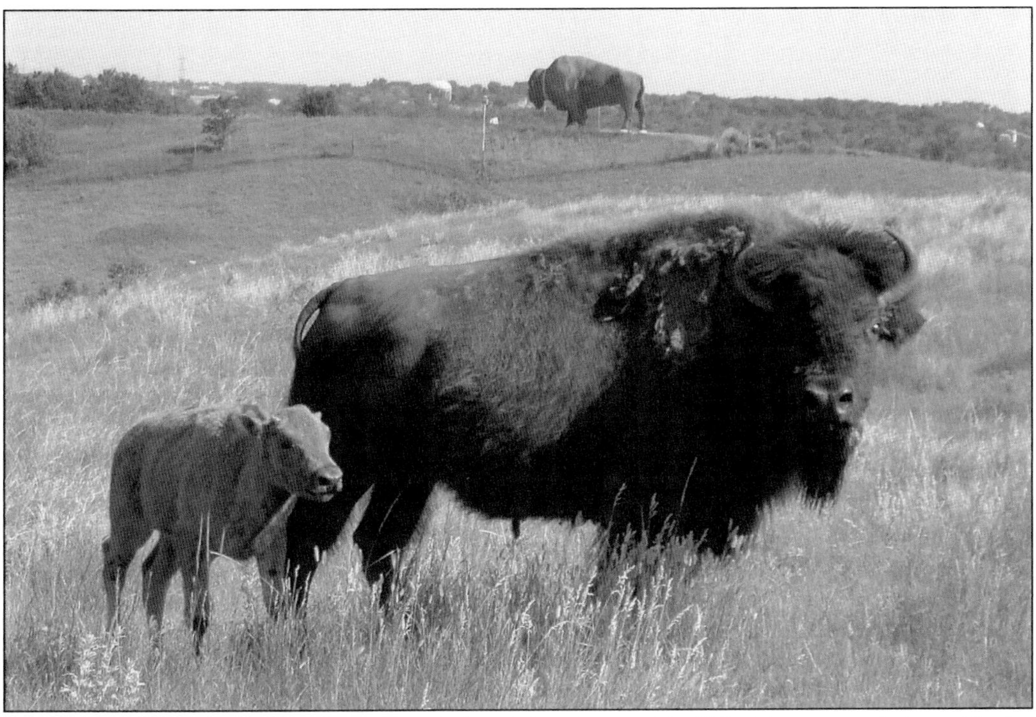

A small herd of bison grazes in a pasture behind the National Buffalo Museum and alongside the *World's Largest Buffalo* on the edge of Jamestown. The live buffalo are part of the draw that brings visitors to the museum. (Photograph courtesy of the National Buffalo Museum.)

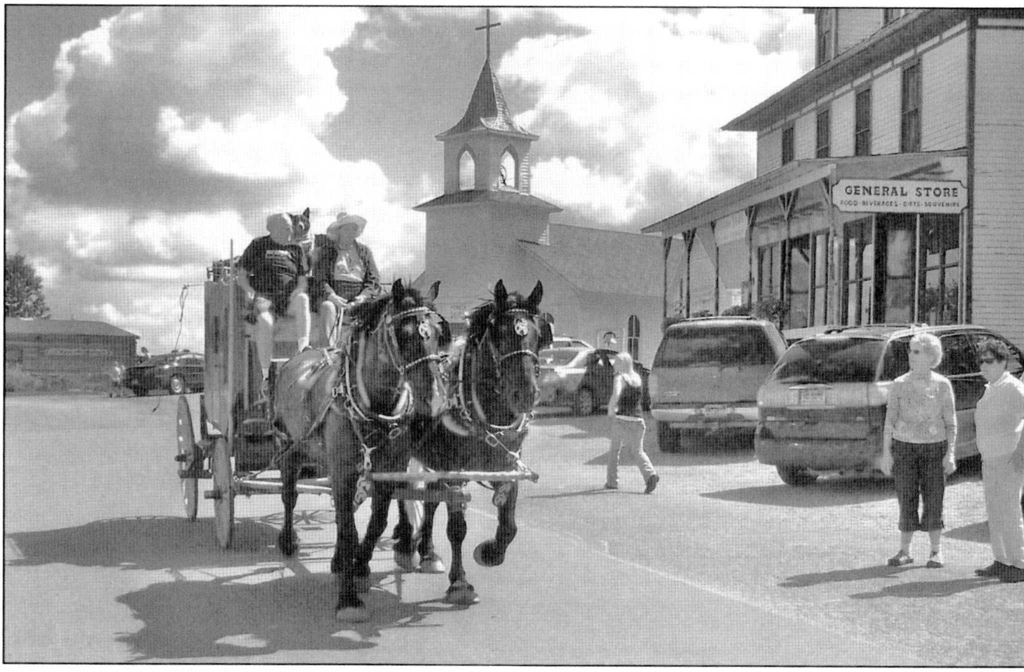

A stagecoach rolls through Frontier Village, the area that grew up around the *World's Largest Buffalo* beginning in the 1960s. The village's main street is lined with vintage-style buildings, including an old-time barbershop and general store. The village is nothing short of an Old West town with all of the amenities of today. For a nominal fee, visitors can ride the stage just like their great-great-grandparents did more than 100 years ago. (Photograph courtesy of the Frontier Village Visitors Center.)

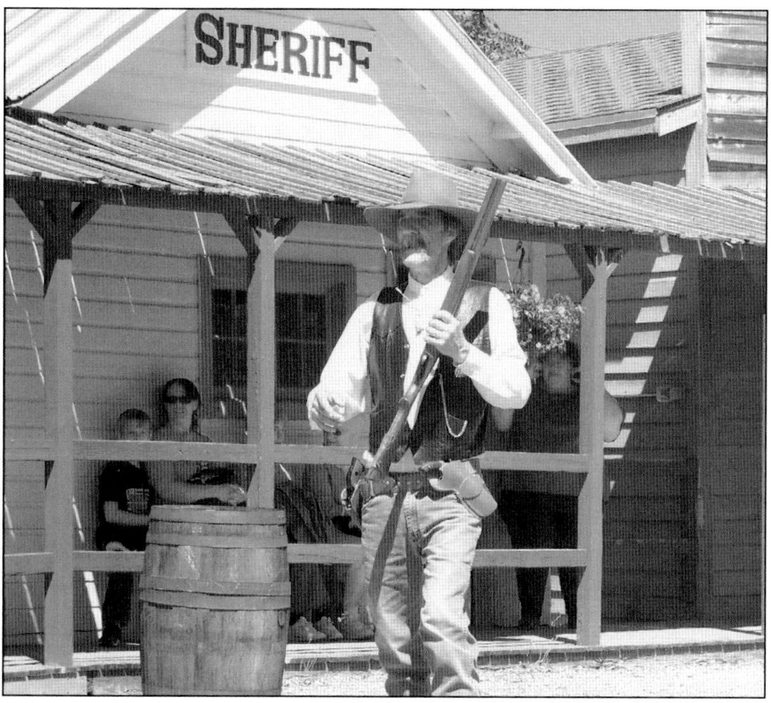

A reenactor dressed as a sheriff steps down the "deadly" street at Frontier Village during a mock shoot-out conducted for the entertainment of tourists. (Photograph courtesy of the Frontier Village Visitors Center.)

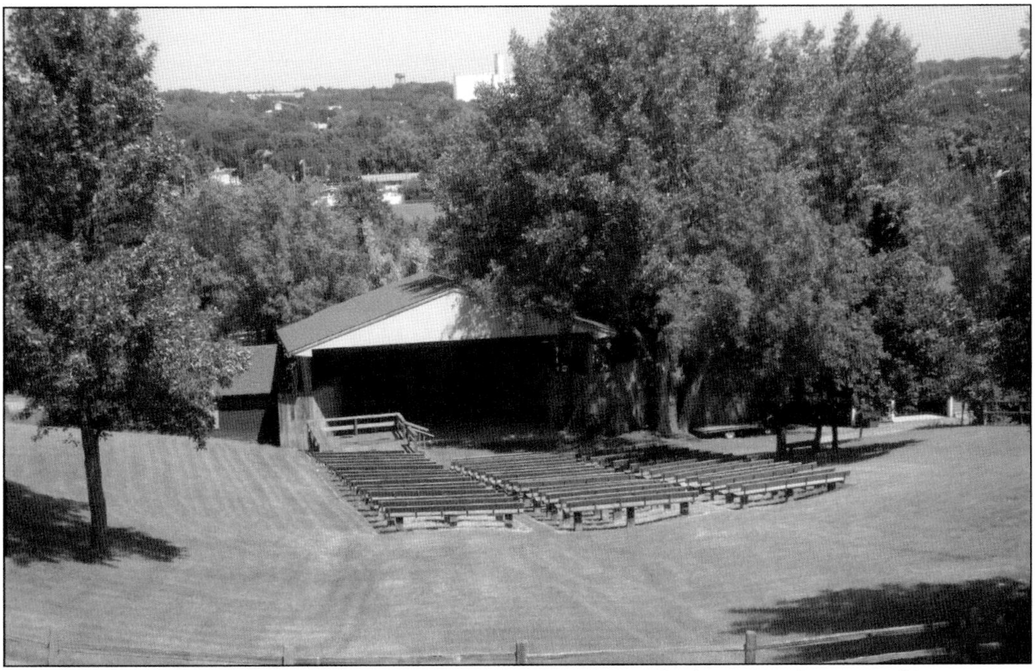

Summer theater comes to life at the Frontier Village amphitheater. The city of Jamestown lies just to the north in the James River valley. (Photograph courtesy of the Frontier Village Visitors Center.)

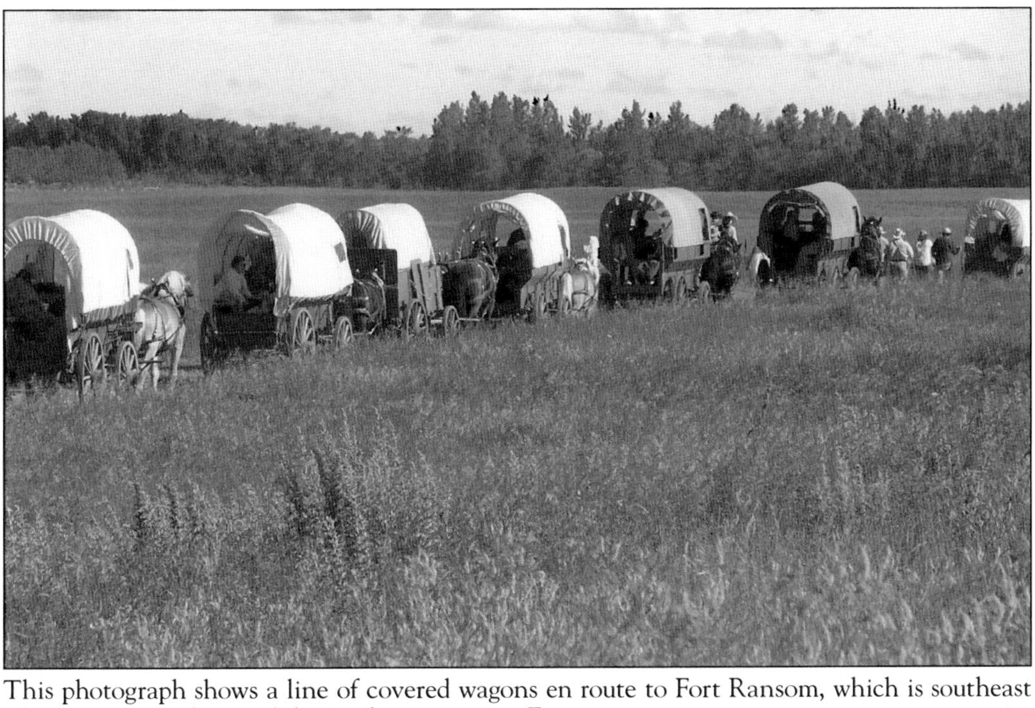

This photograph shows a line of covered wagons en route to Fort Ransom, which is southeast of Jamestown and several days' ride in a wagon. Every summer, participants get an opportunity to experience firsthand what it is like to bump and rattle across the prairie with a wagon train. (Photograph courtesy of the Frontier Village Visitor's Center.)

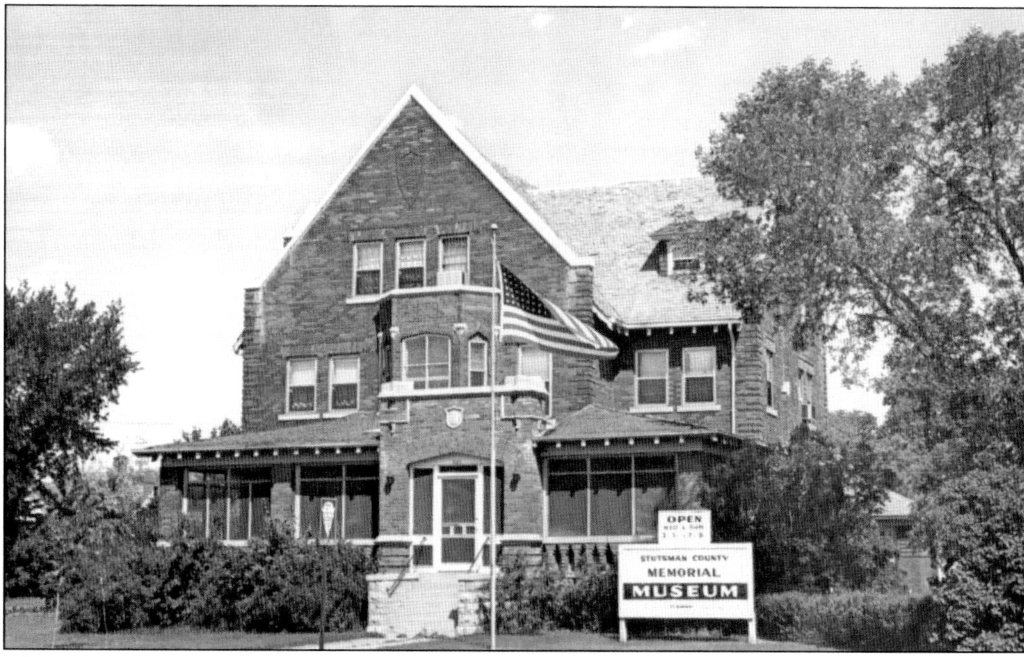

The Stutsman County Memorial Museum offers free public viewing of its exhibits. The museum was first opened by the Fort Seward Historical Society, which purchased the mansion for the purpose. Through the years, Jamestown residents and the Pioneer Daughters of Jamestown have donated to, developed, and written interpretation on the antiques and artifacts housed at the museum. (Picture postcard by King Studios.)

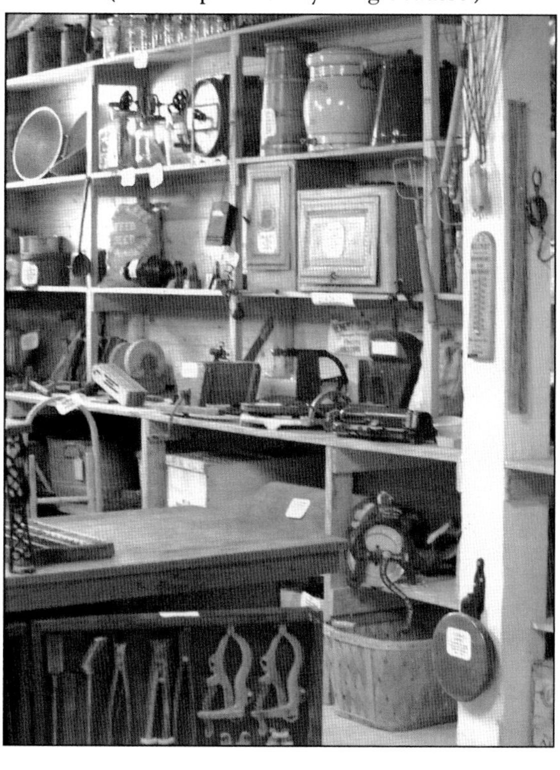

Three full floors and a basement provide thousands of square feet of display space for the collection at Stutsman County Memorial Museum. The museum building was once the home of George Lutz, a German immigrant who settled in Jamestown with his wife and two children. The Arts and Crafts–style home was constructed in 1907 and is still sometimes referred to as "the Lutz Mansion." (Photograph by Journé Domek.)

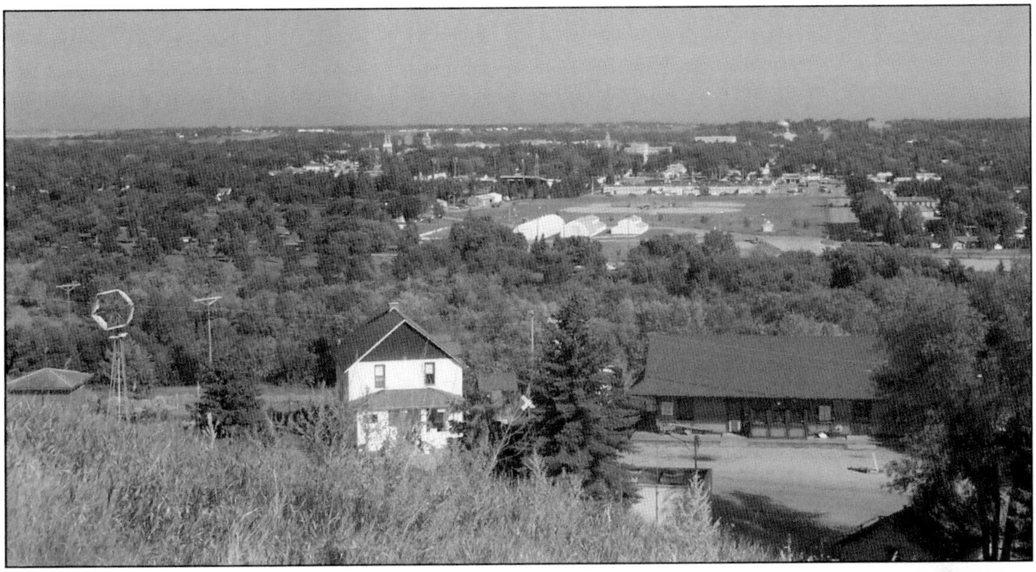

This recent photograph offers a panoramic view of Jamestown as seen from Frontier Village. (Photograph courtesy of the Frontier Village Visitors Center.)

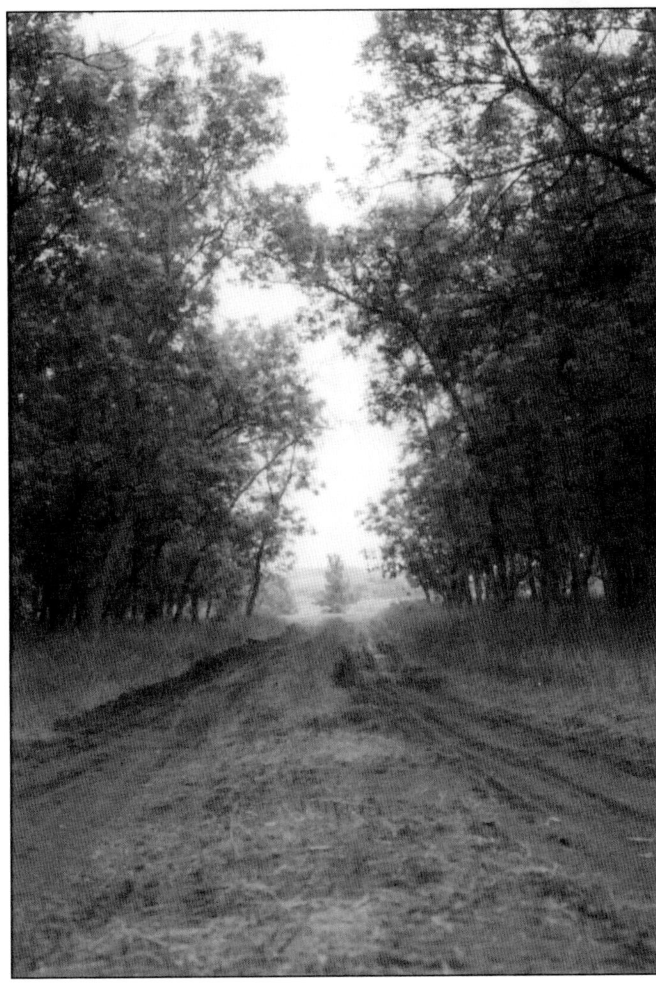

This lonely country road, someplace outside Jamestown, leads into the hidden thoughts and indelible images of a collective past. (Photograph by Tom Domek.)